# Contents

Ken Paterson

with Roberta Wedge

# Oxford Grammar for EAP

## English grammar and practice for Academic Purposes

with answers

OXFORD

UNIVERSITY PRESS

Great Clarendon Street, Oxford, OX2 6DP, United Kingdom

Oxford University Press is a department of the University of Oxford.
It furthers the University's objective of excellence in research, scholarship,
and education by publishing worldwide. Oxford is a registered trade
mark of Oxford University Press in the UK and in certain other countries

First published in 2013

2017 2016 2015 2014 2013

10 9 8 7 6 5 4 3 2 1

ISBN: 978 0 19 432999 6

Printed in China

This book is printed on paper from certified and well-managed sources

ACKNOWLEDGEMENTS

*Illustrations by*: Peter Bull Studios: p.172

*Photographs supplied by kind permission of the following*: Alamy Images
pp.91 (Graphene sheet model/nobeastsofierce), 100 (Cyclists/format4),
106 (Mountaineers climbing Mont Blanc/Images & Stories), 165 (Child
robot/Fernando Cortés de Pablo), 166 (Beach in Cornwall/Kevin
Britland); Corbis pp.13 (Woolworths closing down/Richard Baker/
In Pictures), 16 (Julia Child chopping vegetables/Aaron Rapoport/
CORBIS OUTLINE), 24 (Beijing 2008 Olympics opening ceremony/
Tim de Waele), 38 (Office workers/Ocean), 54 (Woman with baby/
Hannah Mentz), 62 (Tea picking/Gavin Hellier/Robert Harding World
Imagery), 71 (Lab workers/India Picture), 90 (Protesters/Guo Lei/Xinhua
Press), 108 (Family outside new home/H. Armstrong Roberts), 108 (Lab
technician/Douglas Kirkland), 108 (Ice creams on the beach/Hulton-
Deutsch Collection), 108 (US GI in 1943/Bettmann), 108 (Stressed
businessman/LWA/Dann Tardif/Blend Images), 115 (Mountaineer in
storm/Gordon Wiltsie/National Geographic Society), 116 (Farmers
Market/Chris Hills/Demotix), 124 (city at night/George Hammerstein/
Fancy), 132 (Two Chinese men talking/Peter Turnley), 150 (Portrait
of William Shakespeare by Martin Droeshout/Heritage Images),
151 (Margaret Thatcher/Bettmann), 152 (Flood/Gideon Mendel),
178 (Community garden/Mark Bolton); Getty Images pp.12 (Factory
Outing 1923/Topical Press Agency), 14 (Wheelbarrow/Brand X Pictures),
28 (Japan, Mt Fuji, Waves in sea with mountain in background/Machiro
Tanaka), 92 (The well built by the NGO/Pascal Parrot), 159 (Commuters
cycling/Shaun Curry/AFP), 179 (books/Russell Tate/iStock Vectors);
Mary Evans Picture Library pp.6 (Whaling from a small boat/Engraving
in Chatterbox), 88 (Whales fighting a whaler, copper engraving by
Williams James Linton/INTERFOTO/Bildarchiv Hansmann), 89 (Ludwig-
Wilhelm-hospital in Karlsruhe/Mary Evans/Sueddeutsche Zeitung
Photo), 160 (The South Sea Bubble traders/Unattributed illustration
from a set of Cigarette cards (no. 37) for Franklyn's Cigarettes
'Historic Events'); Oxford University Press pp.12 (workers outing),
44 (Smokestack/Photodisc), 46 (Dewy spider's web/Photodisc),
70 (Elephant/PhotoKratky - Wildlife/Nature), 70 (Antelope/Thinkstock),
74 (New York city/Keith Levit), 80 (Eruption at Mount St Helens/
Photodisc), 81 (Surgeon/Digital Vision), 82 (Chrysler Building/Digital
Vision), 130 (Homeless man/BananaStock), 131 (Teens eating burgers/
Stockbyte), 132 (Leopard/Digital Vision), 142 (Wheat fields/Photodisc).

Words in the AWL (Academic Word List) Glossaries are used with
the kind permission of Dr Averil Coxhead of Victoria University of
Wellington, New Zealand, and the accompanying definitions are
adapted from *Oxford Advanced Learner's Dictionary, 8th edition* © Oxford
University Press.

*The authors and publishers would like to thank the following people for their
advice in the early stages of the development of this book*: Maggie Holmes, York
St John University; David Sawtell, English in Chester; Barbara Howarth,
University of Glasgow.

The author would like to thank staff and students at the University of
Westminster for their support throughout many years of teaching.

# Introduction

OXFORD GRAMMAR FOR EAP (English for Academic Purposes) is a study and practice book for international students planning to take or already taking a university course in the medium of English. Focusing on the key grammar of academic English, the book provides clear explanation, appropriate examples and plenty of practice material. It will be of great use to those students who need extra English language support for their studies.

English for Academic Purposes is the kind of English that is required at college or university. Unlike the study of everyday conversational English, the study of academic language concentrates on the more formal language that is generally used in written academic contexts. However, because discussion in seminars and giving presentations are also important elements of academic study, examples of language that is particularly useful in these situations is indicated by this symbol 💬.

Example sentences, texts and exercises in *Oxford Grammar for EAP* are taken from a wide range of subject areas including business, science, creative arts, social studies and law.

*Oxford Grammar for EAP* is designed for self-study, and has a full answer key, but is also suitable for use in classroom situations.

## The structure of the book

The book has 20 units, each one dealing with a different area of grammar. You can work your way through the book from beginning to end, or go straight to units which you see as a priority.

Some units, such as *01 Tense review or 11 Modal verbs*, focus on aspects of grammar that are relevant to any academic situation; others, such as *02 Comparing and contrasting*, concentrate on language that is useful for particular strategies or tasks.

## How the units work

Each unit starts with a simple activity to get you thinking about the main idea. In *04 Being formal and informal*, for example, there are two texts and you are asked to try to identify the kind of language that makes their styles different.

The rest of the unit is divided into short, easy-to-read sections with a *test yourself* practice exercise at the end of each one, so you can check your understanding immediately. Explanation and example sentences are accompanied by *Tips*: key pieces of extra advice on the topic in question.

At the end of every unit, there is a *Challenge yourself* section with a wide variety of longer exercises, giving you the opportunity to test yourself thoroughly on all the grammar points covered. *Challenge yourself* sections normally finish with a short writing task for which there is a model answer in the key.

For the *Challenge yourself* sections there is a reference next to each answer in the key that allows you to check any wrong answers against the appropriate section of the unit.

## Appendices

At the end of *Oxford Grammar for EAP* you will find a brief guide to punctuation, a glossary of the grammatical terms used in the book, and the full Academic Word List, as well as the answer key and a full index.

## Academic Word List

Developed by Dr Averil Coxhead at Victoria University of Wellington in New Zealand, the Academic Word List (AWL) contains a range of the most frequently-used words in academic English. Where these words occur in the *Challenge yourself* sections, definitions are often given alongside the exercises to help you extend your understanding of academic vocabulary efficiently and in context. The definitions are adapted from *Oxford Advanced Learner's Dictionary, 8th edition* © Oxford University Press.

## Introduction

This unit provides an overview of English tenses, focusing on their use in academic English, and on the areas that can sometimes cause difficulties.

**1** Choosing between simple and continuous forms.
- *Painters **see** things that the untrained eye might easily miss.* (present simple)
- *Many countries, both rich and poor, **are** already **seeing** the effects of an ageing population.* (present continuous)

**2** When to use the present perfect.
- *In recent months vegetable oils **have seen** volatility in the spot price more reminiscent of petroleum.*

**3** When to use the past perfect.
- *The conservation of endangered species is safeguarded by the world's best zoos, whose scientists and staff have successfully reintroduced species to areas where they **had died out**.*

**4** The various future forms.
- *Harrison argues that more countries **will be entering** the European Union over the next ten years and, as they do, greater tensions **will arise** between the richest and the poorest.*

**Read the text and then try to name the verb tenses used. Can you say why each tense is used?**

For centuries, people on sea coasts around the world ¹*have hunted* whales. From the mid-nineteenth century onwards, with the advent of modern factory ships, the annual worldwide catch ²*increased* until it ³*reached* a peak in the 1960s. A rapid decline ⁴*followed*, however, because the plastics industry ⁵*had invented* substitutes for most of the products of the whale's carcass. The whale-hunting that ⁶*takes place* today ⁷*is* mostly done for food.

1 _____
2, 3, 4 _____
5 _____
6, 7 _____

Suggested answers: see page 189

Other units that deal with tenses are unit *9 Passives*, unit *11 Modal verbs*, and unit *17 Conditionals*.

## 1.1 Present simple and continuous

### 1.1 study

In academic writing and speaking, the primary use of the present simple is for factual descriptions.

- Almost a billion people ~~are speaking~~ **speak** Mandarin, the official language of the People's Republic of China.
- When you **heat** a substance, its particles **move** faster, and so **collide** more frequently.

This includes:

**1** describing regular activities
- 49,000 people ~~are entering~~ **enter** the underground station at Waterloo every day, during the three-hour morning peak.

**2** describing processes (often in the passive in academic English) or giving instructions (in the active)
- The fabric **is** then **washed, dyed,** and **cut** into patterns.
- Then you **wash** the fabric, **dye** it, and **cut** it into patterns.

**3** summarizing or reporting the main arguments of other academics.
- Steele **explains** that survivors of tragic events often undergo periods of guilt.
(See page 143 in unit 16 Paraphrasing for more examples of reporting verbs.)

**4** talking about the plots of books, films, etc.
- Brooklyn by Colm Tóibín **tells** the story of Ellis Lacey, a young woman who **is sent** by her family from Ireland to the USA to get a good job.

The present continuous is used to describe events or actions that are happening at the moment (now or around now). These might be continuous events/actions or a series of regular events/actions.
- Kayston plc **is advertising** for a new CEO, after Hugh Alexander's sudden departure.
- Chinese construction companies **are securing** a number of major contracts to rebuild Ethiopia's infrastructure.

They include temporary situations and trends in society or the world around us.
- Kingston Enterprises, which **is** currently **operating** from premises in Wandsworth while their new factory outside Cambridge **is being completed,** is one of the UK's leading manufacturers of computer hard drives.
- More people **are shopping** online these days, and the service standards that consumers expect **are rising.**

**TIP** State verbs such as believe, know, mean; like, prefer, want; belong, own, possess; contain, depend, matter, are usually used in the present simple.
- The Church Commissioners' report indicates that the Church of England ~~is owning~~ **owns** around 120,000 acres of rural land.

### 1.1 test yourself

**Circle the correct option.**

**1** Boston College looks for/is looking for an international marketing manager for their overseas recruitment drive.

**2** Social enterprises can be defined as those which are placing/place environmental concerns alongside profit.

**3** Monetary policy is operating/operates by influencing the price at which money is lent.

**4** Smartphones are establishing/establish themselves as the dominant mobile device amongst younger consumers.

**5** David Hare's plays, as Felton (2009) notes/ is noting, provide actresses with some of the strongest roles in modern drama.

**6** According to the Broadcasters' Audience Research Board, the average Briton watches/ is watching just over thirty hours of television per week.

**7** Most people are recognizing/recognize that a respect for the law is the fundamental basis for a civilized society.

**8** When a team works/is working intensively on a project, the team leader should protect them from distraction.

**9** Stevens argues that consumers these days are preferring/prefer to do business with companies that have environmentally-friendly policies.

**10** Babcock suggests that attitudes to work amongst young people are changing/change.

## 1.2 Past simple and continuous

### 1.2 study

The past simple is used, often with dates, times or places, for finished events, whether they are long, short, or repeated.

- *The Mughal Empire* ~~was controlling~~ **controlled** *a large part of the India for more than 300 years.*
- *Boo.com* **was launched** *in the autumn of 1999 as an online clothing retailer. The company then* **spent $35 million** *of venture capital in just eight months, but* **went** *into receivership on 18 May 2000, one of the most spectacular failures of the 'dotcom' era.*
- *During the summer of 2010, Theatrespace* ~~was putting on~~ **put on** *a new show every week for twelve weeks.*

In the second example above, three separate events occurred, one after another, so the past simple was used. But if events overlap or 'interrupt' one another, the past continuous is used for the longer, 'background' event.

- *Brooks Brothers of New York* ~~performed~~ **were performing** *reasonably well when the takeover bid came from Marks and Spencers.*
- *At the time of his death, Einstein* **was** *still* **working** *on his attempt to unify the laws of physics.*

Note, however, that state verbs (see **TIP** on page 007) are not normally used in the continuous form.

As an alternative to the past simple, you can use *used to* and *would* + infinitive without *to* to refer to habitual actions and events in the past.

- *Before the Clean Air Act of 1956, London* **used to/would** *suffer from severe air pollution known as 'smog', a combination of smoke and fog.*
- *Portland Zinc* ~~would~~ **used to** *mine most of its supplies in Brazil. They* **shipped/would ship** *the ore from São Paulo to processing plants further up the coast.*

Note that in the second example above, you could replace *used to* by saying something like *Portland Zinc mined most of its supplies in Brazil in the 1950s*, or *Portland Zinc once mined most of its supplies in Brazil*, but you cannot use *would* until a past context has been established.

Note also that *would* is not normally used with state verbs, and that *used to* is not used with numbers of months, years, etc.

- *Pampas Products* ~~would~~ **used to** *own a subsidiary in Florida, but they were obliged to sell it to recoup their losses during the recession of the early 1980s.*
- *The company's headquarters* ~~used to be~~ **were** *located in Berlin for eight years.*

### 1.2 test yourself

Circle the correct option. If both are possible, circle both.

1 At the moment when the earthquake was striking/struck, most people were sleeping/slept.
2 Phillips asked/was asking her subjects to watch clips of people smiling, and measured their heart rate afterwards.
3 During the 18th century, merchants would/used to transport their goods around England by canal.
4 Audi used to launch/launched their new family saloon in 2010.
5 At the time of the crash, high street banks were investing/invested in some very risky products.
6 The yacht *White Tiger* made/was making excellent progress when an unusually high wave destroyed/was destroying its mast.

## 1.3 Present perfect (and past simple)

### 1.3 study

The present perfect is the tense that connects the past and the present. In the example below, the present perfect is used to describe 'the very recent past up until the present' – with the focus on the present.

- *In acquiring Duogame, Gamesmaster plc* **has become** *a major player in the UK computer games market.*

If the past simple was used, the focus would be on 'when' (i.e. a finished moment in the past), and we might include a date.

- *In acquiring Duogame, Gamesmaster plc* **last week became** *a major player in the UK computer games market.*

The present perfect is the tense to use to describe people or things as they are now (present focus) in terms of their experience in the past.

- *The province of Alsace* **has changed** *hands several times in its history, which explains its cultural heritage.*

Compare the example above with a sentence beginning *Alsace changed hands in 1848 and 1872, ...* which focuses less on the present nature of Alsace and more on specific events in its history.

You can use the present perfect and the past simple to present different aspects of the same subject.

- *In 2005, scientists **measured** a land temperature of 70.7°C in the Lut Desert of Iran.* (past focus)
  → *No higher temperature **has been recorded** on earth since then.* (present focus)
  → *This is the only time scientists **have recorded** a temperature above 70°C.* (present focus)

Note how *just* is used with the present perfect to emphasize that an action is recent.

- *A team of Russian scientists **has just completed** a five-year study of the behavioural patterns of three Siberian wolf packs.*

In academic writing, the present perfect is useful for referring to earlier studies or to generally accepted theories in expressions such as: *Studies **have shown** that ..., It **has become accepted** that ..., Mathematicians **have proved** that ...*
(See page 127 in unit *14 Hedging* for more ways of referring to the work of others.)

You can also use the present perfect to summarize the arguments you have made up to that point in an essay or presentation.

- *The first part of this report **has outlined** the way in which one-way road systems can be beneficial in reducing traffic congestion in town centres. Now, some of the disadvantages will be considered.*

The present perfect continuous is used to highlight the length of an activity (often with *for, since, so far, up until now, all year*, etc.).

- *General Motors* ~~have designed~~ *have been designing their new family saloon for the past six months.*
- 💬 (in a presentation) *The problems that **I've been looking at** so far can all be resolved by an increase in the general level of funding.*

You can also emphasize the effects that the activity has had on the present situation.

- *Neither company has much cash left because both **have been investing** heavily all year in new plant.*

Note again that state verbs are rarely used with the continuous form.

**TIP** As a general rule, contracted forms such as *I've been looking at ...* are normally avoided in written academic English, but may be used in presentations, seminars, etc. (See unit *4 Being formal and informal* for more information on what is acceptable in a formal context.)

## 1.3 test yourself

Complete each sentence with the present perfect or past simple form of the verb in brackets.

1 New research indicates that scientists _____ (discover) a potential cure for some forms of dementia. The key finding _____ (make) two months ago by a team working for Dr Julia Davidson.
2 Construction companies _____ _____ (build) a new village outside Perpignan for past three years.
3 Thousands of UK citizens _____ _____ (emigrate) to Australia to start a new life in the 1950s and 60s. One of them _____ (write) an account in 1976 that _____ (just/film).
4 Currently editor of *The Weekly Business Digest*, Wendy Crozier _____ (have) an interesting career. It _____ _____ (start) in 1976 at the BBC.
5 Research _____ (demonstrate) that people can delay the onset of Type 2 diabetes by losing weight.
6 A million Chinese people _____ _____ (move) to Africa in the past twenty years to take advantage of new business opportunities. More than 250,000 Chinese immigrants _____ (arrive) in South Africa alone since 1994.

## 1.4 Past perfect (and past simple)

### 1.4 study

The past perfect is used to talk about a past event which happened before another past event.

- *Trade union representatives returned* (past) *to the talks on Friday 17 May, but by this time the management team* ~~withdrew~~ *had already withdrawn* (earlier past) *their offer.*
- *G & M Business Machines lost a significant percentage of their market share between 2004 and 2010 because they **had failed** to anticipate the growth in Chinese demand.*

The past perfect is commonly used:

**1** after past simple forms of verbs connected with speaking or thinking such as *admit, agree, believe, claim, confirm, deny, know, realize*
- *A number of MPs **claimed** that Tony Blair **had misled** parliament during the debates over the Iraq war.*
- *Most observers **agreed** that the merger **had taken** place too quickly.*
- *Professor Bernard **knew** immediately that her team **had made** a significant discovery.*

**2** in relative clauses
- *The report **concluded** that no side effects were apparent in the patients who **had received** low doses of the new medicine.*

**3** in third conditional sentences
- *If the company's accountants **had submitted** the tax return by the due date, GM Holidays would not have been fined.*

**4** in past situations where plans did not succeed.
- *Researchers **had hoped** to complete their study by 2010, but found that they did not have sufficient data.*
- *The chairman of the enquiry **had wanted** to question General Armstrong, but the General's legal team refused to cooperate.*

The past perfect continuous is used in the same way as the present perfect continuous - to highlight the length and effects of an activity.
- *The haulage company was prosecuted when health and safety inspectors were able to prove that some of its employees **had been driving** for up to twenty hours without taking a break.*

### 1.4 test yourself

**Correct each sentence by adding *had*.**

**1** The team of scientists just left the laboratory when the fire broke out, so there were no injuries.
**2** James Lott described the trip as a failure as they expected to discover at least three new species of insect.
**3** The regiment made a successful case for all those who participated in the rescue voyage to receive the Distinguished Service Cross.
**4** Petroleum Products finally admitted that crude oil been leaking from their tanker for more than a week.
**5** Many companies signed contracts with competitors by the time Holliwell Carlease offered them the new Fiat.
**6** The government denied that they announced the new proposals before they were ready.

## 1.5 Future

### 1.5 study

There are a number of ways of talking about the future using the following words and structures: *will, be going to*, and present tenses; the future continuous and perfect tenses; *be (due) to, be about to*, etc., and the 'future in the past'.

**1** *Will*, *be going to* **and present tenses**

*Will* and *be going to* can often be used interchangeably with no change in meaning. *Will*, however, is much more commonly used in written academic English than *be going to*.
- *The President **will spend/is going to** spend two days in Moscow, before travelling on to Oslo.*

💬 *Be going to* is more natural when announcing a plan in spoken English, or when describing the announcement of a new initiative in written English.
- *May I start my presentation? Thank you. ~~I will~~ **I'm going to** talk about water conservation today.*
- *A group of private universities in Germany **is going to** introduce a fast-track medical degree course next year.*

In the above examples, you could replace *be going to* with the present simple or present continuous form of a verb such as *intend to* or *plan to* (*A group of private universities in Germany **intends/is intending to** introduce ...*).

The present continuous may be used as an alternative to *will* for fixed arrangements, and the present simple can be used for schedules.

- *The UK **is hosting/will host** a summit in December to discuss the international response to global warming.*
- *The theatre company **begins/will begin** its tour in Chicago in May.*

*Will* is normally used after verbs that express uncertainty about the future such as *doubt, expect, hope,* and *think.*

- *Some critics **expect** that the new scheme **will fail** quite quickly through lack of public support.*

## 2 Future continuous and perfect tenses

You can use the future continuous (*will + be + -ing* form) as an alternative to *will* + infinitive without *to* to emphasize what will be happening at a specific time in the future.

- *Two British astronauts **will join/will be joining** the Russian team at the space station in October.*

When you describe a future activity that will already be in progress at a specific time in the future, however, you must use the continuous form.

- *By this time next year, it is possible that Bailey and Sharp ~~will export~~ **will be exporting** more of their tractors to China than to EU countries.*

The future perfect (*will + have +* past participle) and future perfect continuous (*will + have been + -ing* form) are used to say that something will happen or be achieved before a specific time in the future.

- *Many commentators believe that six or seven of the smaller American merchant banks **will have gone** into receivership by this time next year.*
- *In a year's time, Railton plc **will have been operating** in China for a quarter of a century.*

## 3 Be (due) to, be about to, be (un)likely/certain to

The present tense of the verb *be + to +* infinitive is used as an alternative to *will* to express formal decisions, plans and requirements. *Be due to* is used in a similar way.

- *The UK and Argentina **are to/are due to** sign a new trade agreement in January next year.*

You can use *be about to* + infinitive to describe something that will happen in the immediate future. *Be on the point of* + *-ing* form is used in a similar way.

- *Scientists **are about to test** the prototype of a scheme to cool parts of the atmosphere. (= Scientists **are on the point of testing** ...)*

*Be (un)likely to* or *certain to* + infinitive are normally used to express probability.

- *The government **is unlikely to announce** new reforms to the House of Lords until after the next election.*

In discussing the history of an event, you may want to use 'future in the past' with past forms of *be to* (*was/ were to*), *be about to* (*was/were about to*), *will* (*would*), and *be going to* (*was/were going to*).

- *President Obama **was to attend** the opening event, but a security alert changed the situation.*
- *Keirston plc **was about to go** bankrupt when a new order from Japan came through.*
- *The CEO of Spector Products realized in 2007 that the economic situation **would get** worse.*
- *Some local communities **were going to hold** street parties to celebrate the royal wedding until they discovered that they were legally obliged to get permission from the local authorities.*

*Was/Were to* can also be used with *be* or *prove* to emphasize the importance of a past event or action on future consequences.

- *The opening of a series of branches in the USA **was to prove/be** an expensive mistake for the UK retailer, Bourke and Mason.*

## 1.5 test yourself

**Circle the correct option. If both are possible, circle both.**

1 Tesco doubles/is going to double the number of its hypermarkets in China by 2020.
2 Government cuts mean that life will be/will have been difficult for many people over the next three years.
3 The establishment of an office in New York in 2009 was to prove/would prove to be a very successful move for the UK TV company.
4 If everything goes to plan, at 14.16 this afternoon, a minute after starting his engine, Andy Green will be driving/will drive faster than anyone has driven before.
5 Some economists argue that India is to/will outperform China in the long-term.
6 The new law on the advertising of cigarettes will take/takes effect in April next year.
7 All of the parties would/were about to come to an agreement when news broke of a new rebel attack.
8 A major new aerospace factory is opening/will open in Sunderland in February.

# 01 Challenge yourself

**A** Complete the text with the correct form of the verb in brackets.

The business of tourism ¹_____ (grow) massively over the past century. While extensive foreign travel has always been one of the pleasures of the wealthy, its extension to the mass market ²_____ (be) a phenomenon of the last fifty years. Domestic tourism really ³_____ (begin) in the mid-nineteenth century, as workers ⁴_____ (gain) paid annual leave, at first for one week and then for two. Longer periods gradually ⁵_____ (become) common, in some cases granted by benevolent employers such as Cadbury's, but more often ⁶_____ (fight) for and ⁷_____ (win) by the trade unions. This was made possible as a result of the concentration of the labour force in factories during the Industrial Revolution of the nineteenth century, which ⁸_____ (change) the balance of power between employers and employees.

**B** Match the beginning of each sentence with the correct ending.

1 At the beginning of mass tourism, the whole workforce of a factory would
2 This model of tourism was
3 Workers from the polluted industrial cities of Russia used to
4 For example, they might be told to
5 As much as possible, people wanted to

a travel en masse to the pristine shores of the lakes of the Central Asian republics, where doctors examined them on arrival and prescribed specific food, drink, exercise, and activities for the month.
b spend their vacation building up their strength, socializing with colleagues, and relaxing with their families.
c move to the seaside, a resort town, or a spa, to spend their holiday together with their workmates and immediate family.
d amplified in the Soviet Union.
e walk in the pine forests for an hour a day.

**C** Circle the correct option (a–d) to complete the sentences from a short text about air travel.

**1** The development of larger planes in the 1950s and 60s ___ down the cost of air travel.

   **a** brings   **b** brought   **c** had brought   **d** is bringing

**2** This led to the business of tourism that we ___ today.

   **a** are seeing   **b** have seen   **c** see   **d** saw

**3** The relatively prosperous citizens of northern Europe ___ their holidays within their own country.

   **a** used to take   **b** take   **c** were taking   **d** took

**4** Now they ___ to coastal resorts in Greece and Spain.

   **a** are flying   **b** were able to fly   **c** had flown   **d** had been flying

**5** These sunny holiday destinations ___ popular for decades.

   **a** are   **b** are being   **c** used to be   **d** had been

**6** Previously, however, they ___ a long journey by road or boat, taking several days in each direction.

   **a** had required   **b** were required   **c** were requiring   **d** require

**7** This was not possible for someone with only a couple of weeks' vacation allowance. With the advent of cheaper air travel, foreign destinations ___ accessible in a way they had never been before.

   **a** become   **b** became   **c** are becoming   **d** did become

**D** Complete this paragraph about shopping, using the correct form of one of the verbs in the box. You will have to use the passive for one verb.

be   contribute   need   pose   serve   take

The changing retail landscape ¹_____ a challenge for both business leaders and city planners. Town centres ²_____ as the commercial centre of their communities. This is no longer entirely the case, and there are two main reasons. The first ³_____ the rise of the so-called superstores or big-box stores, usually grouped in retail parks on the outskirts of cities, well provided with parking but poorly served by public transport. The second is the rise of internet shopping. This can ⁴_____ the form of giant web retailers such as Amazon and eBay, or the online presence of long-standing retail chains, or the digitization of content such that no physical product ⁵_____ , and hence no physical shop either. Both these long-term trends, to big out-of-town stores, and to internet shopping, ⁶_____ to the decline of the town centre.

**E** Correct the mistakes in the verb forms. There is one mistake in each numbered section.

1 'There are fewer wheelbarrows waiting to be invented.' This contention appears in a millennial essay on 'The road to riches', which was seeking to develop an explanation for the astonishing rise in living standards in the West over the past couple of centuries.

2 Why did *The Economist*'s anonymous writers choose the wheelbarrow as their exemplar of progress? Because it had transformed construction.

3 The pyramids of Egypt are built without them; nineteenth-century skyscrapers could not have been.

4 A corollary of this argument will be that the pace of technological innovation is bound to slow down, instead of, as was previously assumed, endlessly increasing.

5 Scientific discoveries are likely to continue indefinitely, subject to funding. If blue-sky research is curtailed in one area, for example genetics in the United States, it is going to be certain to migrate to another.

6 Technology, on the other hand, encounters, or is about to encounter, a ceiling, according to this argument.

7 The practical, tangible innovations that have lifted much of humanity from poverty to affluence, from subsistence agriculture through the Industrial Revolution to, in many countries, service-based economies – these innovations were already invented.

8 There will be no more significant, radical new inventions that transform an industry. Instead, gradual and incremental improvements would be the path of the future.

9 The counter-arguments to this are twofold. Firstly, it can be argued that we were not capable of knowing what has not yet been invented.

10 Before the wheelbarrow exists, no one felt the need for one. There may be plenty more such devices waiting in the wings. There is no shortage of intelligent, ingenious people eager to make their mark as inventors.

11 The second argument is pointing to entirely new areas of human activity, for example in personalized medicine and in human–machine interaction.

12 The future may see scientists inventing things we cannot yet imagine. Instead of wheelbarrows – sturdy objects that anyone can use and understand – our future inventors may have been working at a microscopic, or indeed molecular, level.

**F** Complete the text with the correct form of the verb in brackets.

The inter-relationship between diabetes and obesity ¹_____ (be) for some time a matter of interest to researchers and clinicians. The case of the Pima Indians is one that continues ²_____ (be) much studied. They are a group of Native Americans who ³_____ (live) for thousands of years in what is now the southwestern United States and northern Mexico. Their traditional economy was based for the most part on subsistence agriculture, and they ⁴_____ (endure) periods of famine as well as plenty. In the twentieth century, the way of life ⁵_____ (change) dramatically in the former country, but not so much in the isolated rural areas of the latter. By 2000, the American Pima ⁶_____ (become) obese, and ⁷_____ (develop) one of the highest rates of diabetes in the world. However, their Mexican cousins do not suffer these problems to nearly the same extent.

**G** Circle the correct option.

The situation is as close to a scientific experiment as it ¹*is/ will be* possible to find in the field, that is, without direct and deliberate intervention. The American and the Mexican Pima ²*share/are sharing* essentially the same genotype, and until a few generations ago they also ³*shared/were sharing* the same phenotype. In other words, although they ⁴*have/ would have* very similar genetic make-up, the two groups, which once had the same body shape, now ⁵*will look/look* different and ⁶*will suffer/suffer* different health problems. This genotype-phenotype distinction is a fundamental one for any study of genetics.

Neel (1962) proposed that the predisposition towards diabetes ⁷*will be caused/ is caused* by what he called a 'thrifty gene', one that ⁸*has enabled/enables* the body to store fat when food is plentiful, in preparation for the famine that ⁹*will lie/lies* around the corner. This theory has undergone modification in the past half-century. Barker's hypothesis (1997) posits a 'thrifty phenotype': if a pregnant woman is starved of nutrients, her baby ¹⁰*is/will be* born small, and is likely to develop certain diseases later in life. The growing foetus is prepared for a life in which famine ¹¹*is/is going to be* likely. In reality, of course, famine ¹²*has been/is* increasingly unlikely for most citizens in most countries today. We suffer from the opposite problem, overnutrition. Our biology, which ¹³*had evolved/evolves* in slow tiny steps, has not kept pace with the rapid changes in the way we live, and one consequence ¹⁴*had been/is* the epidemic of diseases of affluence, notably obesity and diabetes.

**H** Write 100–200 words about the past, present, and future of the place you come from (village, city, or country).

**AWL GLOSSARY**

**intervention** the act or process of becoming involved in a situation in order to improve or help it

**similar** like somebody/ something but not exactly the same

**distinction** a clear difference or contrast especially between people or things that are similar or related

**fundamental** serious and very important

**undergo** to experience something, especially a change

**modification** the act or process of changing something in order to improve it or make it more acceptable

**evolve** to develop gradually, especially from a simple to a more complicated form

# 02 Comparing and contrasting

## Introduction

Sometimes the only way to show that you really understand something is to compare it with something else. This is why 'compare and contrast' essays are so popular with tutors and examiners.

- *How does the 1978 remake of the* Invasion of the Body Snatchers *differ in its directorial style from the original 1956 film?*
- *Compare the psychological impulses that underpin anorexia nervosa and bulimia.*
- *Contrast, with examples, the situations that produce bear and bull markets.*

In answering this type of essay question you will need to express similarity and difference in a variety of ways, using the following.

**1** Adjectives and adverbs, particularly structures with *(not) as … as, too, enough*, and in the comparative and superlative forms.
- *Adolescents may think that other people will like them* **better** *if they are thinner.*

**2** Modifiers with adjectives and adverbs.
- *Stock prices need to be* **at least** *20% lower for a period of two months for a bear market to be declared.*

**3** Words and phrases for expressing similarity and contrast, such as *like, similarly, unlike, in contrast to.*
- *Kaufman's camera in the later film seems to prowl the streets* **like** *an animal seeking its prey.*

> Identify the key words in the text that enable the writer to make comparisons. Then make notes in two columns showing what ideas or things are actually being compared.

| cookery programmes on TV now | cookery programmes on TV before |
|---|---|
|  |  |

Home cooking in the UK, despite the fact that there are more cookery programmes on television than ever before, is in a long slow decline. While the freshest items in the supermarket remain on the shelves, sales of prepared meals are booming. Without doubt, it is not as easy to cook from a recipe as it is to place a cook-chill meal in the microwave, but is this the only reason why the ready-to-cook section of the supermarket is becoming its single biggest area? In this essay, I will explore the cultural values of two countries where, unlike the UK, home cooking seems to have retained its appeal, and try to understand firstly what they have in common, and secondly, how they differ from the UK.

Suggested answers: see page 190

See also unit *6 Stating facts and opinions* and unit *7 Connectors* for expressing contrast and additional information.

## 2.1 Comparative and superlative adjectives and adverbs

### 2.1 study

Here is a brief reminder of how comparative and superlative forms are made.

One-syllable adjectives and adverbs, and two-syllable adjectives ending in -ow, -le and -er normally add -er to form the comparative and -est to form the superlative.

adjectives:

high → higher → highest
narrow → narrower → narrowest
gentle → gentler → gentlest
clever → cleverer → cleverest

adverbs:

soon → sooner → soonest
fast → faster → fastest
hard → harder → hardest

Two-syllable adverbs and adjectives ending in -ing, -ful, -ed, and -less, and longer adverbs and adjectives normally use more/most or less/least:

adjectives:

boring → more/less boring → most/least boring
careful → more/less careful → most/least careful
talented → more/less talented → most/least talented
ruthless → more/less ruthless → most/least ruthless
spectacular → more/less spectacular → most/least spectacular

adverbs:

regularly → more/less regularly → most/least regularly
seriously → more seriously → most seriously
reliably → more reliably → most reliably

But remember the following.

1 Adjectives ending with a single vowel + single consonant double the consonant and a final y becomes i.

big → bigger → biggest
thin → thinner → thinnest
noisy → noisier → noisiest
happy → happier → happiest

2 There are some exceptions (irregular forms).

good (adj.)/well (adv.) → better → best
bad (adj.)/badly (adv.) → worse → worst
far → further → furthest (farther/farthest is possible but less common)

3 Some adjectives use -er or more/most (both are correct).

common → commoner/more common → commonest/most common

4 Some adjectives and adverbs such as early, hard and late share the same forms.

### 2.1 test yourself

**A Write the comparative and superlative forms. Use more/most where necessary.**
1 hot _____ _____
2 complex _____ _____
3 far _____ _____
4 helpful _____ _____
5 simple _____ _____
6 optimistic _____ _____
7 lucky _____ _____

**B Now do the same for these adverbs.**
1 late _____ _____
2 badly _____ _____
3 realistically _____ _____
4 well _____ _____

## 2.2 Comparisons with adjectives and adverbs

### 2.2 study

The following structures use adjectives and adverbs in their basic form (not in the comparative or superlative form).

1 *As* + adjective/adverb + *as*

- *The World Health Organization has suggested that sunbeds can be **as lethal as** cigarette smoking.*
- *Some researchers have argued that biodiesel does not work **as efficiently as** regular diesel.*

A structure that places an adjective + a/an + noun between as and as is also possible.
- *It was not **as effective a law as** the government had hoped. (= The law was not as effective as the government had hoped.)*
- *Alexander argues that Churchill was not always **as optimistic a leader as** he has been portrayed.*

**2** *Too* + adjective (+ *for someone*) + infinitive with *to*

- *The conditions of the contract proved **too difficult to fulfil**.*
- *Stevens argues that it is **too simplistic for critics to state** that modernism in art was a reaction to realism.*

**3** Adjective + *enough* (+ *for someone*) + infinitive with *to*

- *The proposed changes to the layout of the factory were **easy enough (for the owners) to implement** without causing any significant delays in production.*

---

## 2.2 test yourself

Rewrite the sentences using the word(s) in brackets.

1 The water in Tank A is cloudier than the water in Tank B. (not as)
2 Howton argues that basic products are often cheaper in big cities than in towns. (not as)
3 Changes in microclimates frequently occur so quickly that one cannot predict them. (too)
4 Excel plc did not return a profit last year because they exported so few of their helicopters. (enough)
5 French and English are equally difficult to learn. (as)
6 Some of the roads in this region are very dangerous, and you must not travel on them. (too)
7 The formula was not as complex as most mathematicians had expected. (It was not …)
8 Campbell's *Bluebird* was so fast it broke the water speed record several times. (enough)

---

## 2.3 Comparisons with comparative adjectives and adverbs

### 2.3 study

The following structures use comparative adjectives and adverbs.

**1** Comparative adjective/adverb + *than*

Note, in the examples below, that the verb phrases in brackets are often left out because they are 'understood', and it helps to keep the sentences short.

- *Manufacturing productivity is **lower** in the UK **than** (it is) in France and Germany.*

- *Benson International are failing because they market their products **less successfully than** their competitors (do).*
- *Researchers were looking for figures on homelessness that were **more precise than** the current estimates (are).*

**TIP** It is often possible to present the same information using either a comparative adjective/adverb + *than*, or *not as* + adjective/adverb + *as*.
- *Employment figures are **higher** in Spain **than** (they are) in Portugal. = Employment figures are **not as high** in Portugal **as** (they are) in Spain.*

**2** 'Double' comparatives

You can use -*er* and -*er*, *more and more* or *less and less* to intensify adjectives and adverbs.
- *Joseph points out how motorists under stress tend to drive **faster and faster**.*
- *In the last ten years the market in mobile phones has become **more and more** competitive.*

**3** *The* + comparative …, *the* + comparative

This pattern, in which *the more* or *the less* are sometimes used on their own, can be used to show how situations, patterns of behaviour, etc. may be linked to each other.
- ***The longer** (that) a company has traded, **the more** the public tends to trust it.*
- *It may not always be true that **the harder** athletes train, **the better** they perform.*
- ***The riskier** an investment, **the less suitable** it is for the first-time buyer of stocks or shares.*

**TIP** You can compare something with people's expectations or with the past.
- *Professor Foster concluded that the tests were not as rigorous as they could have been.*
- *The task of selecting a new CEO proved to be more time-consuming than the board had thought.*
- *Skincare products for men are selling much faster than before, as the male population responds to the use of role models in advertising.*

## 2.3 test yourself

Rewrite the sentences using the word(s) in brackets.

1 Critics have complained that school exams are not as difficult as they used to be. (than)
2 As an institution gets closer to a financial crisis, it feels the pain more. (the more)
3 Campaigners hoping for change within the country have become increasingly pessimistic. (and more)
4 The Swiss wind turbines have not worked as efficiently as the Italian ones. (The Swiss ... than)
5 The particles become easier to observe when they gain weight. (The heavier ...)
6 Introverts do not absorb information as quickly as extroverts, according to research. (Introverts ... than)

## 2.4 Comparisons with superlative adjectives and adverbs

### 2.4 study

*The* + superlative adjective/adverb is used to rank things, people, or places in a group of three or more.
• *The turnout for the referendum on the euro was* **the lowest** *ever recorded. (= the lowest of all turnouts)*

A possessive noun/pronoun sometimes replaces *the*.
• *Eurobank's dynamic new CEO, Carol Midgely, is* **their strongest** *asset.*

*The* can be left out before a superlative adverb or when a superlative adjective comes after the noun it refers to.
• *Midgely will now focus on the sectors of the company where it is growing (the) least quickly.*
• *Which department is (the) most productive?*

When present and past participles act as adjectives, they can follow superlatives.
• **The earliest recorded** *evidence of an earthquake was traced back to 1831 BC in eastern China.*
• *The mobile phone company O2 claimed that the Apple iPhone was* **its fastest selling** *product of all time.*

You can use *second, third, fourth* (not *first*) before superlatives.
• *The pronghorn antelope is considered to be the world's* **second** *fastest animal, after the cheetah.*

Note that superlatives are normally followed by:

1 *of* before periods of time, and for specifying the group of things being compared
• *According to folklore, 12 January, St Hilary's Day, is the coldest day* **of the year** *in the UK.*
• *ExxonMobil is the most profitable* **of the multinational corporations** *listed by Forbes.*

2 *in* before singular group nouns (e.g. *the class, the team, the family*)
• *Dr Parr is the most experienced person* **in the team.**

3 *in* or *on* as appropriate (not *of*) before words describing places or areas, i.e. *in the world, in the UK, in the east, on the coast, on the river,* etc.
• *The driest place* **in the world** *is in Antarctica in an area called the Dry Valleys, which has seen no rain for nearly two million years.*
• *The Preluna Hotel is the tallest building* **on the seafront** *at Sliema in Malta.*

TIP In formal contexts the superlative (without *the*) may simply mean 'very'.
• *The conclusion of the study was most surprising.*

### 2.4 test yourself

A Write out the parts of the sentences in italics, replacing the adjectives or adverbs with superlative forms, and adding the correct prepositions where necessary.

1 According to Ito (2012), the Rongai is *easy/the many routes* to the summit of Mount Kilimanjaro.
2 Ürümqi in western China is generally accepted to be *far city/the planet* from the sea.
3 In 2009, film critic Peter Ride nominated 'Mulholland Drive' (2001) as *good film/the decade.*
4 The team that completed the task *efficiently* was found to have pooled its resources at every stage of the process.
5 Carroll (2011) argues that the Bank of Montreal is now one of *socially responsible companies/Canada.*
6 An autocratic approach is criticized by Benn (2008) as being *effective/all leadership styles.*
7 Even *carefully planned/expedition* can encounter a sudden change in weather conditions.
8 Rat snakes are believed by some experts to be *high climbing snakes/North America.*

**B Complete the sentences, using one word in each space.**

1 Jeanne Calment, who died at the age of 122, has been verified as the world's _____ person.

2 At the Vaio X's launch in 2009, Sony claimed that it was the world's _____ laptop, weighing only 655g.

3 Of the three sections reviewed, marketing was performing _____ efficiently, and required an action plan to improve it.

4 Osaka is _____'s third largest city by population after Tokyo and Yokohama.

5 Mongolia, with only 1.8 people per square kilometre, is the _____ densely-_____ country _____ Earth.

6 Iceland's Althingi has _____ strongest claim to be the _____ ancient _____ the world's parliaments.

7 With an average rainfall of 211 mm, July is _____ _____ month _____ New Delhi.

8 Tokyo takes the top position, but immediately afterwards, with a modest lunch costing as much as $43, Oslo is now _____ _____ _____ expensive city _____ the planet, according to ECA rankings.

## 2.5 Modifying adjectives and adverbs

### 2.5 study

Comparative adjectives and adverbs are sometimes modified (i.e. made stronger, weaker, or more precise).

- *Start-up companies face certain difficulties, but while some of these are similar across all industries, others hit manufacturing businesses **much harder** than service enterprises.*

1 Words or phrases that modify *as … as …* structures include *just* (emphasizes the equality); *almost/ nearly*; *not quite* or its opposite *not nearly*; *twice, three times, four times*, etc.
- *Writing a good report can take **almost as long as** carrying out the market research itself.*
- *Vitrack, though successful, is **not quite as profitable** a company as its competitors.* (= Vitrack is slightly less profitable than its competitors)

- *Building costs under the new designs are **not nearly as high** (as under the old designs).* (= the costs are much lower)
- *With some modifications to the operating theatre, procedures could be carried out **twice as quickly** (as before).*

2 Words or phrases that modify structures with *than* include *much, a great deal, far, considerably*, etc., or their opposites *slightly, a little, marginally*, etc.
- *Significantly, it became **far easier** to obtain credit in the 1990s (than it was before).*
- *Swanson plc is **marginally more successful** in the hi-tech sector than its competitors.*

You can also use *three times, four times*, etc. and percentages (but note that we would normally say *twice as heavy as* rather than *two times heavier than*).
- *Steel is **three times heavier** than aluminium.*
- *Growth is expected to be **0.5% higher** in this quarter (than the last).*

**TIP** You can modify *twice, three times*, etc. themselves with words and phrases such as *nearly, more than, slightly more than, exactly*, or *approximately*.
- ***Exactly twice as many patients** were treated in the same period last year (as this year).*
- *Experts believe that the meteor entering the Earth's atmosphere was moving **more than three times faster** than was predicted last week.*

3 To modify superlatives, you can use *one of, almost/ nearly, by far*, or *easily*.
- *The Niger is **one of** Africa's longest rivers.*
- *Arctic sea ice melted at **almost** its fastest pace in 2010.*
- *Bob Hawke is **by far** the longest-serving Labor Prime Minister in Australia.*

## 2.5 test yourself

**Circle the correct option.**

1 The number of holidays taken abroad by UK citizens was more/22%/nearly lower than last year.

2 Private companies are twice/considerably/just more common in the UK than public ones.

3 Despite outperforming all of its competitors in tests, the Samson desktop publishing system is a little/not quite/almost the cheapest available.

4 It is an axiom in business that customers are not nearly/by far/a great deal as interested in describing good experiences as bad ones.

5 With their moveable thumbs, chimpanzees are exactly/just/slightly as capable of grasping objects as humans.

6 The traditional Mediterranean diet is one of/far/twice the healthiest in the world.

7 Observers have claimed that the Antarctic is losing ice by far/twice/a great deal as fast as ten years ago.

8 With the new software in place, companies such as Vasco plc have been able to process considerably/more/approximately twice as many claims as before.

## 2.6 Words and phrases for expressing similarity

### 2.6 study

Specific words and expressions, as well as adjectives and adverbs, can be used to compare and contrast. This section focuses on ways of saying that things are the same or similar (almost the same). (See also page 067 in unit 7 *Connectors* for more structures that express similarity, including *also*, *as well as*, *too*, and *not only ... but also*.)

### 1 (The) same

*(The) same* is frequently used to express similarity.
- *Cats and dogs have almost **the same** capacity to be domesticated.*

*As* is used as a connector.
- *The proposal from Mitchell plc is exactly **the same as** Barker's in its speed of delivery.*
- *When they are observed, people do not behave in **the same way as** they do in private.*

Note in the first two examples above how *the same* is modified by *almost* and *exactly*. Other modifiers include *just* and *precisely*.

### 2 Similar, similarity, similarly

The adjective *similar* is followed by *to* when things are linked with common features, and by *in* before describing the quality that things share.
- *Venus is quite **similar to** Earth **in** mass and size. (= Venus and Earth are quite **similar in** mass and size.)*

Other modifiers, apart from *quite* above, include *slightly*, *superficially*, *fairly*, *remarkably*, *very*, and *extremely*.

Note also that the verb *resemble* means 'is similar to' (*Venus **resembles** Earth in mass and size*), and that *in* can be replaced by *in terms of*, *as regards*, or *with respect to*.

The noun *similarity* is used with *between* to compare two things, and with *in* to describe a shared quality.
- *The main **similarity between** the Senate and the House of Representatives is that both houses are directly elected.*
- *There was a **similarity in** the approach taken to the crisis by all three companies.*

Other modifiers with *similarity*, apart from *main*, include *slight*, *superficial*, *apparent*, *distinct*, *obvious*, *striking*.

Note how *similarity*, *similar* and the phrase *in common* can be used to express the same meaning.
- *All living organisms have several **similarities**. = All living organisms have several **similar** features. = All living organisms have several features **in common**.*

*In common with* can be used to link two or more things together.
- *According to Samuels, the European Union has a great deal **in common with** the United Nations.*

The adverb *similarly* can also be used.
- *Smog is damaging trees in the mountains of south China. **Similarly**, acid rain is harming forests in the north of the country. (or ... south China. Acid rain is **similarly** harming forests ...)*

### 3 Alike, like, likewise

*Alike* means the same as *similar*, and is normally used with the verb *be* after the things being compared.
- *France and Germany are **alike** in that both support a thriving rental sector in their housing markets.*

*Like* is also used with *be*, but between the things being compared (*France is like Germany in that ...*) and it is also used quite often on its own.

- *Dolphins, **like** porpoises, breathe through blowholes on the top of their heads.*

Modifiers with *alike* and *like* include (*very*) *much, rather, somewhat, quite,* and *a little*.

Note that *alike* is occasionally used on its own, when it cannot be modified (*Dolphins and porpoises alike breathe through ...*).

*Likewise* is used just like *similarly* (see **2** above: *Likewise, acid rain is ...*)

⌐TIP Notice how, after words such as *alike* or *different* you can sometimes use *in* + a noun phrase (*Rats and mice are **similar in** their colouring*) or *in that* + a clause (*Rats and mice are **similar in that** they are both grey or brown in colour*).

---

## 2.6 test yourself

**Complete each sentence with one of the words in the box. One word is not needed.**

> like   to   in   similarly   as   that
> similar   similarities   same

1 Indonesian and English are _____ in their word order, but the former language has no tense system.
2 The two colleges are very much alike in _____ both draw in a high proportion of international students, and focus on the subject areas of business and law.
3 Bowson Brothers, _____ Farston plc, export most of their products to Germany and France.
4 EasyJet targets exactly the same type of budget traveller _____ Ryanair.
5 Klein argues that there are distinct _____ between the working conditions in some Third World factories and those of 18th-century slave plantations.
6 Canterbury attracts tourists all year round. Bath _____ manages to maintain a significant number of visitors in summer and winter.
7 All successful leaders share some of the _____ characteristics.
8 A short sleep taken during the day is similar _____ type to non-rapid eye movement sleep at night.

---

## 2.7 Words and phrases for expressing contrast

### 2.7 study

This section focuses on ways of saying that things are different. (See also page 064 in unit 7 *Connectors* for more structures that express contrast, including *although, despite, however,* and *while/whereas*.)

**1** *Different, differ, difference*

The adjective *different* and the verb *differ* normally follow the two things being compared.

- *After working for several months with fellow chemist Stevens, Schenke took a **different** path towards their goal.*
- *The approaches taken by the two companies **are different/differ** in that Brennan and Smith offer an ecologically sustainable solution.*

Notice how *dissimilar* and *unlike* could also be used in the sentence above. (*The approaches taken by the two companies are **dissimilar/are unlike each other** in that ...*)

*Different* + *from* and *differ* + *from* are normally used between the two things being compared.

- *In law, a 'responsive' brief **is different from/differs from** an 'original' brief in that it contains arguments directly responding to positions taken by the other side.*

Note that *dissimilar* + *to* and *unlike* could also be used in the above sentence. (*In law, a 'responsive' brief is **dissimilar to/is unlike** an 'original' brief in that ...*)

*Different* can be modified by *slightly/a little, rather, very, fundamentally, completely/quite, totally,* and *differ* can be modified by placing these words afterwards: *slightly/a little, fundamentally, completely, totally*.

*Difference* is used with *between* to compare two things. *In* + noun may be added to specify the context.

- *Parker explored the key **difference between** 'leadership' and 'management' **in** a series of seminars held in New York in early 2010.*
- *New research from Brown University has identified the **difference in** chewing **between** mammals and fish.*

Note that, as well as *key* above, there are many modifiers that you can use with *difference*, including *slight, minor, considerable, major,* and *significant*.

**2** *In contrast to, contrary to, unlike*

These expressions are all used before noun phrases to point out the contrast between things.
- *An exit poll,* **in contrast to/contrary to/unlike** *an opinion poll, asks members of the public to reveal how they have just voted.*
- *In contrast to/Contrary to/Unlike earlier studies, Professor Cadogan's report found that cholesterol measured in middle or old age showed no link to dementia.*

Note that *in contrast to* and *in contrast with* are both acceptable, with no difference in meaning.

(See **1** above for another use of *unlike*.)

**3** *On the contrary, in contrast, on the other hand*

These are all linking expressions that connect contrasting statements. Note, however, that while *on the contrary* contradicts an element of the previous statement, *in contrast* and *on the other hand* link two different but true situations.
- *Selecting the right PR company is by no means easy;* **on the contrary,** *(contradicts easy) it may involve a great deal of research.*
- *The 1989 earthquake in the Santa Cruz Mountains occurred during an exceptionally dry period, preventing any large-scale landslides.* **In contrast/On the other hand,** *the great 1906 earthquake occurred after an unusually wet winter.*

## 2.7 test yourself

**Correct the incorrect sentences. Some sentences are already correct.**

1 Swans, in contrast to many other species of bird, appear to mate for life.
2 The climate on the coast differs the humid interior in that it is often pleasantly cool and windy.
3 Gregory asserts that shale gas is not an energy solution to be welcomed. On the other hand, he argues, its environmental impact is likely to be devastating.
4 Contrary to northern hemisphere countries with their September start, the academic year in the southern hemisphere normally begins in January or February.
5 A significant political difference from the USA and the UK is that the former has a written constitution.
6 Some politicians support spending cuts as a means of reducing the deficit; on the contrary, others argue for a rise in personal taxation, particularly for wealthier citizens.
7 Steyn concludes that Japanese and British tourists have different expectations while on holiday.
8 Having a job at university provides a useful source of income; on the other hand, it can make life difficult when academic deadlines are imminent.

# 02 Challenge yourself

**A** Complete the text about a new factory with the comparative or superlative form of the word in brackets.

The opening of the new factory, fitted with [1]_____ (up-to-date) equipment in the industry, meant that Ginnorex plc could produce [2]_____ (high) quality goods than its competitors. The premises were located at a motorway intersection, ensuring [3]_____ (fast) delivery times for the finished products, compared to the old suburban factory. Along with the building, Ginnorex invested in IT, for a [4]_____ (integrated) supply chain. These strategic decisions led to increased customer satisfaction; soon, the company was [5]_____ (profitable) than ever before. In addition, the staff were [6]_____ (happy) with their [7]_____ (comfortable) working environment, so employee absenteeism became [8]_____ (problematic).The HR department noted that staff turnover was [9]_____ (low) in the city, when compared with other factories of a similar size. Last year, Ginnorex won an award for being [10]_____ (good) local employer.

**B** Correct the seven mistakes in the text about the Olympic Games. Some sentences are correct.

[1]The Olympics are sometimes described as a greatest show on earth. [2]The Summer Games are certainly the biggest event of the world in terms of the number of athletes involved. [3]However, most spectators do not realize that the so-called 'Olympic family' consists of many more people than just the competitors. [4]In fact, there are many more coaches, national officials, sports journalists, and other accredited personnel as athletes. [5]The Olympics usually end up being one of the most expensive shows on earth, as well. [6]The most popular sports differ than one host country to another; ice hockey is a major game in Canada but not in Brazil, for example. [7]The tickets that are the hardest to get are almost always for the opening and closing ceremonies. [8]The Paralympics, on other hand, until recently were not nearly as higher profile as the Olympics themselves. [9]It used to be easier enough to get tickets to the major Paralympic events. [10]Now, however, the Paralympics have become too popular to guarantee seats for all their fans.

**AWL GLOSSARY**

**equipment** the things that are needed for a particular purpose or activity

**locate** to find the exact position of something

**strategic** done as part of a plan that is meant to achieve a particular purpose or to gain an advantage

**environment** the conditions that affect the behaviour and development of somebody/something; the physical conditions that somebody/something exists in

**C** 🗣 Complete the transcript of a presentation about economic difficultie[s] using the phrases in the box.

almost twice as heavy    fast as    the highest    the best    the sooner, th[e]
in contrast to    three times heavier    nearest    unlike    like    stronger
its worst    highest    more and more    the strongest    by far the longes[t]

Let me begin my talk by saying that this country is in ¹_____
economic situation for a generation. That is the reality. We are enterin[g]
sixth consecutive quarter of negative growth, ²_____ p[__]
recession in the working lives of most of you in this room. ³_____
businesses are going bankrupt. Only yesterday, one of our ⁴_____
and best-loved retail chains went into receivership. Unemployment is
⁵_____ level since the Great Depression of the 1930s. So far the
authorities have declined to take strong action. We need ⁶_____
government, and it must take ⁷_____ possible action.
⁸_____ some of the pessimistic views you heard earlier,
I believe that change is possible. ⁹_____ everyone here,
I deplore the excessive salaries and bonuses of the bankers and the boardroom
elite. ¹⁰_____ paid – those whom society has rewarded the
most richly – must bear their share of the responsibility. However,
¹¹_____ many of you, I think the answer lies with less tax,
not more regulation. Our tax burden is ¹²_____ as our
¹³_____ neighbours, and ¹⁴_____
than some of the newly emerging economies that we are trying to compete with.
¹⁵_____ way forward – the simplest solution – is to unshackle
business, and let the economy grow as ¹⁶_____ it can. And I say,
¹⁷_____ !

**D** Circle the correct options in the text. More than one option may be correct.

Microsoft is ¹*one of/by far* the world's biggest software companies, and its
well-established operating system, Windows, is ²*easily/a great deal/by far* the
most widespread, according to Bernard-Jones (2010). ³*Alike/Likewise/Similarly*,
industry statistics show that its Office suite of products is used by ⁴*many/
much/twice* more people than any other competing product. Microsoft bundled
its web browser, Internet Explorer, with Windows, a practice which proved
⁵*too controversial/controversial enough* to trigger an anti-monopoly court case.
The original judgement required Microsoft to break into two smaller companies,
but a higher court overturned this ruling on appeal.

The position of Internet Explorer following the second round of the browser
wars, circa 2006–2007, demonstrates how it is no longer as influential ⁶*a product
as before/product as it was/a product as it was*. Harperson (2009) argues that
many unsophisticated computer users acted as though IE was the only browser,
especially prior to the middle of that decade. ⁷*On the other hand/On the contrary*,
there are several options. The second ⁸*much/most/more* popular browser after IE
is Firefox, an open-source alternative. (This means that the underlying software
code uses a licence that permits anyone to examine and develop it; this is ⁹*unlike/
dissimilar* to proprietary software where the copyright holder has exclusive legal
rights.) Google brought out Chrome in 2008, claiming that the new product
differed ¹⁰*to/from* other browsers in that it was both faster and more secure.
The dominance once enjoyed by Microsoft is, it seems, less and less apparent.

---

**E** 🗣 Complete the words [...]
students are talking a[bout ...]

Alain    I think [...]
         tha[...]
Maria    ²[...]

[...] or an org[...]
who have the power to
make decisions or who
have a particular area
of responsibility in a
country or region

**decline** to refuse
politely to accept or do
something

**emerge** to start to exist;
to appear or become
known

**AWL GLOSSARY**

**widespread** existing
over a large area or
among many people

**trigger** to make
something happen
suddenly

**underlying** existing
under the surface of
something else

**exclusive** only to be
used by one particular
person or group; only
given to one particular
person or group

**apparent** easy to see
or understand

...it's much [1]e_____ to learn a language as a child
... as an adult. Babies learn languages without any effort, but the
..._____ you get, the [3]m_____ you struggle.
I know what you mean, but look at it this way: babies, [4]u_____
adults, only have to learn to how to speak; they don't have to worry about
reading and writing!

**Alain** Yes, but it's [5]e_____ the same with children studying a second
language at school. They pick up the basics of a new language
[6]m_____ more [7]q_____ than adults do. And the
[8]y_____ they are, the easier it is for them.

**Maria** My own experience is [9]q_____ different [10]f_____
yours, I'm afraid! Children may be [11]b_____ than adults
at pronunciation, but they're not always very motivated at school,
are they? I took English classes all through high school, but it wasn't
[12]n_____ as useful as the time I spent working at my aunt's
hotel in the summer. Every day I could understand a little more than
[13]b_____, and I got [14]m_____ and [15]m_____
confident the [16]l_____ I worked there. By the time I went back
to school, I was [17]e_____ the [18]b_____ in the class.

**F** Correct the description of a corporate headquarters by adding one word to
each sentence.

[1]British Airways, in common many other large international companies, invested
in prestigious, purpose-built headquarters. [2]The Waterside complex, near
Heathrow Airport, is in many respects similar other corporate centres. [3]Its steel
and glass office buildings, for example, look virtually the same hundreds of
others throughout the world. [4]The noticeable innovation is The Street, the long,
covered space that all six office blocks open onto, which includes a supermarket,
a hairdresser's, and a gym. [5]All employees, from the most highly paid senior
managers to most junior clerical workers, share these facilities.

[6]BA commissioned Waterside in tandem with a business re-design process, with
the aim of making working life more efficient it was in its previous headquarters.
[7]The company wanted to use space than it had in its old offices, partly in order
to save money. [8]At the same time, it wanted to find ways to work effectively.
[9]One step was to persuade employees to accept hot-desking, in contrast the
previous system of fixed work stations. [10]One of biggest changes was to remove
the space allocated to archives, first by moving the paper storage offsite, and
then by digitizing all the records.

**AWL GLOSSARY**

**invest** to spend money
on something in order to
make it better or more
successful

**facilities** buildings,
services, equipment,
etc. that are provided for
a particular purpose

**commission** to officially
ask somebody to
write, make, or create
something

**previous** happening or
existing before the event
or object that you are
talking about

**remove** to take
something away from
a place

**allocate** to give
something officially
to something for a
particular purpose

**G** Put the words in italics in the correct order to complete the text about London and New York.

London and New York [1]*common have in much*, in that they are world leaders in the fields of art, design, fashion, music, and much else. Indeed, [2]*are between similarities there obvious* these two cities. However, [3]*difference is there one significant*: London is a political capital, whereas New York is not. Both, of course, are commercial, financial, and retail capitals. [4]*The UK's city London is most populous*; similarly, New York holds that position in the United States ([5]*alike although exactly is not situation the*, given the different legal status of suburbs in each country). There is, finally, [6]*in similarity a striking* the ability of these two cities to attract tourists in every season of the year.

**H** Rewrite the phrases in italics, using the words in brackets, to complete the text about film remakes.

There can be several reasons for remaking an earlier film. Firstly, a director or producer may believe that the central idea of the original film [1]*is so strong that it will draw in* (enough) a new generation of cinema-goers. Secondly, a production company might decide that though the source film was interesting in some way, [2]*it was not realized as successfully as it could have been* (more). A further reason might be that the first film, because of the contemporary censorship laws, [3]*was cautious and did not do justice to its theme* (too). Similarly, it might be that, in terms of creating special effects, [4]technology *today is more advanced than it was at the time of the source film* (not as … as). In both these last two cases, it could be argued that the 'real' film was waiting to be made. In the end, of course, whether [5]*the new version resembles the original film* (similar) or not, the remake has to be judged on its own terms.

**I** Write two short texts (100–200 words), using the language of comparison and contrast.

**1** Compare the advantages and disadvantages for a student of doing a degree at a local college or a university in the capital city. Choose at least three factors to compare (e.g. cost, flexibility of study, quality of qualification).

**2** Compare two cities (*or* two regions of the same country *or* two countries) that you know. Make your point of view clear, whether you are considering them as a resident, a tourist, or a company considering setting up an office there.

## Introduction

The meaning of a noun can be made more precise by the words immediately before (pre-modifying words) or after it (post-modifying words). These words and the noun together are called the 'noun phrase'. Pre-modifying words can help you to describe the noun, and post-modifying words and phrases can be effective in connecting your noun to your next idea. Careful use of noun phrases is an economical way of conveying complex and detailed information.

Pre-modifying words include articles, adjectives and nouns.
- *When **a** famous actor died in 2009, **a** junior reporter was asked to prepare his obituary. Unfortunately, **the** journalist took all her information from **a** page of Wikipedia that contained several serious errors.*
- *In this paper, we propose a **task-driven** approach to software design.*
- *A single case of food poisoning can sometimes produce a regional **health** scare.*

Post-modifying structures include prepositional phrases and noun clauses.
- *An investigation **into the relationship between politicians and the press** is urgently required, in the view of backbench MP Tom Watson.*
- *The argument **that early exposure to alcoholic drinks in young people can be beneficial** comes under attack in a study published by the Drink Awareness Campaign in 2010.*

Note that relative clauses also act as post-modifying structures (see unit *5 Relative clauses*).

> **Read the text, then try to answer the questions.**
> 1 What is the general function of the underlined words and phrases that come before and after the nouns in bold?
> 2 How do the underlined words that come before the bold nouns differ from one another grammatically?

One **cause** <u>of the economic troubles</u> is the 'tsunami effect', which does not refer to a literal tsunami, but rather to the <u>metaphorical</u> **ripples** and shockwaves of the highly <u>globalized</u> **economy**. <u>Resource</u> **extraction** and the **manufacture** <u>of commodities</u> are activities carried out on a worldwide scale: a problem anywhere along the <u>production</u> **line**, from freak weather to bad harvests to **the blockage** <u>of a shipping channel</u>, can cause extensive <u>economic</u> **disruption**.

Suggested answers: see page 192

See also unit *19 Collocation* for selected adjective + noun, and noun + noun collocations (page 169).

## 3.1 Articles

### 3.1 study

#### 1 Articles in general

As the description implies, the indefinite articles *a* and *an* are used to introduce a general idea or to refer to an indefinite example of something, whereas the definite article *the* is used to refer to a definite thing, either when there is only one in existence or when the reader or listener knows which specific thing we are referring to.

• *A new committee is to be set up by **the** government to consider press regulation.*

Particular uses of *a/an* and *the* (or no article) to be aware of are:

**a** geographical names (e.g. countries, mountains, rivers etc.), which need to be learned

**b** expressions such as *miles an hour, times a day/week/month,* etc.

**c** means of transport (*by car/train,* etc.)

**d** places used in a general sense (*the number of people at work or at university*)

**e** *the government, the police, the media, the Italians, the rich* (but *rich people*), etc.

**f** dictionary definitions and generalizations (*a/the bear is an animal that ..., bears are animals that ...*).

(See page 162 in unit *18 Using defining language* for more examples of definitions.)

#### 2 Articles with uncountable nouns

A number of common nouns such as *water, money, information* are described as 'uncountable' because they have no plural form. We can't normally use *a/an* with these nouns or add *-s* to them: ~~an~~ equipment, some advice~~s~~.

**TIP** There is a group of uncountable nouns which already end in *s* and are followed by singular verbs (*news, politics, diabetes, genetics, athletics, mathematics, statistics, linguistics, economics*).
• *Before the era of the 'career politician', **politics was seen** as a profession to enter once you had already followed another form of employment for a number of years.*

Some nouns which are usually uncountable can be countable when used with a different and more specific meaning.

• *Relevant experience is normally required for most jobs.* BUT
*The Roper Poll of 2002 suggested that 14% of Americans had had or knew of someone who had had **an experience** of UFO activity. (an experience = an incident in one's life)*

• *Success in business requires a measure of luck as well as aptitude and hard work.* BUT
*Before becoming CEO of Paige plc, Susan Butterworth owned **a small business** in New Mexico. (a business = a company)*

• *As well as offering a financial reward, work provides an individual with a level of self-esteem.* BUT
*The quality of **a work** should be measured by its beauty or ability to provoke thought rather than its market value. (a work = a work of art such as a play or painting)*

Note that uncountable nouns can be 'counted' or 'separated' by general words and phrases such as *a piece of* (*a piece of evidence/advice*) and *an item of* (*an item of information/clothing*) or specific nouns, (*a **grain** of rice, a **strip** of metal, a **strand** of hair, a **means** of transport*).

• *A conference normally takes place in the newsroom to decide which **item of news** will lead the evening broadcast.*

### 3.1 test yourself

**Correct the articles. Some sentences are already correct.**

1 Google originated in the research project by Larry Page and Sergey Brin.
2 A marsupial is a mammal, such as a kangaroo, that is carried after birth in a pouch on the mother's belly.
3 A good advice for anyone planning to rent a property is to read the tenancy agreement carefully.
4 James Dyson opened a factory and a research centre in Wiltshire in 1993. A factory produced the first dual cyclone vacuum cleaner.
5 Insufficient capital is a common reason for a business to fail.
6 Throughout the 1980s, Marston carried out important research into dying languages.
7 The number of patients in the hospital in the UK has risen once again.
8 The Millennium Bridge across Thames was closed for two years while modifications were made to its structure.

## 3.2 Quantifiers

### 3.2 study

Quantifiers (e.g. *all*, *many*, *some*) describe nouns in terms of quantity. When used with definite noun phrases (e.g. *the answers*) they are normally followed by *of* (*some of the* answers). In this section, they are divided into three groups: the most inclusive (*all*, etc.); large and smaller quantities (*many*, *some*, etc.); and words that are often used negatively (*any*, *neither*, etc.).

**1** *All, both, each, every*

*All* is used with countable and uncountable nouns; *both* is used with plural uncountable nouns. In definite noun phrases, *of* is sometimes left out after *all*, and *the* may be omitted before numbers; with *both*, *of* and *the* may be left out.

- The Labour Party majority was reduced each time in **all** three (of the) elections that Tony Blair won.
- **Both** (of the) bills were defeated by a large majority.

*Each* and *every* refer to individual members of a group and are used with singular countable nouns. *Each* tends to focus on the individual thing in a group; *every* emphasizes the individual as a member of a group or series. In the phrase *each/every one of*, *one* can be left out after *each*.

- **Each** (one) of the symphony's movements depicts a different season in the year. (*Each* because of the focus on separate parts.)
- **Every** student passed the final examination after following this method. (*Every* because of a focus on *all*.)

⌐TIP *Every* can be used with a plural period of time to describe how often something happens.
- The Olympics take place **every four years.**
- Health and safety checks are carried out **every six months.**

**2** *Many, much, some, few, little, enough*

*Many* is used with plural countable nouns and *much* with uncountable nouns. In informal and spoken English they tend to be used only in questions and negative structures, and even in formal writing *much* is often replaced by *a great deal of* or *plenty of* in positive statements (unless it is used with *so*, *too*, or *as*).

- 💬 The artefacts discovered by Howard Carter and his team were able to provide scholars with ~~much~~ **a great deal of** information on the practices of royal burial.

*Some* combines with uncountable and plural countable nouns to indicate a moderate amount or number (*some information, some board members*). In academic English you can use it to suggest a contrast in opinion, and to mean 'approximately' before a number, percentage, etc. In the latter case, it can suggest a figure higher than was expected.

- **Some** psychologists have argued that happiness is governed by factors outside our control. (The implication is that there are other psychologists who take a different view.)
- Cleveland plc now export their weighing machines to **some** twenty countries. (The implication is that this is an achievement.)

*A few* (with countable nouns) and *a little* (with uncountable nouns) have a similar meaning to *some*, whereas *few* and *little* without the indefinite article mean 'not many'.

- **Few** critics were impressed by the staging of the opera, and this was reflected in the following day's reviews.

You can use *enough* before countable and uncountable nouns. It can be modified with *just, more than, (not) nearly*, and *quite*.

- Some commentators believe that there have been **more than enough** opportunities for parliament to debate the death penalty, without introducing a new bill.

(See page 017 in unit *2 Comparing and contrasting* for the use of *more, most, less* and *least* in comparisons.)

**3** *Any, either, neither, no, none*

As well as being used in questions and negative structures, *any* can suggest 'if there is any' or 'it doesn't matter which' in positive sentences with countable or uncountable nouns.

- **Any** opposition to the new water scheme is likely to come from local farmers who have traditionally taken as much water as they like from the reservoir.
- **Any** medicine taken in a very high dosage is likely to have side effects.

In noun phrases, *either* and *neither* are used with singular nouns and verbs to talk about groups of two.

- The river could be dammed or diverted, but **neither** option is without its risks.
- 💬 (in a seminar) We can consider **either** of the two proposals/**either proposal** first. It doesn't matter.

You can use *no* in a noun phrase as a more emphatic form of *not any*.
- *There were **no** heated arguments at the talks, but neither was there a firm agreement on the way forward.*

Note that in formal English, *none of* + plural noun is followed by a singular verb, and you can use *not one of* as a more emphatic alternative.
- ***None of/Not one of** the factories concerned has passed a full health and safety inspection.*

### 3.2 test yourself

Complete each sentence with a quantifier. In two of the sentences two quantifiers are possible.

1 Carston plc had _____ success in extending their business to the USA, and soon had to close all their branches.
2 A late surge in sales produced just _____ income for the company to survive.
3 _____ application received after the deadline will be rejected.
4 _____ of the two candidates made a opening statement before the debate took place.
5 Bywater Ltd will have _____ thirty subsidiaries worldwide after their expansion programme is complete.
6 Becoming self-employed or setting up a limited company: in theory, _____ option is open to the freelancer.
7 Some printers support automatic printing on _____ sides of the paper (known as 'duplex printing').
8 Professor Chalmers claims that a virtual reality helmet that mimics _____ five senses will be ready within five years.

## 3.3 Adjectives + nouns

### 3.3 study

Pre-modifying nouns with compound adjectives (a ***small-scale** experiment*), adverb-adjective combinations (a ***potentially irreversible** decline*) and coordinated adjectives (***strict and systematic** procedures*) are an effective way of conveying information economically, normally avoiding a relative clause.
- *The offices benefit from a **recently-installed** air-conditioning system. (= The offices benefit from an air-conditioning system that was recently installed.)*

### 1 Compound adjectives

Compound adjectives, which are usually hyphenated before nouns, can be formed in a number of ways.

ADJECTIVE + PAST/PRESENT PARTICIPLE (*ready-made, best-selling, longest-serving*)

ADJECTIVE + NOUN (*free-market, hi-tech, right-wing*)
- *The architect Mary Chang was commended for her **cutting-edge** hospice designs.*

NOUN + NOUN, ADJECTIVE OR PAST/PRESENT PARTICIPLE (*smoke-free, fuel-injected, peace-keeping*)
- ***Year-end** bonuses for bankers have become a contentious issue since the banking crisis of 2008.*
- *An element of **performance-led** pay is appropriate to some professional situations.*

PAST PARTICIPLE + ADVERB (*paid-up, screened-off, left-over*)

TIP Note the difference in meaning between adjectives such as *interested, disappointed*, and *frightened* (describing how we feel) and their counterparts ending in *-ing* (describing what makes us feel that way).
- ***Exhausting negotiations** and **tired participants** often lead to poor decisions.*

### 2 Adverb + adjective combinations

Adverbs can combine with adjectives (*highly sensitive, politically independent*); with past participles (*extensively-researched, well-planned, highly-educated*), and with present participles (*slow-moving, rapidly-growing*). The hyphen is optional, but tends to be used with the second two categories.
- *The **relatively low** cost of shale gas makes it an attractive, if controversial, alternative to traditional energy sources.*
- *A hotel in Bordeaux is significantly cheaper to run than a **comparably-sized** establishment in Paris.*

(See page 167 in unit *19 Collocation* for more adverb + adjective combinations that can be placed before nouns.)

## 3 Coordinated adjectives

Coordinated adjectives, which are linked by *and*, give two dimensions to the description of a noun. Sometimes the description is made more inclusive by mentioning opposites (*male and female, old and new, positive and negative*) and sometimes the second adjective is fairly similar to the first (*social and cultural, economic and political, safe and effective*).

- *Long-term unemployment can affect a person's **mental and physical** health.*
- *Juries in fraud cases are often presented with **complex and technical** information.*

⌐TIP If you use more than one adjective to pre-modify a noun, follow this order: opinion, size, age, shape, colour, origin, material, purpose + noun:

- *GlaxoSmithKline plc is a **global** (size) **pharmaceutical** (purpose) company headquartered in London.*

### 3.3 test yourself

**Complete each sentence with one of the words or phrases in the box.**

> -up   -divided   and private   -boosting
> -distance   -fitting   and secondary
> -renowned

1 An interesting model is one whereby public _____ TV channels must contribute a percentage of their turnover to the national film-making industry.
2 The most expensive item on show in the costume collection was a red silk dress designed by the world _____ couturier Hanae Mori.
3 Badly _____ seatbelts can be almost as dangerous as a complete absence of restraint.
4 The writer of a dissertation will normally make use of primary _____ sources in their work.
5 The argument that England is a geographically _____ country gains ground when you notice the higher unemployment figures in the north.
6 Long _____ commuting by train is much more common than it used to be in the UK.
7 Drug abuse amongst pre-teen children is a growing problem in the boarded _____ inner-city areas of some American cities.
8 Some CEOs invite senior managers to confidence _____ weekend retreats.

## 3.4 Nouns + nouns

### 3.4 study

You will be aware from everyday English of the way that a noun can pre-modify another noun by acting like an adjective (*a fur coat, a bathroom door, a horse race*). The same thing happens in academic writing, allowing for the concise expression of complex ideas. It is a technique you should consider using wherever you can.

- *Few **government measures** have raised as much **public opposition** as the poll tax of 1989. (= Few measures taken by the government have raised as much opposition from the public ...)*

You can combine nouns to suggest a variety of relationships.

**1** Source (*shale gas* = gas that comes from shale)

**2** Purpose (*defence systems* = systems that are used for defence)

**3** Specialization (*accounts manager* = a manager who is in charge of accounts)

**4** Composition (*lead walls* = walls made of lead)

**5** Content (*linguistics essay* = an essay on/about linguistics)

**6** Location (*back pain* = pain in the back)

**7** Time (*weekend job* = a job that takes place at the weekend)

(See page 169 in unit *19 Collocation* for more noun + noun combinations.)

The first noun in these combinations is normally singular (~~trains~~ *train timetable*, ~~markets~~ *market crash*), unless it is always plural (e.g. the subject *linguistics*) or generally plural (e.g. *accounts* as part of a company). Nouns that are often used in the plural include *arts* (*arts centre*), *arms* (*arms manufacturer*), and *sales* (*sales figures*).

Sometimes you can use noun + noun + noun (*school trip supervisor, police patrol car, accident research centre, government press release, business opportunities conference, inner-city drugs problem*).

There are a number of common noun + *and* + noun phrases that can act as pre-modifiers, such as *trial and error, health and safety, law and order*.

- *A **trial and error** approach is sometimes the best way forward in scientific research.*

## 3.4 test yourself

Complete each sentence with one of the words or phrases in the box.

> water   European Union member   market
> arts research   protest   cash   family
> law and

1 There are normally maximum limits on _____ withdrawals from ATMs.

2 _____ order debates in Parliament on matters such as the latest crime figures normally attract a full house.

3 _____ movements against government cutbacks are already taking place in the UK.

4 Growth in the number of Vietnam's telecom companies has been so strong that there are now indications of _____ saturation.

5 Since 2007, there have been 27 _____ states.

6 The role of the _____ doctor has been weakened by the transience of local populations.

7 _____ supplies to rural communities have been put at risk by the drought.

8 The Getty Foundation is a major source of _____ funding, particularly in the area of museums and archives.

## 3.5 Nouns + prepositional phrases

### 3.5 study

Nouns are often post-modified by prepositional phrases (phrases that begin with a preposition, e.g. *for*, *in*, or *of*).
* *Public protests can sometimes lead to a **change in** the law.*

Sometimes these phrases can be longer and more complex.
* *There is a **risk of reaching a simplistic rather than useful conclusion** if the enquiry is rushed.*

Certain nouns are followed by particular prepositions (sometimes more than one), and these patterns need to be learned. Here is a selected list of nouns and their prepositions, arranged by preposition. Nouns that are related to each other in meaning are given first in boxes as a memory aid and the other nouns follow in alphabetical order.

(See page 35 at the end of this unit for a list arranged alphabetically by noun.)

1 + *for* appetite, demand  case, motivation, reason  advertisement, application, basis (also *basis of*), need, preference, request, respect, substitute
* *In the latest poll, a majority of those taking part expressed a **preference for** the 'first past the post' electoral system.*
* *If both sides on the negotiating table are looking for a settlement, then there is normally **the basis for/of** a potentially fruitful discussion.*

2 + *in* decrease, drop, fall, reduction, increase, rise  belief, change (also *change to*), interest
* *There was a sharp **rise in** inflation in the first quarter of 2009.*
* ***Changes in/to** the way that export licences are granted are likely to be made at the end of the year.*

3 + *into* inquiry, investigation, research (also *research on/in*) insight (also *insight on*) + *into*
* ***Research into/on/in** social work practice indicates that time spent face-to-face with clients is falling significantly.*
* *Studies of chimpanzees can provide an **insight into/on** human behaviour.*

Note that we use *enquiry about* for smaller or more personal issues (*make an enquiry about the opportunities for doctoral research*).

4 + *of* analysis, examination, exploration (also *examination/exploration into*)  example, type  means, method, way  cause, cost, description, dozens, experience (also *experience in*), idea, importance, knowledge, lack/shortage, level, opinion, part, risk, study (also *study into*), victim
* *An **analysis of** the data shows which illnesses are likely to be exacerbated by stress.*
* *All of the team had previous **experience of/in** high-altitude climbing.*

Note that in **3** and **4** above, the preposition *into* can suggest a deeper analysis (*an examination of the photo*, **but** *an examination of/into the causes of the conflict*).

**5** + **on** *article, assignment, book, dissertation, essay, lecture, project, work* attack (also *attack against*), ban, emphasis, expert (also *in*), tax

- *Some commentators see a **ban on** smoking in open-air spaces such as parks as the logical next step.*

Note that *about* can follow *article, book, essay, lecture,* and *project* but sounds less precise and more informal.

**6** + **to** *approach, alternative, answer, attention, damage, introduction, response, right*

- *Protestors argue that wind farms cause visual **damage to** the environment.*
- *The **right to** silence on the part of a suspect is integral to some legal systems.*

**7** + **towards/to** *move, movement, progress* attitude

- ***Progress towards** meeting the provisions of the Kyoto agreement has been worryingly slow.*
- *Some police forces take a more lenient **attitude to/towards** the possession of 'soft' drugs for personal use.*

## 3.5 test yourself

**Complete each sentence with a preposition.**

1 There have been a number of recent articles _____ what is perceived as abnormal worldwide weather patterns.
2 As an alternative _____ conventional cars, hybrids still have a great deal to prove to the would-be consumer.
3 An investigation _____ the train crash resulted in a substantial fine for the track maintenance company.
4 James Hopper is the second CEO in recent weeks to complain about a shortage _____ young UK entrepreneurs.
5 There is no substitute _____ practical, on-the-job training.
6 A move _____ vegetarianism is particularly prevalent amongst teenagers.
7 Some victims _____ identity theft have found themselves liable for their losses through their personal behaviour.
8 There is a growing interest _____ ecologically-sustainable ways of heating domestic properties.

## 3.6 Nouns + noun clauses

### 3.6 study

Look at these two sentences:
- *The serious issues **that the enquiry has raised** may lead to new laws.*
- *The fact **that the enquiry raises a number of serious issues** should surprise no one.*

The bold part of the first sentence is a relative clause: *that* could be left out or replaced by *which*. Using a relative clause is a useful way of post-modifying a noun (in this case *issues*).

The bold part of the second sentence is different: it is a noun clause, which completes the meaning of the fact. *That* cannot be left out or replaced. A helpful way of looking at these sentences may be to regard the noun and its clause as a single complex idea controlling the main verb.
- *The belief **that an industrial dispute can be resolved without some form of negotiation** sometimes causes long and avoidable delays.*

Sentences with noun clauses are useful in your writing because they enable you to keep the information that you are conveying in the foreground, while at the same time allowing you to make a comment on it through the type of noun that you choose (*fact* or *belief*, as above, or *statement, warning,* or *hypothesis* below).
- *Many of the journalists present at the press conference were dismissive of **the statement that the police had investigated the matter thoroughly**.*
- *The **warning that sea levels could rise significantly even after a small earth tremor** was taken seriously, and several coastal villages were evacuated.*
- *The experiment was designed to test **the hypothesis that members of the public will tend to follow the instructions of authority figures even when these would appear to conflict with their normal values**.*

**TIP** Here are some of the nouns that often precede noun clauses: *announcement, argument, assumption, belief, claim, conclusion, danger, doubt, effect, fact, hypothesis, idea, impression, likelihood, news, possibility, probability, proposition, prospect, risk, rule, rumour, statement, view, warning.*

## 3.6 test yourself

**Circle the correct option.**

1 Halt has criticized the probability/proposition that people with depression have a clearer perception of reality.

2 The news/rule that the Labour Party Shadow Cabinet must be elected needs to change, according to McTernan.

3 The conclusion/claim that Kipling may have wished readers of *The White Man's Burden* to reach was that both the colonizers and the colonized were trapped in the imperial system.

4 Locke argues against the doubt/view that there are such things as 'innate' ideas.

5 Share prices in Comtech plc rose when the risk/news that they had won a major Pentagon contract was released.

6 Most economic theories are based on the effect/assumption that people tend to act rationally.

## Nouns + prepositions

| | | | |
|---|---|---|---|
| advertisement for | cost of | importance of | request for |
| alternative to | damage to | increase in | research into |
| analysis of | decrease in | inquiry into | research on |
| answer to | demand for | insight on | research in |
| appetite for | description of | insight into | respect for |
| application for | dissertation on | interest in | response to |
| approach to | dozens of | introduction to | right to |
| article on | drop in | investigation into | rise in |
| assignment on | emphasis on | knowledge of | risk of |
| attack on | essay on | lack of | shortage of |
| attack against | examination of | lecture on | study of |
| attention to | examination into | means of | study into |
| ban on | example of | method of | substitute for |
| basis for | experience in | motivation for | tax on |
| basis of | experience of | need for | type of |
| belief in | expert on | opinion of | victim of |
| book on | expert in | part of | way of |
| case for | exploration of | preference for | work on |
| cause of | exploration into | project on | |
| change in | fall in | reason for | |
| change to | idea of | reduction in | |

# 03 Challenge yourself

**A** Complete the text about the role of NGOs after conflict, using the nouns and adjectives in the box.

> completion   child   demobilized   financial   government   humanitarian
> long-term   recent   three-year   vocational

Non-governmental organizations (NGOs) have had to reconsider their strategies in dealing with young veterans of conflict. Former [1]_____ soldiers face [2]_____ difficulties in reintegrating into their communities, according to Babush (2009). There used to be an understanding amongst [3]_____ agencies and the relevant [4]_____ authorities that reintegration had a finite [5]_____ date. This model has been reassessed in [6]_____ years and replaced with a more realistic view. In Sierra Leone, for example, Child Safety International reports that the government has revised its [7]_____ deadline for [8]_____ youth to complete [9]_____ training and claim [10]_____ aid to start a small business.

**B** Complete the text about cycling, using the noun clauses (a–f).

a  that traffic patterns will shift for the better
b  that cycling brings many benefits to a country or city
c  that the numbers speak for themselves
d  that cycling can be advantageous for their city
e  that cyclists run a heightened risk of accidents
f  that treating the physical trauma (broken bones, etc.) bears a cost of its own

The proposition [1]\_\_\_ can be measured financially. It is a fact [2]\_\_\_ , and from this it follows [3]\_\_\_ . However, on balance, regular cyclists live longer than people who have a sedentary lifestyle. Another benefit to the community is the likelihood [4]\_\_\_ . In other words, when a critical mass of workers commutes by bicycle, this lowers the number of cars on the road at rush hours. Mayors and councillors all over the world are coming to the conclusion [5]\_\_\_ and therefore [6]\_\_\_ .

**C** Complete the text about data storage, using the words and phrases in the box.

> considerable   comprehensive   any well-run   obvious   of obsolescence
> storage   very little   virtually   paper   well-maintained

To store data effectively is essential to [1]_____ organization. Two [2]_____ systems are paper and electronic. [3]_____ filing systems do not require any power and do not become obsolete. They provide a [4]_____ archive but require a [5]_____ amount of space. Paper files necessitate a [6]_____ catalogue, or they soon become [7]_____ unusable. On the other hand, they do offer the benefit of reliability. The dominance of computer technology means that there is [8]_____ paper storage in the MegaCorp plc offices. Files stored on a computer are easy to access and require no physical [9]_____ space. However, they do run the risk [10]_____ , if hardware or software becomes unobtainable over time.

**D** Rewrite the underlined parts of the sentences, following the instructions in brackets.

1 The 2004 inquiry into the funding of the arts in the regions (use three words) criticized the way in which grants awarded by government (use two words) had been distributed.

2 Stonebridge (2009) explores the phenomenon of riots that take place in the summer (use two words) in UK and American cities.

3 New legislation is unlikely to change beliefs that have been held for a long time (use a compound adjective and a noun) over the place of religion in society.

4 Freedom of the press (use two words) and human rights are often linked, argues Hogg (2010).

5 A documentary that was broadcast recently (use a compound adjective and a noun) suggested that residents in care homes (use three words) are not always treated with the respect they deserve.

6 Allegations of bribery (use two words) have been made against several European companies that trade in oil (use a compound adjective and a noun).

7 Drivers of tankers that carry fuel (use two words) are required to take a test in fire safety (use three words).

8 Trucks that have broken down (use a compound adjective and a noun) are sometimes abandoned in this region because of a lack of spare parts.

9 Products made from plastic (use two words) are rarely biodegradable.

10 Reliable statistics for the length of time that people are expected to live (use three words) are not yet available for the island.

**E** Put the words in each phrase in the correct order. Then use the phrases to complete the text about the response to the banking crisis in the first decade of the 21st century.

a banking bubble of piercing the the
b a higher scrutiny level of public
c average higher much than the were which
d all at levels of protests society
e funds of public this use
f housing collapse market of the the
g banks failing of some these

Let us now turn to the protests following $^1$___ and $^2$___ in 2008–2009, the ramifications of which continue to be felt. $^3$___ were bailed out by the state. $^4$___ has exposed them to $^5$___ than they are used to. When these banks and financial institutions sought to continue paying their executives year-end bonuses $^6$___ annual salary, the public began to take an interest. $^7$___, from polite but firm letters to newspaper editors to window-smashing, have been the response.

**F** Match each word or phrase in box A with its partner in box B. Then use some of the phrases to write 100–200 words about the founder of Apple Inc., Steve Jobs.

| **A** | ground- | the importance | hardware | relatively |
|---|---|---|---|---|
| | customer | demand | | |

| **B** | satisfaction | high cost products | for | breaking |
|---|---|---|---|---|
| | and software engineers | of | | |

## Introduction

> **Look at two texts on the same subject. Where do you think you would see them? What are the main differences between them? Identify at least three specific examples.**

What should you wear when you start your first real job? Obviously, things are different depending on whether you're a guy or a gal, but a lot of the decisions are the same. You're probably worried about the interview and the first few days at work. The interview, of course, is where they decide if they're actually going to hire you. But also, you have to think about the trial period when you and the employer look each other over. It's a two-way street, isn't it? Clothes are a good way of seeing if you'll fit in. It's part of what they call the 'corporate culture'.

Many young people graduating from university are unsure about the clothes they need when they embark on their chosen careers. The details are different for men and women, but the principles are the same. In most cases, the main concern is the job interview itself, and, secondarily, the first week once hired. At the interview, the company assesses the candidate and makes a decision on whether to offer a contract of employment, usually on a probationary basis of six months. This is to see if a candidate will fit in to the corporate culture.

**Suggested answers: see page 193**

Academic language should always be clear and logical, but it should also conform to its own genre or style, otherwise it risks distracting the reader or listener from the main purpose. Academic English, particularly when written, is usually described as 'formal' language. The formality of academic writing is characterized by the following.

**1** An impersonal rather than a personal style, including the use of structures that begin with *it* and *there*, rather than the personal pronouns *I*, *we* and *you*.
* *There needs to be a proper exploration of the causes of the riots.*

**2** A tendency to base structures around nouns rather than verbs (called 'nominalization').
* *The research team made a careful **assessment** of the data. (*Rather than *The research team **assessed** the data carefully.*)

**3** The use of formal vocabulary, such as *resign from* rather than *quit* a job, and *children* rather than *kids*.

**4** A preference for a cautious and objective approach, with evidence to support our ideas, and consideration given to the views of others, along with the avoidance of emotive or subjective language such as *disgusting* or *marvellous*.

In this unit, the first three areas are covered in some depth, but note that, for the fourth, you should refer to unit *14 Hedging* for an in-depth analysis.

See also page 086 in unit *9 Passives*, for the use of the passive voice to demonstrate objectivity.

# 4.1 Nominalization

## 4.1 study

Nominalization is the process of focusing your writing around nouns rather than verbs or adjectives. Not only do nouns make your language more impersonal, they also allow you to add information to your writing more easily and to use structures that place the emphasis on an important event rather than on the agent (the person or thing that made it happen).

- *Severe weather conditions in the developing world often **lead to** short-term poverty.* (verb phrase)
  → *Severe weather conditions in the developing world **are often the cause of** short-term poverty.* (noun phrase)
  → *Severe weather conditions in the developing world **are often the primary cause of** short-term poverty.* (noun phrase with additional information)
- *The council **converted** the disused factory into a community centre ...*
  → *The **conversion** of the disused factory into a community centre ... (provided a much-needed social space for the area).*
  Note that in the example above the important word (*conversion*) is now at the beginning of the sentence.

### 1 Nominalizations from verbs

- *Governments or central banks **vary** (verb) interest rates to **control** (verb) the economy.*
  → ***Variations** (noun) in interest rates are a **key instrument** (additional information) in economic **control** (noun).*
- *To maintain staff motivation, companies need to **consult** with managers before **changing** their job descriptions.*
  → ***Consultation** with managers over **changes** to their job descriptions is vital in maintaining their motivation.*

Note that you can also nominalize by using the *-ing* forms of verbs.

- *If companies continue to **burn** the forests, they are likely to **destroy** much of the local flora and fauna.*
  → *The continued **burning** of the forest will lead to the **destruction** of much of the local flora and fauna.*

**TIP** As you can see in the examples above, nominalized sentences often use the simple verb *be* because the weight of meaning is carried by the noun rather than the verb.

**TIP** Many nouns with verb partners have *-tion* endings, e.g. *clarify/clarification, demonstrate/demonstration, fluctuate/fluctuation, innovate/innovation, legislate/legislation, motivate/motivation, predict/prediction, produce/production, reduce/reduction, resolve/resolution.*

### 2 Nominalizations from adjectives

- *The judge will decide finally on how **long** (adjective) the offender remains in jail.*
  → *The judge will make the final decision on **the length** (noun) of the offender's prison sentence.*
- *The context in which it is exhibited may determine whether or not a painting is **powerful**.*
  → *The **power** of a painting may be determined by the context in which it is exhibited.*

**TIP** Sometimes you can use a completely different noun to express the same meaning as a verb or adjective.

- *Parts of the country's infrastructure have been **getting better** in the last two or three years.*
  → *There have been some **improvements** in the country's infrastructure in the last two or three years.*

**TIP** Here are some more adjective-noun partnerships: *beneficial/benefit, coherent/coherence, enormous/enormity, intelligent/intelligence, logical/logic, relevant/relevance, secure/security, similar/similarity, stable/stability.*

---

## 4.1 test yourself

**Complete the second sentence so that it has the same meaning as the first. Use one noun in each space.**

1 It is essential to communicate regularly but briefly with the sales force in the field.
   Regular but brief _____ with the sales force in the field is essential.

2 Local authorities preserved a wide area of land from being developed, and this allowed them to create a park.
   The _____ of a wide area of land from _____ allowed local authorities to create a park.

3 The presenter questioned whether some of the research into prime numbers was relevant.
   The _____ of some of the research into prime numbers was questioned by the presenter.

4 Orton supports Foster, who predicts slow economic growth led by the service sector.
   Orton supports Foster in his _____ of slow economic growth led by the service sector.

5 The political situation must be stable before it is possible for poverty in this part of Africa to be eliminated.
   The _____ of the political situation is a pre-condition for the _____ of poverty in this part of Africa.

## 4.2 Using *it …* and *there …*

### 4.2 study

Academic writing often involves the balanced discussion of contrasting viewpoints and ideas. It is useful, therefore, to be able to use structures that do not commit you personally to a claim or statement. *It* and *there + be* both offer ways of starting sentences in a way which makes them appear more objective.

**1** *It …*

Starting the example below with *It …* (sometimes called the 'empty' or 'preparatory' subject) allows the writer to avoid using the more direct and personal *I cannot foresee …* It also avoids the clumsy impersonal structure *To foresee a significant improvement in the levels of poverty in Liberia while the fighting continues is difficult*, which places a long clause between the subject (*To foresee*) and its verb and complement (*is difficult*).

- *It is difficult to foresee a significant improvement in the levels of poverty in Liberia while the fighting continues.*

The passive structure below is a less direct way of saying *Educationalists have argued …*, and it also gives more prominence to the argument itself (which is the important thing) rather than to the people doing the arguing.

- *It has been argued by educationalists that a greater number of male teachers at primary school level might improve the performance of young boys in the classroom.*

**2** *There …*

*There* introduces something, or says that it exists.
- *There was some evidence in the survey that British people still feel closer links with the USA than with their fellow citizens in the European Union.*
- *There are a number of conclusions that can be drawn from this comparative study of hospital procedure.*

The example above offers a less direct and personal alternative to *We can draw a number of conclusions …*, but note that you could also say *A number of conclusions can be drawn from …*

**3** *It …/There …* + modal verb

With *it …* and *there …* it is possible to use a modal verb or *seems/appears*.
- *It **must** be remembered that Italy as an entity did not exist until 1861.*
- *There **seems** to have been a disagreement over the exact date of the discovery.*

**TIP** Writing can appear less personal when words such as *essay, report, evidence, research*, etc. are used as the subject of your sentence (*This report focuses on …; The evidence available suggests that …*).

### 4.2 test yourself

**Complete each sentence with *it* or *there*.**

**1** _____ is a persuasive argument for adopting any traffic scheme that reduces town centre congestion.

**2** _____ should be recognized that raising interest rates may not solve the inflationary pressure.

**3** _____ may be preferable for the newspaper industry to regulate itself.

**4** _____ was a difference of opinion within the team about the design of the logo.

**5** _____ may be a case for rewarding drivers who regularly take colleagues to work.

**6** _____ seems to be difficult for larger travel companies to gain the positive feedback that their smaller competitors enjoy.

## 4.3 Using *I*, *we*, *you* and *one*

### 4.3 study

**1** Using *I* and *we*

Although it is best to take a generally impersonal approach to your writing, there are times when it may be appropriate to use *I* and *we*.

When outlining your approach to a subject, either as a single or joint author or presenter.
- *First, **I** will summarize the arguments in support of political sanctions.*
- *In the middle section of our report, **we** have advocated the use of certain types of pesticide.*
- 💬 (in a presentation) ***I** will finish **my** presentation by considering the ways in which some animals migrate to survive.*

When commenting on your own position in verb phrases such as *I (would) accept, I (would) argue, I believe, I (would) consider, I (would) propose, I (would) suggest, I suppose, I (would) think.*

- 💬 (in a presentation) *I would suggest that if the recommendations of the Clarkson report were put into practice, we might see a reduction in the number night-time accidents in rural villages.*
- *In conclusion, I consider it unlikely that we will see a fundamental change in the attitude of most British citizens to immigration, which is why a basic level of equal rights legislation will always be required.*

When people are presenting themselves as members of a wider community.

- 💬 (lecturer) *We know that viruses can adapt to survive.* (*We* = everyone in this lecture hall)
- 💬 (in a presentation) *We are already facing a water crisis in some parts of the world.* (*We* = humanity)

### 2 Using *you* and *one*

*You* and *one* can both be used to refer to people in general. *You* is informal and is more common in spoken academic English. *One* is quite formal.

- 💬 (in a seminar) *If you make any kind of commercial or public enquiry, you'll notice how the organization will use almost any strategy to encourage you to find the answer via their website rather than by phone.*
- *The process of teaching one's own subject can provide new insights into it.*

**TIP** In spoken academic English, you can use a less formal style, but you should still avoid colloquialisms and slang such as *kids, stuff, cute, dead easy,* etc.

- 💬 (in a presentation) ~~How come there are~~ *Why are there so few women in the House of Commons?*

**TIP** In written English, it is normally better to avoid contractions such as *didn't, won't, we'll, wouldn't,* etc.

- *A company that ~~won't~~ will not invest properly in research and development is likely to be overtaken by its competitors.*

## 4.3 test yourself

Complete each sentence with one of the phrases in the box.

> one is   we have   agree   we
> I would   I understand

1. _____ know that many scientific discoveries are made by a process of trial and error.
2. As a researcher, _____ aware that another academic may be investigating exactly the same area.
3. To sum up, _____ argue that the UK would benefit from encouraging a growth in the culture of philanthropy.
4. _____ decided that each member of our team will present a separate model of arts funding.
5. _____ your fears, but I also think you are unlikely to find a new energy source with as much potential.
6. I _____ that there are valid criticisms of this scheme, but, as my last slide shows, the alternatives are all more expensive.

## 4.4 Formal verbs, nouns and adjectives

### 4.4 study

Some words have a more formal 'feel' to them than others. In the selected examples in this section a less formal, but perfectly acceptable, alternative is given in brackets. It is not necessary to always use the more formal words in academic English, but it is useful to be aware that these distinctions exist. (See also unit *15 Phrasal and prepositional verbs.*)

### 1 Verbs

Many verbs have a more formal alternative.

- *Symons argues that there is little point during a time of recession in **calling on** (asking) the government to support further spending in this area.*
- *The company's profits **exceeded** expectations. (The company's profits were greater than expected.)*
- *The oil tanker **incurred/suffered** serious damage in the collision. (The oil tanker was seriously damaged in …)*
- *In the body of our report, we **make reference to** (refer to) the significant contribution in this field of Professors Walters and Marlow at Columbia University.*

- *No self-respecting democracy can **sanction** (permit/ allow) these coercive methods of interrogation.*
- *In his inaugural address Barack Obama **spoke of** (talked about) the long political journey he had made.*
- *None of these important matters were **addressed** (were covered/dealt with) in the work carried out by the Granger inquiry.*

[TIP] Other more formal verbs include *acquire/procure (obtain), assist (help), conduct (carry out), demonstrate (show), dispose of (get rid of), entail (necessitate/require), examine/study (take a look at), investigate (look into), omit (leave out), treat (present/discuss), write of (write about).*

## 2 Nouns

Sometimes more formal nouns are particularly appropriate in law or politics. A *spouse* (husband or wife) and a *sibling* (brother or sister), for example, are useful in being gender neutral. A *dwelling* means 'a place where someone lives' without having to specify whether it is a house or flat, etc., and *premises* means 'a building' or 'buildings', whether it is an office or a shop, etc. Politicians sometimes make *pledges* rather than *promises*, and countries may use an *embargo* rather than a *ban* to prevent some form of trade.

- *Several of the **dwellings** were condemned as unfit for human habitation.*
- *An **embargo** has been placed on all oil supplies destined for the main cities.*
- *Under the current law, a **spouse** must wait for two years after separation, before beginning divorce proceedings.*
- *Police conducted a thorough search of the **premises**, but no drugs were found.*
- *The government has made a **pledge** to review the composition of select committees. (Or The government has pledged to review ...)*

## 3 Adjectives

Some adjectives have more formal partners.
- *Relations between Pakistan and India, rarely **cordial** (friendly) at the best of times, have recently worsened.*
- *The design of the new hospital, with its light-filled social areas, is **exemplary** (ideal).*
- *Mistakes were made by the negotiating team, but these were described by the government as **negligible** (minor).*
- *The **sole** (only) reason for delaying the launch of the new domestic heating system appears to have been a desire to avoid the summer period, when few people are as concerned with cold weather problems.*

[TIP] Other more formal adjectives include *characteristic (typical), correct (right)* and *incorrect (wrong), final (last), justifiable (fair), problematic (difficult), overwhelming (very powerful), substantial (large).*

[TIP] In spoken and written English, there is a tendency to avoid emotive language that shows a personal attitude in the words themselves, such as *mob* instead of *crowd* or adjectives like *appalling, disgusting, wonderful,* etc.
- *It is shameful that refugees in genuine fear for their lives in their home countries are being turned away by immigration services.*
  → *We need to question the moral values that underpin any immigration service that turns away refugees in genuine fear for their lives in their home countries.*

## 4.4 test yourself

**Replace each underlined word or phrase with one of the more formal words in the box. Use a dictionary if necessary.**

administered  catalogued  advisable
occupation  occasions  deteriorated
unacceptable  accelerated  negotiations

1 Medical reports suggested that the trapped miners' physical condition <u>got worse</u> rapidly after the first week.
2 The suspect refused to reveal his <u>job</u> to the police.
3 The enquiry concluded that the drugs <u>given</u> to the patients by hospital staff were inappropriate.
4 The construction company claimed it had informed employees that the wearing of goggles was <u>a good idea</u>.
5 There were at least two <u>times</u> when secret <u>talks</u> were held between the British and Irish Governments.
6 The pace of change within the industry has <u>speeded up</u> over the past decade.
7 The inquiry panel <u>listed</u> the number of accidents that had occurred on that part of the motorway.
8 The opposition argued that the government's cuts to housing benefit were <u>very bad</u>.

## 4.5 Other formal words, phrases, and structures

### 4.5 study

This final section covers the more formal versions of a small group of words and phrases; Latin expressions in current use; and some formal negative expressions.

**1** In this list, words or phrases that are more formal come first: *albeit (although); in excess of (over/ above/more than); in sum (in short/briefly); principally/primarily/predominantly (mainly); somewhat (slightly); virtually (almost)*.

- *There is a distinct, albeit minor, trend for furniture retail outlets to offer customers free refreshments while they browse.*
- *ATMs generally do not permit withdrawals in excess of £500.*
- *Retail turnover, in the period leading up to Christmas, has been somewhat lower than expected.*

**TIP** Using the words *former, latter,* and *respectively* to make references to other parts of a text is also a characteristic of formal English. (See unit *20 Cohesion* page 176 for further information.)

**2** It is not advisable to use Latin phrases simply to make your writing sound more academic, but the following expressions can prove useful: *bona fide* (in good faith); *caveat* (a warning); *de facto* (in reality, but not officially); *in situ* (in its original location); *inter alia* (among other things); *per capita* (per head/ for each person); *pro rata* (in proportion); *quid pro quo* (something in return for a service/favour); *sine qua non* (an essential pre-condition); *status quo* (things as they are); *vice versa* (reversing the order of things just mentioned). You may wish to check if your department has a policy on the use of Latin phrases.

- *Classroom research carried out **in situ** (i.e. in the classroom) can present its own difficulties.*
- *Wilkins argues that companies should take a more flexible approach to employees who request a temporary reduction in their workload for a **pro rata** loss of salary.*
- *It is vital that charities seeking commercial sponsorship understand the details of the **quid pro quo** element of such an engagement.*
- *Mitcham argues that the UK will have to do business with the rebel force, now that it has formed the **de facto** government of the country.*

**3** The negative expressions *no* (instead of *not any*), *little* (instead of *not much*), and *few* (replacing *not many*), all tend to sound more formal, and can be used instead of contractions.

- *(There aren't any) There are no easy solutions available to the problem of drug abuse among teenagers.*
- *(Not many) Few doctors would argue with a system that could reduce the number of inappropriate patient consultations.*

(See also unit *7 Connectors*, page 067 for an explanation of the structure *not only ... but also*, which has a similar, formal feel to it.)

**TIP** In formal English, we tend to limit our use of the terms *etc., and so on,* and *so forth,* replacing them with more precise phrases (*The building of ready-to-rent apartments requires the installation of washing machines, fridges* ~~etc.~~ **and other domestic appliances**).

---

### 4.5 test yourself

**Replace each underlined word or phrase with a more formal alternative.**

**1** There <u>isn't much</u> hope that the opera company will find a sponsor for its innovative programme.
**2** Three of the seven species identified by the team in 1972 have <u>almost</u> disappeared.
**3** Michaels describes an ideal business environment in which confidence strengthens the economy and <u>the other way round</u>.
**4** A new member entering an established group of friends can upset the <u>existing situation</u>.
**5** Brian Talbot is <u>mainly</u> an expert in hydraulics.
**6** Nutritionists generally agree that there <u>aren't any</u> fast-track solutions to sustainable weight loss.

# 04 Challenge yourself

**A** 💬 Three students are discussing their group experiment. Read their conversation and then complete the formal results of their experiment using the words and expressions in the box.

---

A   OK, so we've got our research done. The experiment's finished and we know what happened. Well, mostly, we do. What are we going to write about it?

B   Let's start with the conclusion. What we found out. The results.

C   Yeah. The whole point was looking for what made the bacteria reproduce more quickly.

B   Quickly and successfully. And we found the right level of warmth, 35 degrees, which was what we set out to do. So we've got to say something like 'the optimum temperature'.

A   Remember, it wasn't just the temperature. We had all those different coloured lights too.

C   I know, and they didn't work out so well. So why don't we say we looked at two variables, and one gave us clear results and the other didn't?

B   But they were clear results – they were just negative ones. Nothing happened.

C   You're right, but how can we word that in our report?

---

> set out   namely   optimum   to examine   growth rates   growing conditions
> with regard to   were exposed to   two separate variables   a strong correlation
> the same growth   no matter what   in the range of   showed less influence on

The experiment $^1$_____ $^2$_____ the $^3$_____ $^4$_____
of one particular strain of bacteria, $^5$_____ $^6$_____, $^7$_____
the temperature and the colour of light that the samples $^8$_____ .
The team discovered that there was $^9$_____ between high bacterial
$^{10}$_____ and a temperature $^{11}$_____ 35 to 36 degrees. The samples
kept a degree below this minimum or above this maximum produced about
20% less growth, and those held below 30 degrees produced no growth at all.
Experimentation with a second variable $^{12}$_____ the growth rates.
$^{13}$_____ the colour of light that the bacteria were exposed to,
$^{14}$_____ resulted.

**B** Rewrite the text as one continuous paragraph, following the instructions in brackets. Use more formal language where possible.

- We are burning fossil fuels all the time, and the world's weather is behaving in ways that are more and more changeable. We can try to show the link between these two things, but the connection is not always simple. (use one sentence instead of two, start with the phrase *Demonstrating the link ...,* and use the noun *patterns* instead of the verb phrase *is behaving in ways*)
- Most experts believe that burning these fuels is the main reason for the weather changing. (use *the former* and *the latter*)
- But scientific proof depends on specialists measuring the data accurately, and analysing it in very difficult ways. (use the nouns *measurement* and *analysis*)
- People can make mistakes in the way that they carry out these studies, and some scientists disagree with most of their colleagues, even though the evidence is growing. (start with the word *Mistakes ...* and use the word *conduct* as a noun)

**C** Circle the most appropriate formal phrase (a–c) to replace the underlined phrases in the text about people kidnapped in a war zone.

The abduction of children and women from Kobo District has been a feature of [1]conflict between ethnic groups for the past decade. [2]A man presented a paper at the recent conference on refugees and [3]people who have been internally displaced. [4]He focused mainly on discussion of temporary care for abducted women and children who have been rescued from their abductors and are waiting for their families to be traced; improvement of [5]communication between agencies; [6]the recording of so-called 'spontaneous returns', when the newly rescued choose to transport themselves to their original villages; and exploration of traditional 'reconciliation and return' mechanisms as an alternative to [7]the theoretical model that exists at the moment used by [8]agencies that work internationally.

1  a  group ethnic conflict         b  inter-ethnic conflict
   c  ethnicity conflict
2  a  a paper was presented by someone   b  a presentation occurred
   c  a paper was presented
3  a  internally displaced personalities  b  internally displaced persons
   c  displaced internally persons
4  a  it focused on mainly          b  there was a main focus on
   c  the main focus was on
5  a  cross-agencies communication  b  agency communication
   c  cross-agency communication
6  a  the documentation of          b  the documentary of
   c  the documentation
7  a  the momentary theoretical model  b  the theoretical model in existence
   c  the existing theoretical model
8  a  internationally working agencies  b  international agencies
   c  agencies of international work

**D** In each pair of sentences, which sentence is more formal? Underline the formal features.

1  a  You can interpret the meaning and the substance of corporate social responsibility (CSR) in many ways.
   b  There exist many interpretations of both the meaning and the substance of corporate social responsibility (CSR).
2  a  The disproportionate youthfulness of many developing countries contrasts with the ageing demographics of Europe.
   b  Many developing countries have a disproportionately young population, compared to the ageing populations of Europe.
3  a  The confusion between the voluntary sector and unpaid work is further compounded by the conflation of similar yet distinct working patterns.
   b  The voluntary sector and unpaid work are often confused, and this is made worse when similar yet distinct working patterns are conflated.
4  a  This fails to account for women returning to work after maternity leave, and it assumes that caring responsibilities are solely a female concern.
   b  Not only does this fail to account for women returning to work after maternity leave, but it also assumes that caring responsibilities are solely a female concern.

**E** Write 150–250 words about the changing patterns of transportation in your city or country. Use the different strategies covered in unit 4 to make your paragraph as formal as is reasonable.

---

**AWL GLOSSARY**

**feature** something important, interesting, or typical of a place or thing

**ethnic** connected with or belonging to a nation, race, or people that shares a cultural tradition

**focus** to give attention, effort, etc. to one particular subject, situation, or person rather than another

**mechanism** a method or a system for achieving something

**theoretical** concerned with the ideas and principles on which a particular subject is based, rather than with practice and experiment

---

**AWL GLOSSARY**

**interpret** to decide that something has a particular meaning and to understand it in this way

**disproportionate** too large or too small when compared with something else

**compound** to make something bad become even worse by causing further damage or problems

**solely** only; not involving somebody/ something else

## Introduction

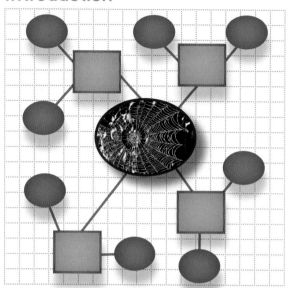

Read the adapted extract from a textbook on organization types and look at the relative clauses (1–4). Then answer the questions (a–c).

The first organization ¹*which we will consider* has a strong leader and a spider web structure: power and influence radiate out from the centre, so what matters is staying close to the hub, ²*where decisions are taken*, and staying close to the individual ³*who matters most*. Growing beyond a certain size is problematic: the leader ⁴*who created a success*, possibly from nothing, is typically reluctant to let go.
(Adapted from *Understanding Organisations* by Charles B. Handy)

a How is relative clause 1 different from relative clause 2?

b Which relative pronouns (in bold) could be replaced by the word *that*? Would it make any difference to the meaning or style?

c Which relative pronoun could be removed from the text altogether? Would it make any difference to the meaning or style?

Suggested answers: see page 194

Relative clauses allow you to include additional information within a sentence in a clear and economical way. They are normally divided into two types: defining relative clauses, where the information 'defines' a noun, and is therefore essential to the meaning; and non-defining relative clauses, where the information may be useful, but the sentence would still be meaningful without it.

• *The National Carbon Company was the first manufacturer **which recognized the potential of the dry cell battery.*** (defining)
• *Claude Monet, **who spent much of his childhood in Le Havre**, was a founder of French impressionist painting.* (non-defining)

The relative pronouns *who* and *whom* (for people), and *which* (for things) can represent the subject or the object of a defining clause.

• *Yves Saint Laurent has been described as the designer **who** changed the world of women's fashion. (= **He** (subject) changed the world ...)*
• *The methods **which** we use to learn languages vary from country to country. (= We use **them** (object) to ...)*

This unit begins by focusing on the two types of relative clause, then looks at the different relative pronouns you can use, and finishes by describing how participles work in relative clauses.

For other units that deal with the adding of information, see unit *3 Noun phrases*, unit *7 Connectors*, and unit *18 Using defining language*.

# 5.1 Defining relative clauses

## 5.1 study

The relative pronouns *which* and *who* can be replaced with *that* in defining relative clauses, and can be left out altogether when they relate to the object of the sentence.

- *The first car **which** I bought was a Honda.*
- = *The first car **that** I bought was a Honda.*
- = *The first car I bought was a Honda.*

However, in academic English, *who* is rarely changed to *that* when it relates to the subject.

- *Yves Saint Laurent has been described as the designer **who** (not ~~that~~) changed the world of women's fashion.*

*Who* and *which* tend to be left out altogether only when they are followed by a pronoun.

- *The scientists **who/that** the Americans hired were originally from Germany.*
- *The methods we use to learn languages vary from country to country.*

**TIP** Remember not to repeat the object in a defining relative clause.

- *We're going to finish the presentation with the slide (that) I showed you ~~it~~ at the beginning.*

### 5.1 test yourself

**Rewrite the sentences to include a defining relative clause, using the information in brackets.**

1 Some doubts were raised about the quality of the questionnaire. (The group used it in the research.)
2 The shoe company was based in Dundee. (It made the largest profits.)
3 The folding bicycle is selling very well. (They designed it at their workshop in York.)
4 Hewitt questioned the experience of the software engineers. (Wentworth plc recruited them.)
5 The director later wrote a memoir. (He pioneered the tracking shot.)
6 The region is crossed by two main roads. (They require substantial repairs.)

# 5.2 Non-defining relative clauses

## 5.2 study

Non-defining clauses are separated from the rest of the sentence by commas.

- *The stethoscope, **which** René Laennec invented in 1816, is used for listening to the body's internal sounds.*

The relative pronouns *who* or *which* can refer to the object of the clause as above, or the subject.

- *Frank Lloyd Wright, **who** designed the Guggenheim Museum in New York, was recognized in 1991 by the American Institute of Architects as 'the greatest American architect of all time'.*

In non-defining relative clauses *who* and *which* cannot be left out or changed to *that*.

**TIP** It may help to think of the commas in non-defining relative clauses as 'protecting' the relative pronouns from being changed to *that* or being left out.

Non-defining relative clauses do not always have to come in the middle of the sentence; they can come at the end, too.

- *A great deal has been written about the naturalist Joy Adamson, **who famously raised a lion cub herself**.*

A relative clause beginning with *which* at the end of a sentence can be useful in referring to a whole idea, rather than a specific noun.

- *In his speeches Martin Luther King often referred to the hope of building a new America, **which** inspired many of the audience to take up active politics for the first time.* (*which* = King's reference to the hope of building a new America)

### 5.2 test yourself

**Rewrite the sentences to include a non-defining relative clause, using the information in brackets.**

1 In a case of gross misconduct an employer may fire an employee immediately. (This includes theft.)
2 Bill Grayson handed his small pharmaceutical business to his daughter. (She transformed it into a multinational corporation.)
3 Turkey has land borders with eight countries. (This has frequently led to a kind of diplomatic balancing act.)
4 Vegetable oils have seen recent volatility in their spot price. (They are traded as commodities.)
5 Barbara Hepworth created *Single Form* for the United Nations building in New York. (Critics regarded her as a key Modernist sculptor.)

## 5.3 Whom and whose

### 5.3 study

**1** *Whom* is the object form of *who*. Because it sounds rather formal, it tends to be replaced in defining clauses by *that*, or to be left out completely (see section **5.1**).
- *The teachers (whom/that) we interviewed all spoke well of the new staff development scheme.*

In non-defining clauses, you can use *who* rather than *whom* to refer to the object, except in very formal styles.
- *The CEO, **who** we met at lunch, was optimistic about the company's long-term prospects.*

You must use *whom*, however, after prepositions.
- *Radovan Karadžić stated at his tribunal hearings that Madeleine Albright was the diplomat **with whom** he had held secret talks.*

**2** *Whose* + noun in defining and non-defining clauses indicates possession both by people **and** things (such as companies, government agencies, committees, etc. and books, plays, films, etc.).
- *A relative **whose** blood type is compatible may be able to donate a kidney if they wish to.*
- *Buyers International is one of the companies **whose** opposition to the deal is well known.*

An alternative to *whose*, when writing about things (not people), is the preposition *of* + *which*.
- *Alice Miller wrote an important book on the psychology of childhood, **whose title/the title of which**, The Drama of Being a Child, indicates the strength of her views on our early years.*
- *An international conference on intellectual copyright, the details **of which** have not yet been announced, is likely to be held later this year.*

**Complete each sentence with one or two words. If no words are necessary, write –.**

**1** New employees should have a mentor from _____ they can obtain advice.

**2** Coca-Cola is an example of a company _____ brand has undeniably passed the worldwide recognition test.

**3** All of the scientists _____ she met expressed their doubts over the viability of cold fusion as an energy source.

**4** The government has proposed an amendment to the legislation, the aim _____ is to restrict the number of local radio stations that can be owned by one person.

**5** Sharon Olwyn, _____ the Prime Minister promoted to the Cabinet, resigned in protest over the issue in 2005.

**6** All the staff on patrol at the reserve are in radio contact with the head keeper _____ they make hourly reports.

## 5.4 In which, from which, to whom, etc.

### 5.4 study

In spoken English, relative clauses may end with a preposition.
- 💬 *And here is a photo of the project team and the local villagers who we worked **with**.*

In academic writing such prepositions are normally placed before the relative pronoun.
- *Langham (2009) argues that Alan Turing is the mathematician **to whom** computer science owes the greatest debt.*
- *HM Prison Maze is the prison **from which** thirty-eight prisoners escaped on 25 September 1983.*
- *Simón Bolívar, **in whose** honour statues have been erected in many of the towns and cities of Venezuela, played a significant role in the Latin American struggle for independence.*

Notice how a determiner such as *many, each, some, neither*, etc. or a number, percentage, etc. can be placed before *of* + relative pronoun.
- *There are hundreds of small businesses in the area, **many of which** are interdependent.*
- *The company has a staff of 1,200, **60% of whom** work on a part-time basis.*

Two prepositional phrases that you will find useful are *the way in which* and *the extent to which*.

- *Most observers agree that **the way in which** Nelson Mandela handled his former political enemies after he took up the presidency of South Africa was exemplary.* (This avoids two *that*-clauses: *... agree that the way that Nelson Mandela ...*)
- *No one can be sure of **the extent to which** the search for water in parts of Africa will become the key source of conflict over the next fifty years.*

Two other useful expressions are *at which point* and *in which case*.

- *A fight may break out amongst the players, **at which point** the referee is entitled to bring the game to a close.*

(This avoids writing *... the players, and at this point, the referee ...* or *... the players, and if this happens, the referee ...*)

- *There is a risk that water levels in the reservoir may fall again, **in which case** the local authorities will have to consider a system of rationing.*

## 5.4 test yourself

**A Complete each sentence with one of the phrases in the box. Two phrases are not needed.**

> from whom   with whom   three of which
> in which   to which   at which
> neither of which   from whose

1 Several charities have criticized Westminster Council for the way ＿＿＿＿＿＿＿ it has cut funding to the shelter for homeless people in Charing Cross.
2 If these types of fault occur in a bridge, there are two options for repair, ＿＿＿＿＿＿＿ is cheap.
3 The rebel leaders ＿＿＿＿＿＿＿ the negotiations were conducted seemed unwilling to make any concessions.
4 A break-even analysis determines ＿＿＿＿＿＿＿ point sales cover the production costs.
5 John Loudon McAdam was a Scottish engineer ＿＿＿＿＿＿＿ name the road-surfacing material tarmac (or tarmacadam) is derived.
6 The hospital then carried out a routine check of the emergency generators, ＿＿＿＿＿＿＿ were found to be defective.

**B Use a preposition + relative pronoun (e.g. *with whom*) to join the two pieces of information below into one sentence.**

1 a jury may have to listen to several expert witnesses/some of them may seem to contradict each other
2 the oil leak may destroy the local fish stocks/the coastal villages depend on them
3 the newspaper chain was inherited by Forster's daughter/one of her first actions was to sell two of the titles
4 several of the paintings were owned by Massine/Picasso collaborated with him in a number of projects
5 the Pianura Padana is the plain in northern Italy/the river Po flows through it to the Adriatic sea
6 the fear is that thousands of local people will begin to move out of the area/in this case refugee camps will need to be established

## 5.5 *Where*, *when*, *why*, and *what* in relative clauses

### 5.5 study

It may sometimes be more economical to use *where*, *when*, or *why* instead of a preposition + *which*.

1 *Where* is common in academic English and often follows the words *place* (or *region*, *country*, etc.), *area*, *situation*, *point*, and *case*.

- *Assisted suicide is **an area** of medical care **in which** many doctors disagree.*
  = *Assisted suicide is **an area** of medical care **where** many doctors disagree.*
- *A **situation** may occur **where** the police need to 'kettle' or contain a group of demonstrators.*
- *Negotiations often reach **a point where** one side feels it has conceded too much ground.*
- *India is **a continent where** we are likely to see substantial economic growth over the next fifteen years.*

**TIP** In relative clauses with *situation*, *point* or *case* + *where*, *where* is sometimes replaced by *when* (without a change in meaning).

- *Zoologists have described cases (where) **when** a shark will attack a vulnerable member of its own species.*

**2** *When* is used with dates, and with words such as *time*, *day*, *year*, *occasion*, *moment*, and *period*.
- *In 2004, when the Sumatra-Andaman earthquake occurred, few expected it to trigger a tsunami of such overwhelming power.*
- *The recession began at **a time when** many British businesses were hoping for a period of extended growth.*
- *On **the day when** the agreement was signed, many people felt that the country would enter into a new period of long-term stability.*

**3** *Why* is used with the word *reason*, sometimes in the phrase *there is no reason why*.
- *What are the major **reasons why** we are losing so much biodiversity?*
- ***There is no reason why** green technology cannot be competitive.*

**4** *The thing(s) which/that ...* can be replaced with *what*.
- *Most of the delegates seemed to disagree with **what** the minister said. (= the things that the minister said)*
- ***What** we expect from a good business leader is a sense of long-term vision for the company.*

## 5.5 test yourself

**A** Replace the underlined phrases with *where*, *when*, *why*, or *what*.

**1** Some start-up businesses seem set on entering areas <u>in which</u> there is already a great deal of competition.

**2** There are several reasons <u>for which</u> Jaguar Land Rover may close its factory at Castle Bromwich.

**3** Mergers are situations <u>in which</u> staff naturally feel that their jobs may be at risk.

**4** Deciding <u>the things that</u> should be included in a questionnaire is sometimes a difficult task.

**5** Staff cuts at the charity became necessary after a period <u>in which</u> corporate and individual donations both fell.

**6** There are several cities <u>in which</u> exhibitions of surrealist art have been particularly successful.

**7** The English Civil War can be said to have started on 22 August 1642, the day <u>on which</u> Charles I raised his standard at Nottingham.

**8** <u>The thing that</u> the marchers were hoping for was a swing in public opinion against the government's proposals.

**B** Complete the sentences with *where*, *when*, *why* or *what*.

**1** March is the month _____ moles begin to appear above ground, having spent much of the winter lining their tunnels with fallen leaves.

**2** Grier (2008) suggests that in the early 1990s, the company car phenomenon was the reason _____ prices in the UK car business stayed consistently higher than those in the rest of Europe.

**3** Tonga is the only island nation in the region _____ formal colonization has never taken place.

**4** Experts noticed that the video footage had been edited at precisely the point _____ government tanks arrived at the demonstration.

**5** Patients who do not respond to hypnotherapy may fear being unable to cope with _____ will emerge during a session under hypnosis.

**6** In the sentencing of rioters, most judges felt that there was no reason _____ maximum penalties should not be applied.

**7** Ronald Reagan's election to the White House occurred at a moment _____ the credibility of the American presidency was at a particularly low point, according to Shah (2010).

**8** The aim of the conference was to consider _____ makes one local community work better than its neighbour.

## 5.6 Participles in relative clauses

### 5.6 study

In defining relative clauses, you may be able to improve your sentences in terms of economy and flow by using a past participle or a present participle form of the verb instead of a relative pronoun + verb. This structure is called a 'participle clause' or a 'reduced relative clause'.

These past participles are commonly used in participle clauses: *based, caused, concerned, given, involved, made, obtained, produced, required, taken*, and *used*.
- *The team studied the results (which were) **produced** by the survey for some weeks before publishing their conclusions.*
- *According to the police, all the people (who were) **involved** in the incident were interviewed at the time.*

- *Statements (which are) **taken** from witnesses many weeks after the event are likely to be unreliable.*
- *It is reasonable to question the accuracy of information (which is) **obtained** through torture.*

These present participles are commonly used in participle clauses: *arising, concerning, consisting, containing, involving, relating, requiring, resulting,* and *using*.

- *The newspaper argued that it was publishing a story **concerning** the public interest. (= which concerned the public interest)*
- *All the data **relating to** individuals is destroyed after the results of the survey are established. (= which relates to individuals ...)*
- *A search **involving** more than a thousand police officers was unable to find the missing girl. (= A search which involved ...)*

Note that present participles can't be used if the relative pronoun represents the object.

- *The methods ~~using~~ **which we use** to learn languages vary from country to country.*

⌐TIP Reduced relative clauses are also used with adjectives such as *available, necessary, possible, responsible,* and *suitable*: *The official ~~who was~~ responsible for leaking the document later resigned.*

---

## 5.6 test yourself

**Complete each sentence with the present or past participle of one of the verbs in the box.**

> consist   arise   use   base   cause   give

1 A key issue _____ from the report is the extent to which politicians put undue pressure on civil servants.
2 The speech on race _____ by Barack Obama in Philadelphia is considered to be one of his best.
3 Peterson describes some of the innovative techniques _____ by Monet to capture light in his paintings.
4 In his article, Ichikawa discusses five recent films _____ on computer games.
5 *Paradoxes* was an art installation _____ of eight individual paintings and sculptures.
6 Coughs _____ by viral infections usually disappear within a few days.

# 05 Challenge yourself

**A** In the text about economic development, match the beginning of each sentence with the correct ending.

1 Zuleika Gubbins (2007) proposes three models of economic development,
2 The country that follows a Spring model has a strong kick-off point, usually
3 Growing beyond a certain size is problematic: the industry
4 The Summer model is that of a healthy ecosystem, with many sectors to the economy,
5 The implication is that even if one of these contracts, others will be in a position to expand, although in a recession,
6 The Autumn model is one of long investment
7 An Autumnal economy might consist of several large industries
8 The difficulty with Autumn, of course, is that Winter,
9 In other words, even industries
10 It would be intriguing to speculate

a providing substantial results.
b one which starts with the growth of one particular industry.
c which is finally bearing fruit.
d which are long-standing and highly successful will not last forever, so economic planners need to have their eye on the next cycle of growth.
e which she names Spring, Summer, and Autumn.
f what a Winter economy might look like.
g a season of hardship, is around the corner.
h each of which is interdependent on the others.
i when the whole economy shrinks, this may not hold true.
j which led the way may not be able to make a successful transition.

**B** Complete the text about encyclopedias by adding relative pronouns to all the sentences except two.

[1]One obvious difference between the two models is the speed with they can update information. [2]However, it would be incorrect to assume that Britannica, used to wait 25 years between editions, failed to move with the times. [3]As early as the 1930s, in a time businesses around the world had to reshape or go bankrupt, it moved to a system of continuously updating its articles. [4]The limitations of the printing process meant that the article writers, are experts in their fields, have to wait years to see the fruits of their labours reach the shelves. [5]It is clear that an online encyclopedia – the most ground-breaking of is Wikipedia – is much better placed to serve readers' needs, not least by correcting its errors swiftly and keeping up to date with advances in knowledge. [6]This shift in how the public accesses and uses information was behind Britannica's 2012 decision to stop producing printed books, and focus all of its attention on digital delivery.

[7]Wikipedia is also free to access, makes it more attractive than spending real money on the full set of paper or CD encyclopedias, or on access to their online versions. [8]However, this radical openness can also be perceived as a weakness – because anyone can update its pages, Wikipedia is regularly accused of inaccuracies. [9]There have been examples of journalists, told to write a profile of a public figure, copy material from Wikipedia, including errors about the individual in question. [10]What should be included can also be controversial: obscure topics would never grace the pages of the Encyclopædia Britannica find a space on Wikipedia.

**C** Cross out the phrases in italic if they are not needed, or replace them with the present participle form of the verb.

**1** Up to 90% of the indigenous population of the Americas died from diseases such as smallpox and syphilis, *which were* introduced by the European explorers and colonizers.

**2** The new generation of smart phones *which contain* a substitute for coltan will be released next year.

**3** South African safaris are dominated by local businesses, *which are* owned and operated by people who live in the area.

**4** The pollutants *that are* generated by internal combustion engines have a major effect on the breathability of city air.

**5** The agricultural techniques *that require* the most external inputs tend to require more machinery as well.

**6** Vegetable oils *which are* traded internationally as commodities have seen volatility in the spot price more reminiscent of petroleum trading.

**7** Ecosystems *which use* certain animals to carry out a particular function may be destroyed if that species becomes extinct.

**8** Political scandals *which* involve governments can often be impenetrable to foreign observers.

**D** Add a defining or non-defining relative clause to each sentence, using the information in brackets.

**1** Klein writes about adbusters and culture jammers. (Adbusters and culture jammers add graffiti to billboards or create their own fake advertisements.)

**2** British banks were bailed out by the government. (The government considered their rescue as the least worst option.)

**3** The inquiry reported on the mechanical failures. (The failures had caused the accident.)

**4** According to a report from Goldman Sachs, the so-called 'next eleven' countries have now been identified. (These countries have the potential to become the world's largest economies.)

**5** The two factories boosted their production. (They introduced a flexi-time policy.)

**6** The polar bear is threatened in its habitat because of global warming and rising sea levels. (The polar bear is a vulnerable species.)

**E** Complete the text about the lack of support for the UK manufacturing industry with *whose*, or a preposition and *whose*, *which*, or *whom*.

There has been strong criticism of UK business leaders for the way ¹_____ they have given precedence in the last 30 years to marketing and promotion over manufacturing. Clements and Walter (2009), ²_____ opinion engineering and the production of goods are now seen as second-rate pursuits, believe, however, that it is not too late to change the commercial and industrial landscape. They argue that, as the recession deepens, a new breed of manufacturers may be the people ³_____ we turn for economic solutions. Howton (2010), ⁴_____ articles in the *Observer* complain about the extent ⁵_____ government initiatives fail to ease the bureaucratic barriers faced by start-up factories, agrees. She suggests that the manufacturing entrepreneurs ⁶_____ UK business leaders could learn their lesson have yet to be given their voice in the financial press.

**F** Write 150–250 words about a profession that might attract a student who is looking for job security and financial reward, describing the type of work involved. Use at least six relative clauses.

**AWL GLOSSARY**

**substitute** a person or thing that you use or have instead of the one you normally use or have

**dominate** to control or have a lot of influence over something

**generate** to produce or create something

**technique** a particular way of doing something, especially one in which you have to learn special skills

**external** happening or coming from outside a place, an organization, your particular situation, etc.

**commodity** a product or a raw material that can be bought and sold

**function** a special activity or purpose of a person or thing

**AWL GLOSSARY**

**precedence** the condition of being more important than something else and therefore coming or being dealt with first

**promotion** activities done in order to increase the sales of a product

**pursuit** something that you give your time and energy to

**initiative** a new plan for dealing with a particular problem or for achieving a particular purpose

## Introduction

A fact is a piece of information that is generally accepted as true and which can be supported by scientific or other evidence or research.

• *The cheetah is the animal capable of the fastest speeds on land.*

An opinion, on the other hand, is a personal statement of belief.

• *It seems to me that Spanish is an easier language to learn than English.*

Academic writing needs to be able to express both facts and opinions, sometimes using facts to support opinions, and sometimes supplying evidence to substantiate facts that are not widely known.

To assist you in expressing your own facts and opinions, and in recognizing the difference between them when listening and reading, the following areas are covered in this unit.

**1** The language used to express facts, focusing on a group of key words such as *data* and *evidence*, and the phrases that explain the statistics found in graphs and diagrams.

**2** Ways of bringing others' views into your writing as evidence.

**3** Expressions for presenting opinions both in writing and in speaking.

> **Read the text and then note separately the three facts and two opinions that it contains.**

Data evaluated by the Office for National Statistics indicates that the number of adoptions in England and Wales has fallen by 4.1% in the past two years. In the same period, statistics confirm that the number of couples applying to adopt has risen. Unless the number of children in care has fallen significantly, it seems plausible that the process of adopting in the UK currently presents an unreasonable barrier to parents who would like to start or enlarge a family in this way. Government figures also show a rise in the number of UK adoptions of children from developing countries (known as 'intercountry adoption'). Most people examining this evidence would agree that changes in the way that UK adoption agencies operate are overdue.

Suggested answers: see page 195

The following units are also relevant to the topic of expressing facts and opinions: unit *2 Comparing and contrasting*, unit *8 Being emphatic*, unit *10 Arguing and persuading*, unit *14 Hedging*, and unit *16 Paraphrasing*.

## 6.1 Key 'fact' words

### 6.1 study

This section presents a selection of words and phrases that frequently collocate with five key 'fact' words: *data*, *evidence*, *fact(s)*, *information*, and *statistics*.

### 1 Data

This is an uncountable noun. It can be used with *some* or with *a piece/an item of*.

> VERB + NOUN: we can *access, acquire, assess, capture, collate, collect, compile, enter, evaluate, examine, gather, obtain, process, retrieve, store* **data**

> NOUN + VERB: **data** can *demonstrate, indicate, (dis)prove, show* **something** or **that** ...

> ADJECTIVES: **data** can be *(in)accurate, current, empirical, financial, out of date, preliminary, recent, relevant*

### 2 Evidence

This is an uncountable noun. It can be used with *some* or with *a piece/an item of*.

> VERB + NOUN: we can *assemble, attack, challenge, collect, consider, demand, dispute, disregard, evaluate, examine, falsify, gather, interpret, present, provide, question, quote, reject, scrutinize, suppress, throw doubt on, weigh up, withhold* **evidence**

> NOUN + VERB: **evidence** can *conflict with, point to, support* **something**; **evidence** can *confirm, demonstrate, disprove, indicate, prove, show* **something** or **that** ...

> ADJECTIVES: **evidence** can be *abundant, ample, circumstantial, compelling, (in)conclusive, conflicting, damaging, documentary, extensive, flawed* (containing a mistake), *flimsy* (= weak), *fresh, growing, hard, incontestable, insufficient, irrefutable, mounting* (= growing), *new, overwhelming, reliable, solid, widespread*

### 3 Fact(s)

> VERB + NOUN: we can *check, distort, establish, examine, explain, ignore, (mis)interpret, misrepresent, present* fact(s); we can *emphasize* **the fact that** ...

> NOUN + VERB: **fact(s)** can *disprove, prove, show, suggest* **something** or **that** ... ; **fact(s)** can *emerge*

> ADJECTIVES: *basic, disturbing, hard, interesting, little-known, relevant, salient, undeniable, well-known* **fact(s)**

### 4 Information

This is an uncountable noun. It can be used with *some* or with *a piece/an item of*.

> VERB + NOUN: we can *absorb, access, demand, disclose, disseminate, exchange, gather, have access to, leak, obtain, record, release, share, store, supply, update, withhold* **information**

> ADJECTIVES: **information** can be *(in)accurate, additional, (un)biased, confidential, detailed, extensive, important, latest, misleading, out of date, public, relevant, sensitive, timely, up to date, valuable, vital*

### 5 Statistics

This is normally a plural noun, which can be used with *some*.

> VERB + NOUN: we can *analyse, compile, gather, issue, produce, release* **statistics**

> NOUN + VERB: **statistics** *demonstrate, disprove, indicate, reveal, show, prove, suggest* **that** ...; *support the idea*, etc. **that** ...

> ADJECTIVES: **statistics** can be *important, (in)accurate, (ir)relevant, latest, misleading, out of date, revealing, reliable, surprising, up to date*

TIP As an academic subject, *statistics* takes a singular verb (*Statistics* **is** *the study of large quantities of information*), and a singular form of the noun is also possible (*A poll has produced the surprising* **statistic** *that as many as 32% of voters make up their minds in the half hour before they actually vote*).

## 6.1 test yourself

**Complete the words in the sentences.**

1 Fr_____ evidence de_____ that some non-avian dinosaurs were able to swim.

2 The company is_____ st_____ to their shareholders that indicated slight but significant growth in three new markets.

3 After the team had ev_____ the em_____ data, it became clear that none of the animals had moved further than 500 metres from the river.

4 Hogue att_____ the evidence in both reports, arguing that it was fl_____ and inconclusive.

5 When all the re_____ facts had em_____ , it was apparent that human error rather than mechanical failure was responsible for the accident.

6 If Howells had not le_____ vi_____ information to the press, the mismanagement of these funds might have continued for years.

## 6.2 Talking about facts and figures

### 6.2 study

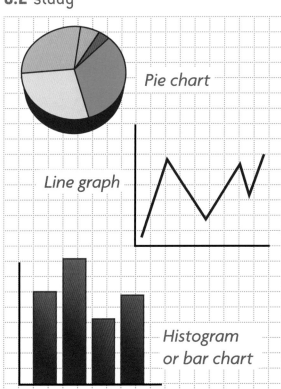

Pie chart

Line graph

Histogram or bar chart

## 1 Referring to visual information

💬 Some useful phrases to be aware of when referring to diagrams and other visual information such as graphs, charts, and tables are:

*This diagram shows/illustrates/displays ...*
*As can be seen from/in the diagram, ...*
*It can be seen from/in the diagram that ...*
*We can see from/in the diagram that ...*
*From the diagram, it may be seen/concluded that ...*
*According to the diagram, ...*
*As (is) shown in the diagram, ...*

- ***This diagram illustrates** the regions that are most affected by drought.*
- ***As can be seen from the diagram**, the greatest proportion of American debt is actually owed to the country itself, in the form of government bonds.*
- ***As shown in the diagram**, share value rose sharply in 2007, when the merger with Stanleys plc was announced.*

## 2 Describing recent/past trends

There are two useful sentence patterns for describing trends in facts and figures.

**a** Present perfect/past simple of *be* + adjective + noun + *in*

| ADJECTIVES: *dramatic, gradual, slight, small, steady, rapid, sharp, steep, sudden* |
|---|

| NOUNS: *decline, decrease, drop, fall, increase, reduction, rise* |
|---|

- ***There has been a dramatic reduction** recently in the number of loans to small businesses.*
- ***There was a steady rise** in the 1990s in UK births to unmarried mothers.*

**b** Noun + present perfect/past simple of verb such as *rise* + adverb

| VERBS: *decline, decrease, drop, fall, grow, increase, rise* |
|---|

| ADVERBS: *dramatically, gradually, slightly, steadily, rapidly, sharply, steeply, suddenly* |
|---|

- *Profits have **increased gradually** for the electronics company Sheldon plc.*
- *Leisure spending **fell sharply** in the last quarter of 2009.*
- *The price of computers has been **dropping steadily** for the last ten years.*

You can use the following verbs and verb phrases to describe the state of figures or statistics at particular periods:

*to peak/reach a peak, to trough/hit a trough*
*to remain stable/constant, to stabilize, to level off/out, to reach a plateau*
*to fluctuate* (= to go up and down)

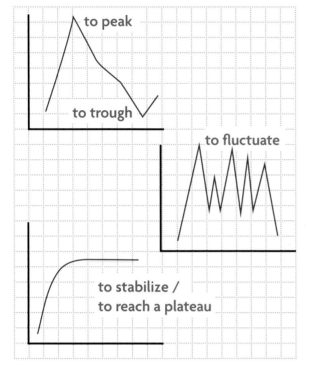

- *Sales of properties in Spain to UK residents **reached a peak** in the early 1980s.*
- *UK unemployment figures **stabilized** at 1.8 million in late 2008 after **fluctuating** in the previous two years.*

### 3 Making comparisons

Facts and figures for one country, company etc. are often compared with those for others, or with the way they used to be in the past. When talking about amounts, percentages, etc. the preposition *by* comes between a verb and the number, and *of* comes between a noun and a number.

- *Economic growth in the UK fell/declined **by** 0.2% in the second quarter of 2010.*
- *Spain enjoyed an increase/rise **of** 10% in its tourist trade in 2007.*

Structures with *more* (or *higher/lower*, etc.) ... *than* or ... *as* ... *as* .... are useful.

- *The Labour Party gained 3% **more** of the public vote **than** the Conservatives in the local elections of 2009.*
- *Manufacturing productivity was not nearly **as** high in France **as** it was in Germany in 2009.*

You can use the superlative form (*highest/lowest*, etc.) to describe peaks and troughs.
- *Birth rates in southern Europe reached their **lowest** level for six years in 2005.*

(You could also write *Birth rates ... hit a trough/troughed in 2005* or *Birth rates ... hit a six-year low in 2005.*)

You can also use expressions describing multiple amounts (*two/three*, etc. *times* or the verbs *double, treble, quadruple*).
- *Nearly **three times** as many Irish citizens work in the construction industry as in agriculture.*
- *The number of Norwegians with access to high-speed broadband **doubled** between 2005 and 2006.*

(See page 017 in unit *2 Comparing and contrasting* for more on comparative and superlative structures.)

---

## 6.2 test yourself

**Correct each sentence by adding one of the words in the box.**

| constant | highest | tripled | risen |
|---|---|---|---|
| from | by | in | of |

1 Clifton plc increased their exports to North America 11% in 2008.
2 In 2009 Portugal suffered a decline 22% in its gross export figures.
3 The number of graduates obtaining employment within six months of leaving university reached its level for a decade in 2007.
4 It can be seen the pie chart that Brazil produces twice as much coffee as Colombia.
5 There has been a gradual increase births by Caesarean section in the USA over the past thirty years.
6 According to the British Antarctic Survey, mean annual temperatures on the Antarctic Peninsula have rapidly since records began fifty years ago.
7 Since its abolition, UK public support for the restoration of the death penalty has remained at around 65%.
8 UK sales of Freedom Food products between 2007 and 2009 to reach £122 million.

## 6.3 Using others' opinions

### 6.3 study

The views of other writers can be used as evidence in your writing. You can paraphrase (see unit *16 Paraphrasing*), or you can make a direct quotation.

As a rule, quotations should be short and not over-used within your writing. Your own university or college should be able to give you a style guide on the technical aspects of citation (different systems are preferred in different institutions), but here are some words and phrases for introducing the opinion of another author.

**1 Using reporting verbs** such as *comment, point out, observe, state, suggest, write*

> *As* (name) + reporting verb
> (Name) + reporting verb + *that ...*

- *As Grover observed*, 'Several categories of question can be distinguished in market research questionnaires' (2007: 45).
- *Grover points out that* several categories ...

Note that verbs such as *point out, observe*, etc. can be used in the past, present and the present perfect tense.

**2 Using nouns** such as *view* or *opinion*

> *The view/opinion of* (Brown) *is that ...*
> (Brown)'s *opinion/view is that ...*
> *In* (Brown)'s *view/opinion, ...*

- *Steele's view is that*, 'The popular reaction to a controversial new building often turns quite quickly from dislike to a kind of affectionate respect' (2004: 62).

**3 Using** *according to* (Brown)

- *According to Wooller*, 'The temperature at which a material will ignite is, of course, of primary concern in the construction industry' (Wooller: 78).

## 6.3 test yourself

**Reorder the words in brackets to make correct sentences. Add punctuation where necessary.**

1 (Escher according to) It should be possible to stabilize this chemical reaction for commercial exploitation.
2 (has out that Stevens pointed) Mexican politics are little understood outside the region.
3 (maintains Nikura as) Some species of insect may die out before they have even been recorded.
4 (that Bostock's is view) Crime statistics are frequently manipulated to support political arguments.
5 (opinion Metstrom's in) Corporate lawsuits may have no other purpose than to delay competitor launches.

## 6.4 Giving your own opinion

### 6.4 study

**1 In writing**

If you do not give a reference for an idea, the reader will normally understand that it is your view. There is therefore little need in academic writing to use expressions such as *in my opinion* or *I think*. If you want to use a phrase, you could consider expressions such as:

*It is likely/probable that ...*
*It seems plausible that ...*
*The evidence indicates/suggests that ...*
*It can/could (in fact) be argued that ...*
*One possible view is that ...*
*On balance, it seems that ...*
*One of the main arguments in favour of (a change in the law) is ...*

- *It could be argued that* the internet is forcing us to engage with new concepts of copyright.

If you feel that your opinion is widely shared, you could write:

*It is generally accepted that ...*
*Most people would agree that ...*

- *It is generally accepted that* there is a strong case for encouraging consumers to become more responsible in the way that they dispose of rubbish and unwanted goods.

## 2 In speaking

💬 Opinions in seminars, tutorials, and presentations are expressed in a less formal style. Here is some language that you might find useful, followed by a short dialogue featuring some of the phrases.

### a Giving an opinion

> I think ...
> I feel that ...
> I'd say that ...
> It seems to me that ...
> What I think/believe is ...

### b Giving an opinion more emphatically

> It seems obvious to me that ...
> As far as I'm concerned ...

### c Giving an opinion more formally

> I believe ...
> I take the view that ...
> It is my view that ...

### d Disagreeing

> Yes, but (on the other hand) ...
> I see what you mean, but ...
> I agree (with you) to some extent, but ...
> Well, you may have a point, but ...
> But what about the fact that ... ?
> Are you sure?
> That may be so, but ...

### e Disagreeing more emphatically

> I disagree. In my view, ...
> I can't agree with that. In my view, ...
> I don't agree, I'm afraid. In my view, ...

### f Agreeing

> I think you're right.
> That's right/true.
> I think so, too.
> I agree.

### g Agreeing more emphatically

> (That's) my view, exactly.
> (That's) absolutely right/true.
> That's exactly what I think.

Tutor:     *Have you any ideas about the kind of business you'd like to set up for your project?*
Student A:  *Well, **I think** we should invent and manufacture a new product. A chair or something.*
Student B:  ***Are you sure?** I mean, it gets complicated if we have to, you know, create a factory ...*
Student C:  ***I agree.** It would take up a lot of time.*
Tutor:     *OK. Well, what about the service sector? Any ideas there?*
Student B:  *An online ticket agency? For festivals and shows and things.*
Student A:  ***Yes, but** there are so many already.*
Student C:  ***That's right.** We'd have a real problem finding a gap, or a USP.*
Tutor:     ***That may be so, but** do any of you use these sites regularly?*
Student B:  *I do, and some of them are terrible.*
Student C:  ***My view, exactly.** They're really frustrating.*
Tutor:     *Well, that's a starting point then. What normally goes wrong when you use them? ...*

(See also unit *10 Arguing and persuading* for ways of presenting and supporting your arguments, and units *8 Being emphatic* and *14 Hedging* for showing the strength of your opinion.)

### 6.4 test yourself

**Complete each sentence with the correct form of one of the verbs in the box.**

> indicate   may   agree   concern
> seem   believe

1 As far as I'm _____, the UK needs to ask itself why it locks so many of its citizens up.
2 Most people would _____ that technological innovation is the key to long-term manufacturing success.
3 On balance, it _____ that there is a desire in the general public to see the benefits system reformed.
4 Well, you _____ have a point, but what would a group live on if all its music could be downloaded for free?
5 What I _____ is that the National Health Service would actually benefit from more competition.
6 The evidence _____ that molecular water exists across the surface of the moon.

# 06 Challenge yourself

**A** Rewrite the sentences using the words in brackets.

**1** Spot prices for metals did not rise or fall in this period despite the turbulence in the oil and textile markets. (stable)

**2** Visitor numbers at the Sizewell education centre increased by 14% in the period 2007–9. (increase – noun)

**3** It can be imagined that modern medicine will continue to extend human life. (plausible)

**4** The sales totals for fine art at the auction house were at their highest level for twenty years in 2009. (peak – noun)

**5** There was a slight fall in house prices in Cumbria in the first half of 2012. (slightly)

**6** 'What you say may be relevant, but I disagree with your order of priority.' (a point)

**7** Payday loan companies reported that there was three times as much demand for their services during the Christmas period in 2012. (trebled)

**8** The number of complaints to the BBC over offensive language rose steeply throughout the 1990s. (rise – noun)

**B** 💬 A group of students is discussing a statistics project on undergraduate sleeping patterns. Complete the conversation.

A   It seems ¹ob_____ to me, just from looking at the amount of data we've ²col_____, that we must have some ³val_____ information to present.

B   That's ⁴abs_____ right, but selecting the most ⁵in_____ facts may not be so easy. Has anyone actually had a chance to ⁶ex_____ their data?

C   Well, I was ⁷com_____ statistics on the average number of hours slept in different years, and the evidence I've got ⁸in_____ that second years sleep the ⁹l_____. If my ¹⁰in_____ is accurate, the amount of time you sleep increases ¹¹_____ 9% from year one to year two. But then afterwards, there's a drop ¹²_____ 17% when you get into the third year.

A   That's a reasonably ¹³sh_____ ¹⁴f_____ between years two and three, isn't it? It must be stress, mustn't it, when you go into the final year?

B   Yes, that ¹⁵m_____ be so, but it could also be that you simply have to put in more hours of work.

C   I ¹⁶a_____. But why do people sleep 9% ¹⁷m_____ in the second year? Can anyone ¹⁸ex_____ that fact?

A   Well, ¹⁹w_____ I think is that in your first year, you're still a bit unsettled. You've got a lot of new information to ²⁰ab_____, haven't you? By the time you get to the second year, you're more relaxed perhaps?

B   Good point. I think you're ²¹r_____. It's a hypothesis, anyway, isn't it, and there's some evidence to ²²su_____ it. OK, what else have we got?

**AWL GLOSSARY**

**select** to choose something from a group of things, usually according to a system

**stress** pressure or worry caused by the problems in somebody's life

**final** being or happening at the end of a series of events, actions, statements, etc.

**hypothesis** an idea or explanation of something that is based on a few known facts but that has not yet been proved to be true or correct

**C** First identify adjectives, verbs, and phrasal verbs that do not sound appropriate in the sentences. Then replace them with the words in the box.

> disturbing   emerge   extensive   hard   preliminary
> produce   retrieve   support   timely   withhold

1 Companies that keep back information from health and safety inspectors may be fined.
2 Everett (2008) maintains that the evidence does not assist the conclusions drawn by Follett in his report.
3 Iqbal (2010) argues that there is no tough evidence to support Kozyrev's claims.
4 Punctual information from the event organizers would have allowed the police to control the situation.
5 The committee insisted that the Department of Work and Pensions should make statistics that the public could understand.
6 The documentary revealed some scary facts about young people involved in online gambling.
7 The first data released by the panel suggests that the oilfield has very limited supplies.
8 The facts did not become visible until two key witnesses were summoned to give evidence.
9 There was wide evidence that some of the officials judging the contest had been bribed.
10 Users found that the new computer system did not allow them to bring back data quickly enough.

**D** Circle the most appropriate option.

As the Knight Foundation [1]*notices/observes/sees* (2007), there continues to be very little [2]*right/truthful/accurate* information on identifying and addressing the needs of girls who have dropped out of education, despite the fact that there has been a [3]*cautious/gradual/graded* increase in their number over the past ten years, as can be [4]*seen/viewed/regarded* in Table 1.2 below. The one exception to this is a report which [5]*got/gathered/saved* evidence on the situation of elder children of large families who were kept at home to help with younger siblings. Statistics [6]*support/express/show* that, once attendance figures were disaggregated by gender, these stay-at-home children were [7]*twice as/double as/more than* likely to be girls as boys. The report [8]*writes/suggests/discusses* that several partial solutions could be adopted, including, for example, the payment of tuition fees and provision of school uniforms. The foundation's [9]*thought is/opinion shows/opinion is* that the distribution of direct financial assistance to families should also be carefully considered.

**E** Look at the two graphs. For each graph, write at least two factual statements, and then interpret the statistics by giving your own opinion. Finally, make a comment on the period from 1971 to 2001, based on the information in both graphs.

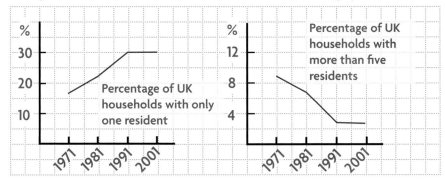

## Introduction

Look at the sentences about Sri Lanka. First, underline the key words (excluding *and*) that connect together the ideas in each sentence – words that could be used for the same purpose in a text on something completely different. Then put the words into three groups, according to whether they add information, express reason and result, or express time.

1 Sri Lanka was colonized first by the Portuguese and the Dutch, and then by the British.
2 Due to its location, Sri Lanka is a strategic naval link between West and South-East Asia.
3 As strong winds meet the mountain slopes of the island's Central Highlands, monsoon rains are unloaded on the slopes and south-western parts of Sri Lanka.
4 Not only does Sri Lanka export tea, coffee, and cinnamon, but it also produces some of the most valuable woods such as mahogany and teak.
5 Sri Lanka has been called 'the pearl of the Indian Ocean' because of its astonishing natural beauty.
6 The island's national parks support elephants, deer, and peacocks, as well as preserving the habitats of storks, pelicans, and spoonbills.

Suggested answers: see page 196

The effective use of connectors such as *also*, *so*, *because*, *while*, and *in spite of* gives a logical flow to your writing, linking ideas within and between sentences. Connectors normally come at the beginning or in the middle of sentences.

• *In spite of* the poor performance of the economy, the government managed to retain a small majority in the general election.
• Some doctors oppose the planned changes to the health service *because* they believe that the new system will require them to spend too much time managing resources rather than treating patients.

In this unit, a wide range of useful and common connectors is divided into seven types.

### Unit contents

Other units that deal with connectors are unit 2 *Comparing and contrasting*, unit 5 *Relative clauses*, unit 8 *Being emphatic*, unit 12 *Cause and effect*, unit 17 *Conditionals*, and unit 20 *Cohesion*.

TIP Connectors are also known as 'connectives', 'linking' or 'connecting' words, and 'conjunctions'.

# 7.1 Expressing reasons and results

## 7.1 study

**1 Reasons**: *because (of), as, since, due to, owing to*

Words like *because*, *as*, and *since* are used to give reasons for actions and events. *Because* is normally placed in the middle of the sentence, where it tends to introduce new or important information.

- *The company website failed **because** visitors found it too difficult to navigate.*

*As* and *since* often come at the beginning of sentences, introducing a reason that may be known already, and leaving the more important information for the end of the sentence.

- *The first fire occurred on a weekend. **As/Since** the office was empty at the time, there were no injuries.*

Before nouns you can use *because of* or, particularly at the beginning of sentences, *due to* and *owing to*.

- *The car was recalled **because of** a design fault in its braking system.*
- ***Owing to/Due to** the recession, most retailers have a recorded a sharp downturn in quarterly profits.*

**2 Results**: *as a result, consequently, therefore*

*As a result*, *consequently*, and *therefore* all have the same meaning. They are used to introduce the results of actions, decisions, etc.

- *The government was hoping that listeners would switch from analogue to digital radio well in advance of the deadline of 2012. **As a result/Consequently/Therefore**, a series of advertisements were planned to highlight the advantages of digital transmission.*
- *Sales rapidly declined and **as a result/consequently/therefore** Bailey Brothers were forced to close their factories.*

Note that it is also possible to place *consequently* and *therefore* in the middle of sentence. In the example above, you could write: *... the deadline of 2012. A series of advertisements were **consequently/therefore** planned ...*

See unit *12 Cause and effect* for more examples of *as a result*, *consequently*, and *therefore*.

**TIP** There are more emphatic alternatives to some of the words and phrases above:

1. *As*, *since*, and *because* may be replaced by *due to the fact that* or *owing to the fact that*.
2. *As a result*, *consequently*, and *therefore* may be replaced by *for this reason* and *that is why*.

It is advisable, however, not to overuse these alternatives.

**3 Results**: *so ... (that)..., such ... (that)*

You can use both of these structures to express results; *so* comes before an adjective or a quantifier (e.g. *many, few*), and *such* before a noun, or adjective + noun.

- *The discussion on the location of the new factory took **so** long **that** there was no time left to agree on its design.*
- *The conference organizers employed **so** few staff **that** delegates had to queue for at least an hour to register.*
- *The online ordering system created **such** confusion **that** a consultant was brought in to redesign it.*
- *There was **such** a high demand for the new product **that** supplies to retailers soon ran out.*

It's also possible to use *so* on its own, but it may sound a little informal in the context of an essay. Here is an example from a presentation.

- 💬 *In fact, the first attempt to change the law on copyright was unsuccessful, **so** the Labour government of the time redrafted their bill.*

---

## 7.1 test yourself

**A Complete each sentence with one or two words.**

1. Rises in the price of oil cause inflation and, as _____, there is upwards pressure on pay.
2. Due _____ the increase in rents, many of the area's tenants are being forced to move out.
3. Older information is stored offsite _____ of a lack of space within the main office.
4. A small business might not have an HR department; the owner may _____ have to take care of personnel issues.
5. Internet marketing can automatically measure its own success _____ websites provide convenient access data.
6. Owing to _____ that the first few performances attracted very small audiences, the show was cancelled at the end of its first week.

**B** Rewrite the information as one sentence, using the connecting word(s) in brackets.

1 The pressure of water was very great. The dam broke. (so ... that)
2 The nuclear facility was damaged by the tsunami. The local area had to be evacuated. (for this reason)
3 Most of the bridges in the region have a very strong structure. They can survive serious earthquakes. (such)
4 The business had made a late surge in sales. The redundancy programme was cancelled. (since)
5 Her first novel was very successful. She immediately gave up her job. (such)
6 There were many complaints. The company withdrew the product. (so ... that)

## 7.2 Expressing purpose

### 7.2 study

You can use all of the following structures to express purpose: *to* + infinitive, *in order (not) to* + infinitive, *so as (not) to* + infinitive, and *so (that)* + clause.

*To* + infinitive can be used in the middle of a sentence, and also, in spoken English, at the beginning. In written English, however, *in order (not) to* is preferred at the beginning of a sentence.
• *The expedition was equipped with tools **to build** bridges across the smaller rivers.*
• 💬 ***To demonstrate** the decline in the rate of these major illnesses, I'm going to show you two graphs.*
• *In **order to** understand the causes of the infection, a team of scientists began a series of laboratory tests.*

*In order (not) to* and *so as (not) to* are often used in spoken and written English as more formal and emphatic connectors than *to*. *So as not to* is less common.
• *We need to develop a new product **in order to** extend our market reach. (= ... **so as to** extend ...)*
• *You will need to wear a mask and gloves **in order not to** contaminate the evidence. (= **so as not to** contaminate ...)*

You can use *so that ...*, often with a modal verb such as *can*, *could*, *will* or *would*, to replace any of these structures with no change in meaning. Note that the subject needs to be restated and can change after *so that*.
• *We will need to launch the product by October in order to gain an edge on our competitors.*
  *= We will need to launch the product by October **so that we can gain** an edge on our competitors.*
• 💬 *I'll finish my presentation by 10.45 **so that you'll be able to** start the meeting at 11.00.*

TIP When using *in order to* when there is a change of subject, *for* goes before the subject.
• *I'll finish my presentation by 10.45 in order **for you** to be able to start the meeting at 11:00.)*

### 7.2 test yourself

Correct each sentence by adding one word.
1 Paper files need to be organized and labelled that staff can find what they need easily.
2 Moresby has taught two chimpanzees sign language in to communicate with them.
3 Meerkats use a special type of call let other members of the group know that a predator is nearby.
4 In order demonstrate the safety of a new car, a number of tests are carried out.
5 The machinery was switched off in order mechanics to repair a number of minor faults.
6 The team had to carry out their observation with caution so as to disturb the nesting birds.

## 7.3 Expressing contrast

### 7.3 study

**1 *But, although, even though, though***

*Although* and *even though* link ideas that seem to contrast with each other. They are both more emphatic than *but*.
• *The team carried out a series of experiments, **but** they were unable to isolate the genetic material.*
• ***Although/Even though** the company has expanded, it hasn't yet increased its profit margin.*
• *Our staff is having difficulty with the new computer program, **although/even though** they have received extensive training.*

In written English, *though* is normally only used in the middle of a sentence. In spoken English *though* can go at the beginning, middle, or end of sentence. When it goes at the end, the two contrasting ideas occur in separate sentences.

- *Strindberg is mainly known as a playwright, **though** he also produced a number of innovative paintings.*
- 💬 *Though I'm enjoying my course, it's hard work.*
  = *I'm enjoying my course, though it's hard work.*
  = *I'm enjoying my course. It's hard work, though.*

### 2 *In spite of, despite*

*In spite of* and *despite* are similar in meaning and position (beginning or middle of a sentence) to *although/even though/though*, but the grammar is different. You can use them with a noun/pronoun or *-ing* form of a verb.

- *Aaron Brothers are on track to break even **despite/in spite of making** losses in the first quarter.*
- ***Despite/In spite of the evidence** presented by expert scientists, some commentators still question the existence of global warming.*

However, you can make them act in the same way as *although* by adding *the fact that*.

- ***In spite of the fact that/Although** he was already profoundly deaf, Beethoven continued to compose.*
- *The company made an overall profit **despite the fact that** sales fell sharply in the autumn.*

### 3 *However, while/whereas*

*However* is useful at the beginning or the end of a sentence in writing or formal speaking to present an argument against something.

- *The Dictionary of the English Language was not Samuel Johnson's only major work, **however**. More than twenty-five years after it appeared, for example, Johnson published the six-volume Lives of the Great Poets.*
- *The UK has certainly built more roads. **However**, it is the train system that has a greater need for new investment.*

Note that it is also possible to place *however* in the middle of a sentence. In the example above, you could write *The UK has certainly built more roads. It is the train system, **however**, that has ...*

*While* and *whereas* are both rather formal, and are often used for making comparisons.

- ***While/Whereas** NATO was created as an alliance against Communist power, the UN was established to keep the peace between nations.*

See unit *2 Comparing and contrasting* for words and phrases for expressing contrast, including *dissimilar, differ, difference, in contrast to*, and *on the contrary*.

---

## 7.3 test yourself

**Circle the correct option.**

1 In spite of/Although we doubled our order from the wholesaler, we still ran out of supplies.
2 Official attendance figures for the protest stand at 5,000. It is clear, whereas/however, that the true figure is much higher.
3 Despite/Even though the product winning design awards, few people seemed to know about it.
4 Several economists have recommended a cut in interest rates, however/though this may cause inflation.
5 While/However children clearly incur medical costs to the state, the care of the oldest members of the community is considerably more expensive.
6 A number of breach of copyright cases have been brought to court. Although/Despite this, the amount of illegal online copying seems to be rising.
7 The interest rate on UK government bonds is 2.2% even though/whereas the rate for French bonds currently stands at 3.2%.
8 Some people refuse to accept that global warming is a threat to our wellbeing, in spite of/however the scientific evidence.

---

## 7.4 Expressing time

### 7.4 study

#### 1 Time words and phrases

The time words *when, whenever, while, before, after, until, as, as soon as, once, by the time, by/in + date*, and *since* come at the beginning or in the middle of a sentence.

- ***Whenever** there is excess supply in a market, we expect to see prices falling.*
- *Van Gogh painted many of his masterpieces **while** he was living at Arles in Provence.*
- ***As soon as** the strength of the bridge has been tested, we can begin planning the opening ceremony.*

In sentences referring to the future with two clauses you must use a present, not a future, tense after the time words.

- We will try to set up some meetings when we ~~will~~ **get** to New York tomorrow morning.
- As the public ~~will~~ **leave** the museum, they will be asked to make a small contribution to its upkeep.

Note that when the word *since* expresses time (rather than a reason, see page 063), you will normally have to use a present perfect tense before it.

- This hospital ~~was inspected~~ **has been inspected** five times since it was opened in 1994.

## 2 Sequencing events

You can use a number of words to order information by time. Some of the most common are: *first(ly)*, *second(ly)*, etc., *then*, *next*, *after that*, *at the same time*, *finally/lastly*.

- *First*, you start the engine. **Then/Next** you press the accelerator. **Then/Next**, you press the clutch pedal with your left foot, and hold it fully down. **After that**, you move the gear lever into first gear, and let the clutch pedal up until you hear the engine noise change slightly. This change means that you are at the biting point. **Finally**, after checking that it is safe to move, you release the handbrake and, **at the same time**, let the clutch pedal come up a little more. The vehicle will begin to move off.

## 3 Other words and phrases

*In the meantime* (which is common in spoken English) and *meanwhile* both mean 'while something else is happening'. *Afterwards* and *subsequently* mean 'after that' and *eventually* means 'after a longer period of time'.

- 💬 *Jeff will now prepare the room for his presentation.* **In the meantime**, *shall we take a coffee break?*
- *Caroline Carman became the Marketing Director in 2005, and the CEO shortly* **afterwards**, *overseeing the merger with Stapleton plc.* **Subsequently**, *she was appointed as a non-executive director of several charities.* **Eventually**, *on retirement, she began a second career as an author and management guru.*

**TIP** *At first* (= *in the beginning*) is different from *first/ly* (= *first in a list*).

- ~~First~~ **At first** *the company's prospects looked good, but things rapidly began to go wrong.*

*At last* (= *after a long delay*) is different from *lastly* (= *last in a list*).

- *When technicians were* ~~lastly~~ **at last** *able to identify the computer virus, the network could be protected.*

*Finally* can mean 'at last' or 'lastly'.

---

## 7.4 test yourself

**A** Circle the correct option.

1 The engineering team continued to test the engine by the time/until they found the fault.
2 We will have a question-and-answer session before we finish/will finish.
3 The government received/has received six offers since the centre was turned over to the private sector.
4 Elcron's sales figures declined in the UK during the second quarter. Subsequently,/Meanwhile, export income for the same period rose dramatically.
5 The construction of the new museum was eventually/afterwards completed in 2009.
6 When the new wing of the hospital will be/ is opened, it will provide bed space for 300 additional patients.

**B** Complete the text, using one of the words or the phrase in the box in each space. One word/phrase is not needed.

> at last    then    same    first    lastly
> next    after

### From wood chips to paper

¹_____ , the wood chips are mixed with water and acid. ²_____ they are heated and crushed to a heavy pulp. ³_____ that, the wood pulp is cleaned, and, at the ⁴_____ time, chemically bleached to whiten it. ⁵_____ it is passed through rollers to flatten it, producing sheets of wet paper. ⁶_____ , the sheets are dried to make the finished paper.

## 7.5 Expressing additional information

### 7.5 study

**1** Apart from *and*, the commonest words which express additional information are *also*, *as well (as)*, and *too*.

The most frequent of these in writing is *also*.
- *We will discuss the decline in Britain's manufacturing base, and we will **also** consider some of the measures the government is taking to arrest this decline.*

*As well* and *too* are normally used at the end of sentences in spoken English.
- 💬 *Although most of my presentation will focus on English cathedrals, I'll discuss one or two examples from France **as well/too**.*

The phrases *as well as* and *in addition to* are followed by the *-ing* form of a verb or by a noun.
- ***As well as/In addition to** eating smaller fish, the tiger shark has been known to consume weaker members of its own family.*
- *Barrow and Wilson sells antique furniture **as well as/ in addition to** rare and first edition books.*

**2** These other connectors all have the same basic meaning, and can add emphasis and variety to your writing: *in addition*, *moreover*, *furthermore*, *what is more*, *not only ... (but) also*.
- *Learners of second languages often have to fit classes around their full-time jobs. **In addition,/Moreover,/ Furthermore,/What is more**, they may be required to show evidence of their progress by taking exams.*
- *Fridtjof Nansen was **not only** an explorer and scientist, **but also** a renowned humanitarian.*

In order to give greater emphasis, you can begin your sentence with *not only ...* If you do this, you need to invert (= change the order of) subject and verb and, if there is no auxiliary verb (*be*, *have*, *will*, etc.) present, you must use a form of *do*.
- *Not only **was Fridtjof Nansen** an explorer and scientist, but also a renowned humanitarian.*
  Or ... (but) he was also a ...
- *Not only ~~succeeded Nansen~~ **did Nansen succeed** in crossing Greenland from east to west, (but) he also managed to gather information on the Eskimos.*

(See page 076 in unit *8 Being emphatic* for more information on emphatic inversion.)

### 7.5 test yourself

**Rewrite the sentences, following the instructions in brackets.**

**1** Charles I lost the Battle of Naseby, and was also forced to give up his crown. (start with *As well as ...*)

**2** The company was declared bankrupt, and the CEO was imprisoned for fraud. (use *moreover* and write two sentences)

**3** Edison patented many new inventions, and he also developed systems for the mass distribution of electricity. (start with *Not only ...*)

**4** The University of Nottingham has its main site in the UK, and campuses in Semenyih, Malaysia and in Ningbo, China. (start with *In addition to its ...*)

**5** The centre's research will increase our understanding of the brain, and it may also help to fight diseases such as cerebral palsy. (start with *Not only ...*)

**6** The National Theatre's production of *Hamlet* ran for two years in the West End, and it toured in India, Australia, and Canada, winning several awards. (use *what is more* and write two sentences)

## 7.6 Using participles to connect ideas

### 7.6 study

For economy, and to maintain the flow of your sentences, you can use participle clauses to link two ideas that have the same subject.
- *Lincoln's Electricals needed to expand abroad to maintain their market share. They bought a small factory outside Paris.*
  → ***Needing** to expand abroad to maintain their market share, Lincoln's Electricals bought a small factory outside Paris.*
- *Lab workers began their tests, **hoping** that they would find the source of the food poisoning by the weekend.*

The perfect participle is used for completed actions.
- ***Having read out** a statement, the Chief Superintendent invited questions from journalists.*

You can use a past participle to replace a passive verb.
- *Penicillin was discovered in 1929. It provided a cure for many serious diseases.* → ***Discovered** in 1929, penicillin provided a cure for many serious diseases.*
- ***Written** around 1600, Hamlet became Shakespeare's most famous tragedy.*

Present participles can replace subject + main verb after the time words *after, before, since,* and *while.*
- *After **investigating** (= after they had investigated) the causes of the accident, flight engineers recommended withdrawing the remaining Concordes from service.*
- *You should talk to the tutor before **changing** (= before you change) your course again.*
- *Since **leaving** (= since they left) college, 20% of graduates have been unable to find work.*
- *While **travelling** (= while he was travelling) with the British navy, on the ship* HMS Surprise, *the naturalist Maturin was able to collect rare species of wild plant.*

If the meaning is clear, you can also replace connecting words such as *because, so,* and *therefore* with a participle.
- ***Not being** (= Because it isn't) far from the centre of the city, the museum attracts many visitors.*
- *The new model of bank opens on a Sunday, **making** (= so it makes) it easier for customers to visit.*
- *A video link may be set up in court for vulnerable witnesses such as children, **preventing** them (= and therefore they are prevented) from having to give evidence in person.*

## 7.6 test yourself

**Rewrite the sentences, using the present, past, or perfect participle of the underlined verb.**

1 The Democrats <u>needed</u> to regain California, so they launched a series of aggressive TV ads.
2 Before he <u>began</u> his expeditions, Amundsen always made meticulous preparations.
3 Hans Blix and his team were <u>refused</u> access to the nuclear facility, so they had to return to their hotel.
4 Because Professor Ancram had <u>worked</u> through the night, she was able to announce her results before the midday deadline.
5 After they had <u>exploited</u> known reserves around the world, oil companies began to look to the Arctic for new sources of petroleum.
6 The bridge rises automatically on the approach of tall ships, and therefore <u>allows</u> them to pass safely through.

## 7.7 Giving examples and rephrasing

### 7.7 study

Some connecting words and phrases may be useful to you in indicating that the next part of the text will give an example, an explanation, a paraphrase, or a summary.

1 You can use *for example, for instance, e.g.,* and *such as* to introduce an example or examples. *For example* is more common than *for instance; e.g.* tends to be used for a series of short examples.
- *Grierson plc made many attempts to enter the American market. **For instance**, it acquired a small mail order company in Wisconsin in 2009.*
- *Another solution is to digitize information, and give coded access to those who need it. This would mean, **for example**, that the sales team would have access to all the information they might need while on the road contacting clients.*
- *One can save files on a physical object **such as** a hard drive or on a memory stick, or one can save them on a server hosted elsewhere.*
- *Micronutrients (**e.g.** chromium, iodine, and zinc) are found in such small quantities in the body that their presence may need to be detected by spectrographic methods.*

2 *That is to say, i.e., in other words,* and *namely* are sometimes used to introduce a definition, paraphrase or a particular example.
- *Many countries depend on primary industries, **that is to say**, industries that take directly from the earth or sea.*
- *The kangaroo is a marsupial, **i.e.** an animal that suckles its young in a pouch on the mother's belly.*
- *Cars contribute to, and are symbolic of, what has come to be called the 'obesogenic' environment we now find ourselves in. **In other words**, society and our cities are now shaped in a way that makes us likely to become fat.*
- *We will look at four management models, and we will then examine how they fit, or fail to fit, one organization, **namely** a university.*

**3** *In brief, to sum up,* and *in conclusion* can be used to introduce restatements in summarized form.

- ⬤ (in a presentation) ... *and these are no more than a few examples of the airborne pollution that now afflicts the mega-cities we have allowed to develop. We are,* **in brief,** *poisoning the very air that sustains our urban lives.*

- **In conclusion,** *it seems clear that in times of recession a significant proportion of investors will revert to traditionally safer holdings such as gold.*

## 7.7 test yourself

**Circle the correct option.**

**1** The first works of many writers, that is to say/ such as D. H. Lawrence and James Joyce, derive almost entirely from the experience of their own early lives.

**2** The list price, i.e./e.g. the price of an article as listed by the manufacturer, may be subject to discount by the retailer.

**3** Some peoples, for example/in other words, the French, are renowned for the quality of their restaurants.

**4** An individual has two options when confronted with a problematic situation, for instance/ namely to change the situation, or to change themselves so that the situation becomes tolerable.

**5** Namely/To sum up, authenticating paintings has become a much more reliable process, but can perhaps never be perfected.

# 07 Challenge yourself

**A** Complete the text, using the connectors in the box.

> but   consequently   in brief   in other words   namely   since
> subsequently   that is to say

Legal tourism, [1]_____ , the practice of bringing a case to court in whatever jurisdiction is deemed most favourable, has increased markedly over the past ten years. It is particularly noticeable in two areas of law, [2]_____ divorce and libel.

Although a couple may both be citizens of a certain country, and may meet and marry and [3]_____ live in that country, there is little to stop the aggrieved party ([4]_____ , the spouse who wants the divorce) from initiating legal proceedings wherever that person thinks the case is most likely to succeed. International legal disputes tend to be expensive, [5]_____ in the case of very rich people (or, as the jargon has it, 'high-net-worth individuals'), the gamble can prove worthwhile.

[6]_____ the laws surrounding marriage break-up vary widely around the world, some lawyers and their wealthy clients shop around. English divorce laws are perceived to favour the less wealthy spouse, usually the wife, and [7]_____ the English courts are seeing more and more divorces in which neither party has a strong connection to England. [8]_____ , the system is being abused.

**AWL GLOSSARY**

**legal** connected with the law

**couple** two people who are married or in a romantic or sexual relationship

**initiate** to make something begin

**proceedings** the process of using a court to settle a disagreement or to deal with a complaint

**vary** to change or be different according to the situation

**perceive** to understand or think of something in a particular way

**B** Correct the underlined phrases if necessary in this description of African safaris. Some phrases are correct.

[1]Due to the steep drop in the numbers of big game ([2]i.e. elephant, rhino, lion), hunt organizers had to take drastic action in the 1960s and 1970s. [3]Since local extinctions gathered pace, they saw their livelihoods at risk. [4]In order to preserve the habitat, they pressed for legal changes, [5]such that the establishment of national parks. [6]Meanwhile as the decline in big game hunting came the increase in non-lethal pursuits. The purpose of these journeys was [7]to track and shoot the animals, [8]but no longer with rifles. These 'camera safaris' began as an organized activity in Kenya and South Africa. [9]As 2010 the industry was valued globally at hundreds of millions of dollars. This branch of eco-tourism, carried on mostly at the level of small-scale businesses, has larger political ramifications in that governments and local authorities may choose to support it, [10]for example, by building up the infrastructure, providing financial encouragement, producing tourist material, and so on.

**C** Match the beginning of each sentence with the correct ending.

**1** Before the discovery of antibiotics, ___
**2** As soon as these naturally occurring compounds had been isolated in the lab, ___
**3** At first, this was difficult, ___
**4** Eventually, the correct protocols were established, ___

**a** because competing varieties contaminated the samples under investigation.
**b** scientists attempted to produce them to order.
**c** simple infections killed untold thousands of people a year.
**d** so the commercial process speeded up.

**D** Match the beginning of each sentence with the correct ending.

**1** After the first antibiotic compound proved effective at treating a human illness, ___
**2** The discovery and development of these drugs took place ___
**3** In addition to funding new weapons technology, ___
**4** As a result, when war broke out, army doctors were able to use antibiotics to treat battlefield injuries, ___
**5** Penicillin, for instance, was widely used, ___
**6** Moreover, it was well tolerated (that is, few patients had a negative reaction to it); ___

**a** as it killed many types of bacteria.
**b** as well as infections acquired off-duty.
**c** by the time its drawbacks were known, the war was over.
**d** many countries wished to support biomedical research with military applications.
**e** other scientists redoubled their investigative efforts.
**f** while Europe was gearing up for World War II.

**E** Correct the connectors. There is one mistake in each numbered sentence. Do not change any punctuation.

[1]Information needs to be recorded and stored safely, as well as all who need it have access to it in a timely fashion. [2]The organization's old paperwork is a valuable historical resource and, as our offices are small and our history long, we do not have the space to keep it all. [3]We have whereas taken steps to store it offsite. [4]In this way the documents are fairly accessible, however they do not take up room in the office.

**F** Circle the correct option (a–d) to complete the six short texts.

One of the quirks of the MegaCorp employment process is that existing employees are encouraged to act up, ¹___ to perform roles on a temporary basis at a level slightly more senior than their experience and qualifications would normally allow. An employee may do a job ably for months, if not years. ²___, when the position is formally advertised and filled, that worker may well be passed over. Until that process began, the employee had had a reasonable level of job satisfaction. ³___ the permanent member of staff is appointed, the long-term employee may have become resentful towards the organization. ⁴___, they may leave, and in the meantime their productivity is likely to suffer.

The choice is apparent: either the two partners demarcate the sides of the business entirely (⁵___ one deals with suppliers and the other with customers), or they find ways of sharing more than the minimum of information. When a micro-enterprise hires its first employee, the lines of communication triple: ⁶___ what previously existed, we must factor in A to C, C to A, and also B to C and C to B.

Some householders with ample storage space choose to bulk-buy their food from out-of-town superstores. Once the costs of driving there and back are taken into consideration, ⁷___, it is not clear that this represents a real savings.

⁸___ American companies stripmine parts of their own country, they are subject to criticism and protest. The protesters, ⁹___, are not in the main calling for the overthrow of the capitalist system – even the terminology seems dated. Instead, they are attacking one company or one industry, and trusting to the legal system and public opinion to help win their case.

It is necessary to have watertight proof of wrong-doing ¹⁰___ firing a staff member for gross misconduct such as theft, or their dismissal could ¹¹___ be deemed unfair by an industrial tribunal. There also remains the issue of error; if it turns out that the employee was not, after all, involved in the theft, then the employer has lost a valuable employee for nothing. ¹²___, there is the bad PR that such a move may generate.

¹³___ multinational agribusiness is thriving, it is difficult for family farmers to survive. Government subsidy goes to big producers with clout; lobbyists for meat and dairy ensure that their industries do well, ¹⁴___ orchards continue to be dug up and heritage vegetable varieties lost. However, there are tendencies working against this centralization, ¹⁵___ the Slow Food campaign, and the movements for organic produce and free-range animal products, for traceability and provenance, for farmers' markets, and for locally-grown food.

**AWL GLOSSARY**

**role** the function or position that somebody has or is expected to have in an organization, in society, or in a relationship

**partner** one of the people who owns a business and shares the profits, etc.

**communication** the activity or process of expressing ideas and feelings or of giving people information

**issue** an important topic that people are discussing or arguing about

**survive** to continue to live or exist

**subsidy** money that is paid by a government or an organization to reduce the costs of services or of producing goods so that their prices can be kept low

**ensure** to make sure that something happens or is definite

1 a nevertheless    b on the other hand    c i.e.    d subsequently
2 a Finally    b Even though    c As well    d However
3 a By the time    b Whereas    c Additionally    d Because
4 a Eventually    b So that    c In order to    d Whenever
5 a at first    b e.g.    c at last    d in order to
6 a in addition to    b also    c but also    d afterwards
7 a moreover    b as well as    c even though    d though
8 a In the meantime    b Whenever    c At the same time    d Subsequently
9 a on the other hand    b while    c however    d whereas
10 a as soon as    b while    c before    d after
11 a meanwhile    b in the meantime    c on the one hand    d subsequently
12 a Next    b At last    c Finally    d Apparently
13 a On the one hand    b Even though    c But    d Despite
14 a nevertheless    b whereas    c in spite of    d despite
15 a that is to say    b namely    c as well    d such as

G Look at the seven categories of connectors covered in unit 7. Try to use at least one
from each category in a brief description (100–200 words). Write about, or write
the script for a talk about, either the economy of your country or an organization
you know well.

## Introduction

> Read the two texts and underline five differences in the second text. What effect do these changes have?

For the first time in history, more people live in cities than in the country. This has been true of industrialized countries for a century at least, but now it is also true for the rest of the world. As these conurbations grow ever larger, their transport infrastructures need to keep pace. These days we see cities grinding to a halt too often under the pressure of traffic jams. By stepping back and taking a fresh approach to our transport systems we will be able to ensure that the places where most of us now live can actually function.

For the first time in history, more people live in cities than in the country. In fact, this has been true of industrialized countries for a century at least. Now it is also true for the rest of the world. As these conurbations grow ever larger, it is vital that their transport infrastructures keep pace. What we see too often these days are cities grinding to a halt under the pressure of traffic jams. Only by stepping back and taking a fresh approach to our transport systems will we be able to ensure that the places where most of us now live can actually function.

Suggested answers: see page 198

Although academic writing is often characterized by the need to be cautious (see unit *14 Hedging*), there are times when, for the sake of argument or clarity, you may want to be emphatic, either in expressing your own point of view, or in representing the emphatic views of others. Being emphatic means stressing the importance of something (often in contrast to another thing or other things) or expressing a strongly-held or extreme view or opinion.

The following techniques for giving emphasis to your ideas are covered in this unit.

1  Using emphatic sentence structures.
* *What governments and the scientific community need to find in the area of embryonic stem cell research is a compromise that will allow medical advances and public opinion to coexist in relative harmony.*

2  Using emphatic inversions.
* *Only by increasing its budget will the Serious Fraud Office be able to fight online deception effectively.*

3  Using emphatic adverbs.
* 💬 (in a presentation) *In the view of our group, it remains entirely unacceptable for a democratic country to consider torture as one of its intelligence gathering options.*

4  Using emphatic expressions.
* *In Frayling's view there can be no doubt that child poverty is a significant barrier to educational achievement.*

## 8.1 Emphatic sentence structures

### 8.1 study

There are two key ways in which you can restructure your sentences to give greater impact to parts of them.

**1** *It + be* + relative clause

By using this structure, you can place a greater emphasis on the first part of your sentence (underlined in the example below).

- *It is <u>the Cabinet</u> that should be the main forum for agreeing policy within the government.*

This sentence might be criticizing a prime minister who took decisions without consulting his or her Cabinet, and is more emphatic than saying *The Cabinet should be the main forum for agreeing policy within the government.*

In the following example, the writer wants to draw attention to Skerritt's opinion on 'constant practice' in language learning.

- *According to Skerritt, it is through constant practice rather than memorization that you ultimately master a second language. (Compare with You ultimately master a second language through constant practice rather than memorization.)*

If you are emphasizing a personal subject, you can replace *that* with *who.*

- *It is only the monarch who can dissolve parliament under the British constitution.*

(See also unit *5 Relative clauses*)

**TIP** Sometimes you can be emphatic just by using short sentences. This is particularly effective in academic English where short simple sentences contrast with the normal style of long sentences with complex structures.

- *It has been argued that land that has been 'strip-mined' can be reclaimed for agricultural purposes. **This is rarely the case.***
- *Hasty inquiries produce poor conclusions. In 2003 the Bastow inquiry spent just ten days examining the evidence submitted by a parliamentary select committee and two police investigations.*

**2** *What*-clause + *be*

With this structure you can place the emphasis on the second part of your sentence (underlined in the example below).

- ***What** we need is an advertisement <u>that will capture the public's imagination</u>. (Compare with We need an advertisement that will capture the public's imagination.)*

Note that additional information that would normally be placed at the beginning or end of a sentence is included between *what* and *be*, and that a plural noun would require the plural form of *be.*

- ***What** we need <u>in order to succeed</u> **are** advertisements that will capture the public's imagination. (Compare with We need advertisements that will capture the public's imagination in order to succeed.)*

In the example above, the focus is on a noun phrase (*advertisements that* ...). To emphasize a verb phrase (e.g. *gain full security clearance* ... below), the verb *do* can be used, followed by an infinitive, normally without *to.*

- *What a candidate for a post at the UN must **do** is (to) gain full security clearance before they can proceed.*

Note, however, that you would not normally emphasize a reporting verb (e.g. *assert, think*).

- *What Fonseca ~~does is believe~~ believes is that fictional heroines still tend to be stereotypes more often than their male counterparts.*

**TIP** To emphasize a noun, you can place a reflexive pronoun after it (normally the third person singular *itself* or plural *themselves*).

- *The symptoms of the disease cannot always be recognized, and the disease itself is notoriously hard to treat.*
- *It was found in the report that contact needed to be made with the senior managers themselves before a satisfactory response could be obtained.*

## 8.1 test yourself

**A** Rewrite each sentence to emphasize the underlined phrase, starting with the word(s) in brackets.

1 A business requires <u>a healthy reserves account</u> for its long-term viability. (What ...)
2 The Americans were seeking <u>a fundamental change</u> in the presidential election of 2008. (It was ...)
3 The advocates of a traditional encyclopedia contend that <u>its research is more objective than that of Wikipedia</u>. (What ...)
4 <u>The police</u> were accused of breaking the law during their investigation. (It is ...)
5 None of the focus groups <u>placed priority on the privacy rights of celebrities</u>. (What ...)
6 Travellers are generally looking for <u>value for money</u> rather than luxury in an airline operator. (It is ...)

**B** Add one or two words to each sentence to make them correct.

1 What the journalist Hongkyu Choe saw first when he arrived hundreds of refugees attempting to leave the city.
2 Colm (2007) suggests that was Isaac Asimov's profound knowledge of chemistry and physics enabled him to become one of America's most influential science fiction novelists.
3 Layard (2008) argues that some economists do not understand is that people's idea of a sufficient income grows with their actual income.
4 What the festival organizers failed to do provide enough car parking space for the extra participants arriving for the final night.
5 As He (2009) explains, the tropical climate in the Nanling region of China that allows two crops of rice to grow per year.
6 According to Nahm (2010), it was William Ramsay first appreciated the medical potential of radiotherapy.

## 8.2 Emphatic inversions

### 8.2 study

If you want to emphasize the negative or limited nature of a situation, you can place certain negative or limiting words or phrases at the beginning of a sentence or a clause.

When you do this, you must invert (= reverse or change) normal word order by placing the auxiliary or modal verb (*be, have, will*, etc.), if there is one, or a form of *do*, in front of the subject.

- ***Rarely*** ~~there has~~ **has there been** *a time, argues Patel, when so many demographic and medical changes were occurring simultaneously.*
- ***No sooner*** ~~the company reported~~ **did the company report** *record earnings in 2009,* **than** *it sold its factory in Northampton and changed direction completely.*

**1 Limiting words and phrases:** *only + -ing, rarely, seldom*

By placing these words at the beginning of your sentence or clause you can limit or restrict the action or event, and therefore put emphasis on it.

- ***Only by holding*** *a referendum will the government be able to resolve this issue.*
- ***Rarely/Seldom*** *do we see a collection of paintings as innovative and wide-ranging as those currently on display at the National Gallery's exhibition 'The Modernists'.*

Note that *only by* is normally followed by *will* or *can*. Other prepositional/adverbial phrases are possible after *only*.

- ***Only after teaching*** *for twenty years did Hilbrandt turn to composing.*

**2 Time phrases:** *hardly ... when, no sooner ... than, not since/until, at no time, never*

By placing these words and phrases at the beginning of your sentence or clause (and using *when* or *than* in the middle with the first two structures), you can emphasize the speed or unique nature of an event or action.

- ***Hardly*** *had the committee reconvened* **when** *the chairperson declared that they could proceed no further.*
- ***No sooner*** *did the advertisement appear* **than** *it was reported to the Trading Standards Authority.* (It is also possible to say *No sooner had the advertisement appeared than ...* without changing the meaning.)

- *Not since the Second World War, concludes the report, has air travel experienced the kind of disruption caused by the volcanic ash cloud.*
- *At no time during the investigation did any of the senior managers offer their resignation.*
- *Never had pharmaceutical companies seen such a period of growth as the 1980s.*

3 **Negative phrases:** *on no account, under no circumstances, neither/nor*

By placing these words and phrases at the beginning of your sentence or clause you can emphasize the negative nature of your meaning. Note that *on no account* and *under no circumstances* are often followed by *should*.

- *On no account/Under no circumstances should infants younger than six months be vaccinated against yellow fever, according to practitioners.*
- *The UK had not experienced this level of industrial dispute before, and neither/nor had it prepared itself for the resulting shortage of coal and therefore electricity.*

(See page 067 in unit *7 Connectors* for more information on the use of *not only ... but also*.)

---

## 8.2 test yourself

**Rewrite the sentences, starting with the word(s) in brackets.**

1 Prime Minister Eden never appeared to be in control of the Suez crisis. (At no time ...)
2 Business confidence has not been so low since the recession of the early 1990s. (Not since ...)
3 The capital has rarely witnessed such a large protest march. (Rarely ...)
4 The amount of food transportation will decline when people buy more local produce. (Only when ...)
5 Doctors should never be employed without a full check of their qualifications. (Under no circumstances ...)
6 The moment the talks broke down, fighting began once again in the region. (No sooner ...)

---

## 8.3 Emphatic adverbs

### 8.3 study

Note that most of the adverbs in this section take a mid-position (just after the auxiliary verbs *be* and *have* and just before other verbs), but some, such as *in fact*, *undoubtedly*, and *invariably*, can also come first in a sentence, and a few, such as *categorically* and *emphatically*, may come after the main verb.

1 *Especially, essentially, even, in particular, only,* and *particularly* can all be used to focus attention on particular parts of a sentence, which are underlined in the examples below.
- *It is difficult, **especially** during a recession, for small companies to persuade their banks to lend them money.*
- *Collins argues that there are **essentially** two forces that motivate people: self-interest and fear.*
- *Riverside property **in particular** needs to be protected against flooding.*

2 *Actually, indeed, in fact,* and *of course* emphasize that something is true.
- *None of the evidence **actually** confirms that humans suffer injury as a result of regular exposure to these low temperatures.*
- *The majority of new employees within the civil service are drawn from the ranks of the temporary or contract staff. **In fact**, the available statistics demonstrate that the most common way to secure a job is to begin as a casual employee.*

3 *Absolutely, categorically, completely, entirely, utterly,* and *wholly* all share the core meaning of *completely. Absolutely* is the most flexible, collocating with many adjectives and verbs. *Utterly* tends to be used when being critical or disapproving of someone or something.
- *Angry travellers **absolutely** refused to wait calmly as the number of cancelled flights increased.*
- *Craigson denied **categorically** that he had been involved in insider trading.*
- *Samson argued that it was **utterly** irresponsible for local councils to subcontract services to providers with civil court actions against them.*

⌐TIP Note that the adverb *quite* can have the same meaning as the adverbs in 3 above when combined with ungradable adjectives such as *absurd, certain, different, false, impossible, right, sure, true, useless,* and *wrong.* ( = completely wrong).
- *The argument that children from privileged backgrounds are innately more intelligent is **quite wrong**.*

**4** Clearly, emphatically, indisputably, obviously, undeniably, undoubtedly, and unquestionably are used to emphasize that there can be little argument or doubt about the facts, and they should therefore be used with care.

- There are **clearly** several options when a company is perceived to be failing.
- She was **indisputably** the best candidate for the job, according to the chair of the interview panel.
- **Undoubtedly**, there are still questions to be asked about the siting of nuclear reactors.

**5** Invariably and unfailingly share the meaning 'always'.
- **Invariably**, consumers in focus groups will express ideas that advertisers had not predicted.

(See also section **8.4** below for the use of certainly and definitely to express the idea that there is no doubt.)

## 8.3 test yourself

**Circle the more appropriate option. In one sentence both options are correct.**

1 Bolivia has had to deal with political instability, and absolutely/indeed revolution, in some of the countries that surround it.
2 Only/Completely half of the companies investigated had filed their annual statements with Companies House.
3 Food purchasing habits in the poorest communities are even/completely different from those in affluent areas.
4 Political polls unfailingly/wholly show a decline in the popularity of a new leader after a year in power.
5 The situation in the south of the country is, however, entirely/quite different.
6 Producers argued emphatically/utterly that the new legislation would damage their businesses.
7 Only/Even successful companies can undergo periods where they question their key goals.
8 Categorically/Obviously, confidential information needs to be stored with care.

## 8.4 Emphatic expressions

### 8.4 study

There are a number of expressions that you can use to add emphasis to your own point of view or to describe the emphatic views of others.

**1** It is/was + clear/obvious/indisputable/inevitable/undeniable that or It is/was + clear/obvious (to someone/something) + that …

- **It was obvious** to the panel **that** the project lacked sustainability.
- **It is undeniable that** there is an immediate need for improvements in the city's infrastructure.

**TIP** Verbs that present clear evidence (such as demonstrate, prove, reveal, show), especially when used without cautious or tentative language, can sound emphatic by themselves.
- These results **demonstrate** that the high stress levels produced by sudden loud noises return to normal in a relatively short space of time. (Compare with These results **may** demonstrate …)

**2** It is/was + necessary/imperative/crucial/vital that … or It is/was + necessary/imperative/crucial/vital for someone/something + infinitive with to …

- As Hoskins points out, **it is imperative for small businesses to have** good credit with suppliers.
- **It was crucial that** the fire was stopped before it reached the chemical factories on the outskirts of the city.

**TIP** Some verbs have more emphatic alternatives with a similar meaning (should → must, state → assert, ask → insist/demand, dislike → detest, criticize → condemn).
- The solutions that are proposed **must** include some investment in programmes of education. (Compare with The solutions that are proposed **should** include …)

**3** There is/was/can be + no doubt that …

- **There is no doubt that** large sections of the Amazon rainforest will be destroyed within the next five years unless some form of concerted action is taken.
- **There was no doubt** at the time, according to the accountants that were called in, **that** the company had to be closed down rapidly to prevent further losses.

Note also the expression *without doubt*.
- *It is **without doubt** the case that surrealism would not have emerged as a movement without the activities of the Dada movement during the First World War.*

[TIP] Expressions using *certain*, *certainly*, and *definitely* can also express the idea that there is no doubt.
- *Allowing sixteen-year-olds to vote is **certain** to be a controversial proposal.*
- *There will **definitely** not be any new investment this year in the city's half-built leisure centre.*

## 8.4 test yourself

**Complete the sentences, using one word in each space.**

1 It _____ clear _____ observers that the peace process cannot be restarted while fighting continues.
2 There _____ certain _____ be a high demand for a cheaper, eco-friendly family car.
3 It _____ vital _____ developing countries continue to submit cases to the International Court of Justice in The Hague.
4 There _____ be _____ doubt, in Fisher's view, that all reasonable steps to prevent the spread of the disease were taken.
5 It _____ crucial _____ a company facing significant losses to establish and follow a clear action plan.
6 It _____ undeniable _____ some of the evidence collected on the trip was overlooked.

# 08 Challenge yourself

**A** In the text about volcanic ash, rewrite the phrases in italics to emphasize the words in bold. Use the words (1–6).

One of the by-products, when a volcano erupts, is volcanic ash. As Pieterson (2008) points out, [1]*the ash from a volcano often causes more damage to human life than the heat and fire.* He cites the eruption of Mount Pelée on the island of Martinique in 1902; [2]***as soon as*** *the residents of St Pierre had emerged from their houses, believing they were safe, they were enveloped in a cloud of poisonous ash,* resulting in 29,000 fatalities.

Dencott (2011) describes the more recent difficulties caused by clouds of volcanic ash. [3]***She focuses*** *on the fine ash that is drawn up into the atmosphere,* where it becomes a danger to aircraft. Damage to a plane's engines can occur quite rapidly when it enters an ash cloud. [4]*A pilot can hope to limit the risk only by* ***decreasing power***; any attempt to 'outfly' the cloud is likely to worsen the situation.

After the eruptions in Iceland sent volcanic ash into the atmosphere in 2010, the relevant authorities came to the conclusion that [5]***they had to*** *close the airspace over much of Europe,* thus preventing commercial flights from taking off. Khan (2011) criticizes this decision, believing that rather than a balanced assessment of the risks, [6]***our health and safety culture*** *makes us overreact in situations such as these.*

| | | |
|---|---|---|
| **1** it ... rather than | **3** What ... is | **5** what ... was |
| **2** no ... than | **4** Only ... can | **6** it is ... that |

**B** Circle the most appropriate option to complete the text about internet fraud.

As the years pass, there is [1]*certain/definitely/obvious* to be an increase in the amount of internet fraud, according to Stapleton (2011), [2]*particularly/actually/indeed* in the area of online banking. It is [3]*certain/obvious/crucial* to the financial authorities, he explains, that as more transactions are completed electronically, a greater number of criminals will move into this field of activity. [4]*Especially,/Indeed,/Even,* statistics released by the Office of Fair Trading (2012) already indicate a significant rise over the last two quarters in online banking fraud.

It is [5]*obvious/certain/crucial*, as Gower and Lutz (2011) maintain, for authorities dealing with online fraud to realize that there are two [6]*even/quite/only* distinct tasks required for the fight against this type of illegal activity. The first, they suggest, [7]*clearly/utterly/quite* involves a continual updating of expert technical knowledge by the authorities, in order to keep one step ahead of the fraudsters. The second task, however, may be [8]*only/even/quite* more important: the patient checking of an almost endless supply of financial data for patterns of abnormal behaviour.

**AWL GLOSSARY**

**indicate** to show that something is true or exists

**significant** large or important enough to have an effect or to be noticed

**task** a piece of work that somebody has to do, especially a hard or unpleasant one

**technical** connected with a particular subject and therefore difficult to understand if you do not know about that subject

**abnormal** different from what is usual or expected, especially in a way that is worrying, harmful, or not wanted

**C** In the text about people who impersonate doctors, rewrite the phrases in italics, using the introductory words (1–6).

Gray (2007) describes a second type of imposter, which she refers to by the commonly used term 'fake doctor'. [1]*She discovered a pattern of behaviour* that should act as a warning to health service managers. Typically, these impostors begin their career as support staff in large hospitals. [2]*Qualifications are seldom required* for such posts, as Gray notes. [3]*They only make their first attempt to act as doctors when they have spent at least six months in these positions.*

[4]*However, the behaviour of members of the public and senior staff towards these impostors is the most interesting aspect*, according to Gray. [5]*Without doubt* the fake doctor's ability to inspire confidence prevents patients from questioning their medical judgments. And, as far as senior staff are concerned, she cites the case of the imposter Thomas Baxter. [6]*He was never asked during his two-year period as a hospital doctor* to produce proof of his status, an error that Gray can only explain by reference to his self-confident attitude.

| | | |
|---|---|---|
| **1** What | **3** Not until | **5** There |
| **2** Rarely | **4** However, it | **6** At no time |

**D** In the text about 'sofa government', circle the most appropriate options. In two cases more than one option is correct.

According to O'Donnell (2009), it is [1]*entirely/undoubtedly/invariably* the case that the practice of Cabinet decision-making has changed in the last fifteen years. She argues that this is [2]*even/quite/essentially* due to the personal style of Tony Blair, Prime Minister of the United Kingdom from 1997 to 2005. Blair, it seems, was [3]*absolutely/only/quite* convinced that his party's vision could not succeed unless key decisions were made outside the forum of regular Cabinet meetings.

O'Donnell [4]*only/in fact/utterly* credits Blair with the invention of what has been described as 'sofa government', the process by which major decisions are [5]*completely/invariably/absolutely* taken by a small group of ministers and advisers and then referred to Cabinet for official approval. Constitutional experts may believe this to be [6]*wholly/even/utterly* wrong, as O'Donnell points out, but Blair's colleague and adviser Mandelson (2010) argues that it was [7]*necessary/important/inevitable*, at least in the early years of government, that new premier Blair would require this form of control. Mandelson goes on to assert that sofa government [8]*actually/particularly/absolutely* produced some of the administration's greatest policy achievements.

**AWL GLOSSARY**

**style** the particular way in which something is done

**convinced** completely sure about something

**vision** the ability to think about or plan the future with great imagination and intelligence

**credit** to believe or say that somebody is responsible for doing something, especially something good

**E** Make the text more emphatic by using some of the language from unit 8.

The electric car should not be dismissed as the vehicle of the future. Despite its low sales, it can be argued that the long-term case for an alternative to the internal combustion engine remains convincing. Petrol prices are rising year on year, and most observers feel that the need to reduce greenhouse gas emissions is still a global priority.

The government should, as environmentalists point out, offer greater incentives to the potential buyers of electric cars. This must include an increase in the number of re-charging points throughout the country, further subsidies on price at the point of purchase, and greater support for the research that could lead to cheaper battery technology. By taking these measures, the government can play its part in creating a system of sustainable public transport.

## Introduction

Verbs can be in the active or the passive voice. When we use the passive voice we begin the sentence with the thing or person being acted on (or being affected by the action) and not with the thing or person carrying out the action (the agent). The subject of a passive sentence would normally be the object of an active sentence. The passive is formed by using a form of *be* with a past participle. If an agent is mentioned in the sentence, it comes after *by*.

- Passive: *One of the earliest accounts of the Nuremberg trials was written in 1945 by Robert H Jackson, the US Chief Prosecutor.*
- Active: *Robert H Jackson, the US Chief Prosecutor, wrote one of the earliest accounts of the Nuremberg trials in 1945.*

The passive is fairly common in academic writing, where an impersonal or neutral tone is often preferred, and where the emphasis may be on results, events or processes, rather than agents.

- *When the vaccine **had been produced**, it **was stored** in airtight containers and **transported** under military escort to the main hospital in the region.*

This unit looks at when to use the passive, how to form the passive in different tenses and with prepositions, and the passive with reporting verbs.

Other units that deal with passives are unit *1 Tense review*, and unit *4 Being formal and informal*.

> Read the two versions of the text. Then underline the passive verb forms in the second one. Why do you think the writer decided to use the passive in the second version?

The Chrysler Building is currently the third tallest skyscraper in New York City. William Van Alen designed it in Art Deco style, and building contractors started work in September 1928. They completed the tower less than two years later, after bricklayers had laid nearly four million bricks manually. In 2007, the American Institute of Architects ranked it ninth on the 'List of America's Favorite Architecture'.

The Chrysler Building is currently the third tallest skyscraper in New York City. It was designed in Art Deco style by William Van Alen, and work was started in September 1928. The tower was completed less than two years later, after nearly four million bricks had been laid manually. In 2007, it was ranked ninth on the 'List of America's Favorite Architecture' by the American Institute of Architects.

**Suggested answers: see page 199**

# 9.1 Avoiding the agent

## 9.1 study

The passive is often used when the agent is obvious, very general, unimportant, or unknown.

- *70% of the operations **were carried out** within two days of the patients **being admitted** to the hospital.* (It's obvious that doctors or surgeons would carry out the operations, and hospital staff would admit the patients.)
- *Passports **can be renewed** online or at a post office.* (The agents are 'people' in general.)
- *An opinion poll **was conducted** in Scotland to find out how much support there currently is for independence.* (The agent – a market research company in this case, presumably – is unimportant.)
- *Two students **were attacked** on their way home from a town centre club.* (The agent is unknown. No one knows who attacked the students.)

The agent is usually obvious, general, unimportant or unknown when processes are being described. It is very common to use the passive in this case, particularly when there are a number of stages to mention.

- *To ensure their freshness, peas **are shelled**, **sorted**, **washed**, and **frozen** within two hours of being picked.*

(See section **9.6** below for information on including the agent.)

### 9.1 test yourself

**Rewrite the sentences so that the underlined phrase is the subject. Do not include the agent.**

1 A company launched <u>a new device for measuring the purity of water</u> at a conference in Manchester last year.
2 Factories abroad make <u>most of the spare parts for the car</u>.
3 Construction companies build <u>some new urban roads</u> without pavements.
4 Someone stole <u>four laptops</u> from the offices of the research team.
5 People can obtain <u>copies of the company's annual report</u> from reception.
6 Staff print, pack, and distribute <u>the new brochures</u> to all the retail outlets.

# 9.2 Ordering information

## 9.2 study

You can use the passive to put information in the order that best suits the text. You may wish to mention the action, idea, or event itself first, for example, rather than the agent or agents.

- *A potential cure for Alzheimer's has been discovered by scientists working at the Hays Laboratory in Texas.*

In the text below, the writer introduces *the President* as the main topic in the first sentence, and then uses the passive to keep him as the subject of the next two sentences.

- *At around 4.30 p.m., the President arrived in Lagos. **He was shown** a new building project before **being taken** to the restored Museum of Ancient Art. Later **he was offered** tea at the Mayor's residence on Princes Street.*

Notice what the alternative in the active voice might look like.

- *At around 4.30 p.m., the President arrived in Lagos. His hosts showed him a new building project ...* (*His hosts* is distracting and doesn't add any important information.)

**TIP** There are some common intransitive verbs (i.e. verbs without an object) such as *arrive, be, come, go, happen, look* which do not have a passive form.

### 9.2 test yourself

**Rewrite the sentences so that the underlined phrase is the subject. Include the agent unless it is in brackets.**

1 A team of Swiss naturalists identified <u>twelve new species of Peruvian insect</u> last year.
2 Pablo Picasso painted <u>Guernica</u> in 1937 as a direct response to the bombing of the Basque town. (The artist) first exhibited <u>it</u> as part of the Spanish display at the World's Fair in Paris in 1937.
3 Hi-tech companies have created <u>10,000 new jobs in the UK electronics industry</u> since 2008.
4 (A construction company) converted <u>the Menier Chocolate Factory</u> into a theatre in 2004. Over the last few years, (its artistic director) has staged <u>a number of award-winning productions</u> there.

## 9.3 The passive in different tenses

### 9.3 study

The passive voice is formed with *be* + past participle. Here are examples in all the tenses.

**present simple:**
- *In Sylvia Plath's poetry, her personal concerns are transformed into something almost mythical.*

**present continuous:**
- *A new system of 'tolerated drug zones' is currently being established in five inner-city areas.*

**present perfect:**
- *New measures to combat the selling of illegal drugs have recently been put in place by the government.*

**past simple:**
- *In the investigation, five deaths in custody were linked to a small group of prison officers who all belonged to the same golf club.*

**past continuous:**
- *New trade agreements were being drafted right up until the moment that the talks collapsed.*

**past perfect:**
- *It took more than a decade after penicillin had been discovered for scientists to find a way of stabilizing and mass-producing it.*

**will future:**
- *Nothing will be achieved unless the recommendations of the panel are implemented within the next year.*

**going to future:**
- *A massive effort on the part of local councils is going to be required to meet the recycling targets.*

**future perfect:**
- *The sponsors are hoping that the construction of the stadium will have been completed by the time inspectors arrive at the beginning of next year.*

**TIP** If you decide to re-order information using the passive voice, you will no longer need an object pronoun if the thing that the pronoun represents is now the subject of your sentence.
- *Geologists carefully removed the rocks and placed them in sample bags.*
  - → *The rocks were carefully removed and placed them in sample bags.*

### 9.3 test yourself

**A** Complete the sentences with the correct passive form of the verb in brackets.

1 It is difficult for Barton plc to do any forward planning, because the company _____ (restructure) at the moment.
2 A pop festival _____ (plan) to raise money for charity when the backers suddenly withdrew their funding.
3 By April next year, the wasteland next to the army base _____ (occupy) by protestors for five years.
4 The prisoners _____ (release) by the time the negotiators arrived to begin talks.
5 When a commercial sponsor can be found, the project _____ (carry out).
6 Most scientists accept that the climate change that _____ (observe) in the last forty years is due at least in part to human activity.

**B** Rewrite the sentences to make the underlined part the subject. Leave out the agents.

1 Guards were transporting the hostages to the airport when they made their escape.
2 Local authorities are going to demolish six of the region's smaller clinics and replace them with two new hospitals.
3 Medical science characterizes emphysema by enlarged lungs and breathing difficulties.
4 For hundreds of years, people named hurricanes in the West Indies after the particular saint's day on which the hurricane occurred.
5 Botanists are discovering new species of plant such as the *Berlinia korupensis* every year in Cameroon's rainforest.
6 Scientists have used 'atomic time' since 1972 as the primary reference for all scientific timing.

## 9.4 Passive modal verbs, infinitives and gerunds

### 9.4 study

#### 1 Modal verbs

You will find the passive voice with modal verbs (modal verb + *be* + past participle) useful in ordering information effectively and leaving out unimportant agents. The verbs most frequently used are *can* and *could* (expressing possibility), and *must* and *should* (expressing obligation).

- *Wikipedia **can be edited** by anyone with access to the internet.*
- *Exporting to a new market **could be described** as one of the key challenges facing an expanding business.*
- *Any incident involving staff trained in first aid **must be reported** to a senior manager.*
- *Local radio is a medium that **should not be overlooked** when planning an advertising campaign.*

Past forms are less common.
- *Alternative proposals **should have been explained** in detail before the committee reached its decision.*

#### 2 Infinitives with *to* and gerunds

You can also use infinitives with *to* and gerunds in the passive. A passive infinitive is formed by verb + *to be* + past participle.
- *Most clients **expect to be met** at the airport.*
- *The staff who **had hoped to be given** a pay rise were offered a bonus scheme instead.*

A passive gerund is formed by verb + *being* + past participle.
- *No managing director **enjoys being criticized** by shareholders.*
- *Curators at the gallery **denied being influenced** by negative reviews when they closed the exhibition two weeks early.*

### 9.4 test yourself

**A** Correct the incorrect sentences. Some sentences are already correct.

1 Health and safety checks must to be carried out by qualified staff.
2 Officials from the trade delegation resented being meet by a junior member of staff.
3 None of the files can be accessed without a password.
4 The equipment in a laboratory should not touch until a member of staff is present.
5 Burton argues that a council without a published 'green agenda' deserves be criticized.
6 Early types of rifle could not be fired without significant risk of injury to the soldier.

**B** Using the passive form of the underlined verb phrases, make the necessary changes to the sentences. Include the agent unless it is in brackets.

1 Local communities <u>can make</u> simple changes to aid biodiversity, according to Shalmi (2012).
2 Most people would prefer (the relevant authorities) <u>to consult</u> them before a flight path is permanently re-routed over the area where they live.
3 Middleton (2011) argues that better quality healthcare <u>could prevent</u> more than 100,000 deaths per year in the UK.
4 Holstein (2009) describes (an official) <u>questioning</u> him for three hours in a threatening manner at Los Angeles International Airport.
5 BAA are piloting a system that will allow (officials) <u>to examine</u> hand luggage more efficiently.
6 If an accident victim is unconscious, (someone) <u>should check</u> his or her breathing regularly.

## 9.5 Passive reporting verbs

### 9.5 study

An important way of achieving the impersonal style that academic writing often requires is to use the passive form of a small group of reporting verbs (*believe, claim, estimate, expect, feel, know, report, say, think, understand*).

- *It is estimated that Saudi Arabia holds 18% of the global reserves of oil.*

Sentences using this type of structure can start either with *it* ... (sometimes called an 'empty' subject), or with the third person singular or plural (*the American President* ... , *BP* ... , *experts* ... , etc.) The examples below demonstrate the variety of tenses that can be used.

**1** *It* + *be* + past participle + *that* ...

- (People believe that =) *It is believed that* computer science, despite the progress of the last twenty years, is still in its infancy.
- (Someone has said that =) *It has been said that the* prison system does very little to rehabilitate prisoners.
- (People understood that =) *It was understood that a new trade treaty between Japan and China would be signed in December last year, but the two negotiating teams could not reach agreement.*

**2** Third person singular/plural + *be* + past participle + infinitive with *to*...

- (People think that Alex Rodriguez earns =) *Alex Rodriguez, the American baseball player, is thought to earn $7.5 million a year.*
- (They had expected that the Prime Minister would stop over =) *The Prime Minister had been expected to stop over in Berlin on his way to the Moscow summit, but his schedule was changed at the last moment.*

In the following example, a continuous infinitive with *to* is used because the action (children working) is taking place at the time of writing.

- (People know that children are working =) *Children are known to be working in the silk-weaving industry of Kanchipuram in India.*

In the example below, a past infinitive with *to* is used because the action (buying a controlling share) has happened already, if the reports are true.

- (Someone reports that Banco Do Brasil has bought =) *Banco Do Basil is reported to have bought a controlling share of the Florida-based Eurobank.*

**TIP** You can achieve an effect similar to that of the passive by the structure *have + something* + past participle. It is used to say that we have arranged or are planning to arrange a professional service or professional help.

- *We're having our new factory designed by a team of award-winning architects.*
- *We had all our staff trained in presentation skills.*

### 9.5 test yourself

Rewrite the sentences, starting with the word(s) in brackets. Do not include the agent.

**1** Officials have estimated that the cost of repairing the fire damage to the port will be £60m. (It ...)

**2** There are reports that oil companies are exploring parts of Antarctica. (Oil companies ...)

**3** Most people believe that Athens in Ancient Greece is the site of the first democracy. (Athens ...)

**4** People think that Juan Olmo, who died in 2009, was Europe's most skilful brain surgeon. (Juan Olmo ...)

**5** A journalist claimed that the drug had been tested on soldiers without their knowledge. (It ...)

**6** Commentators say that passengers on the new jet experience a slight feeling of weightlessness. (Passengers ...)

## 9.6 Passives with prepositions

### 9.6 study

**1 By**

*By* introduces agents in passive sentences.

- *Liverpool FC was bought by American billionaire John Henry.*
- 💬 (in a seminar) *Was The Golden Bowl written by William Faulkner or Henry James?*

**TIP** Sometimes, if the order of the information is not important (see section **9.2** above), and the description of the agent is long, it may be appropriate to use the passive voice. This way your reader doesn't have to read a lot of detail before getting to the action or event that is being described.

- *The bridge **was designed by a small group of highly-experienced engineers from a company in Glasgow**.*

You can use *by* with a non-human agent.

- *Mudslides may be caused **by heavy rainfall**.*
- *Rare languages are sometimes preserved **by recordings**.* (*by* = by means of)

**2 Other prepositions**

There is a group of verbs + prepositions that are more commonly used in the passive than the active voice in academic English. These include *associated with, attributed to, based on, classified as, composed of, confined to, diagnosed as/with, entitled to,* and *located at/in/on.*

- *Apple's success **has** largely **been attributed to** the creative energy of its late CEO, Steve Jobs.*
- *From its discovery in 1930 until 2006, Pluto **was classified as** a planet.*
- *Clearsight plc's marketing drive **was** initially **confined to** domestic sales.*
- *All workers in the UK **are entitled to** the minimum wage.*

**TIP** *Diagnosed as* is normally followed by an adjective or by *having* + the name of a disease; *diagnosed with* is normally followed simply by the name of the disease.

- *Two of the children in the group were diagnosed as dyslexic/as having dyslexia/with dyslexia.*

### 9.6 test yourself

**Complete each sentence with a preposition.**

1 The Little Neath River Cave is located _____ South Wales.
2 The risks of contamination can be reduced _____ temperature control.
3 Healthier diets in pregnant women are associated _____ reduced risks of birth defects.
4 Defendants in some trials have to be separated _____ glass shields from the court.
5 Before being formally diagnosed _____ diabetic, a person may have suffered from the disease for a number of years.
6 The spread of some diseases can be controlled _____ vaccination.
7 Two of the films that won awards at the Cannes Film Festival were based _____ true stories.
8 The United Arab Emirates is composed _____ seven sheikdoms.

# 09 Challenge yourself

**A** Complete the text about whaling with the correct passive form of the verb in brackets.

For centuries, or even millennia, whales ¹_____ (hunt) offshore from small boats such as canoes and kayaks. From the mid-nineteenth century, with the development of the Industrial Revolution, this fairly limited activity ²_____ (join) by pelagic, that is, deep sea, whaling, culminating in modern factory ships. In the 1960s, £20 million ³_____ (generate) annually by the global whaling industry. In spite of the worldwide ban on commercial whaling that ⁴_____ (impose) in 1986, it is worth noting that small-scale shore-based hunting of cetaceans continues in several countries from the Arctic to Polynesia. It ⁵_____ (justify) on the grounds of continuing a long cultural tradition, and usually the meat and other products ⁶_____ (consume) within the same community.

**B** Complete the text about a form of mental illness, using the phrases in the box and a form of *be*. Two of the phrases are not needed.

> associated with   admitted to   based on   classified as   composed of
> confined to   diagnosed as   entitled to   located at

Patients who ¹_____ bipolar often face a frustrating search for suitable treatment. Serious side effects ²_____ some of the most frequently prescribed medications, and this leads some patients to discontinue the drugs. In trying to take control of their lives, they may ³_____ non-compliant, especially by doctors without specialist training. Patients ⁴_____ a free consultation with a psychiatrist, but often this entails a long wait, during which the condition can worsen. In the worst cases, the person may need ⁵_____ an in-patient facility, and perhaps even ⁶_____ a secure ward in a psychiatric hospital. These psychiatric hospitals tend ⁷_____ some distance from the patient's home, increasing the sense of isolation and betrayal.

## AWL GLOSSARY

**revolution** a great change in conditions, ways of working, beliefs, etc. that affects large numbers of people

**impose** to introduce a new law, rule, tax, etc.; to order that a rule, punishment, etc. be used

**justify** to show that something is right or reasonable

**cultural** connected with the culture of a particular society or group, its customs, beliefs, etc.

**tradition** a belief, custom, or way of doing something that has existed for a long time among a particular group of people

**consume** to eat or drink something

## AWL GLOSSARY

**consultation** a meeting with an expert, especially a doctor, to get advice or treatment

**secure** guarded and/or made stronger so that it is difficult for people to enter or leave

**isolation** the state of being alone or lonely

**C** In the text about a public health pioneer, match the beginning of each sentence with the correct ending.

1 The observation that infections were being transmitted between patients

2 The physician who first deduced the link

3 He is now known to be

4 Dr Semmelweis was working in the obstetric clinic at Vienna General Hospital,

5 He discovered that the number of cases of this so-called childbed fever

6 The scientific papers that he wrote about this

7 His ideas

8 Some doctors

9 Still only in his 40s, Semmelweis experienced a mental breakdown, and

10 Later, when Louis Pasteur explained his germ theory, Semmelweis

a could be dramatically reduced by the use of hand disinfection.

b were turned down by many publishers.

c were offended at the implication that they were unclean.

d was shunned by his colleagues and his findings were ignored.

e was committed to an asylum for the mentally ill, where he died two weeks later.

f were rejected by his medical peers.

g was hailed as the 'saviour of mothers'.

h by the doctor who was treating them was a radical one for the mid-nineteenth century.

i one of the most visionary scientists of his age.

j where many women died of infection within days of giving birth.

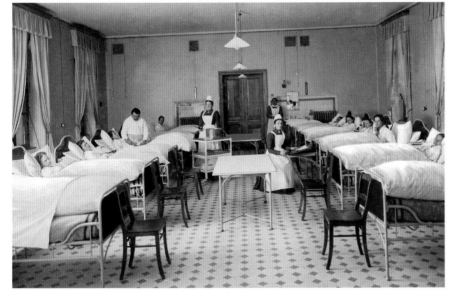

**D** Correct the mistakes in the underlined verb forms in the text about dementia. Some verb forms are correct.

According to recent reports, the threat posed by dementia [1]was growing as societies age. To start with, dementia [2]can be defined as a decline in mental functioning over time, beyond what [3]might be being expected from the natural effects of aging. A recent survey that [4]is being conducted by the Dementia Alliance revealed that the costs to health services [5]are increased twice as fast as inflation, and within twenty years [6]are expecting to outrun the amounts spent on cancer treatment.

As with other cognitive disorders, higher or more complex mental functions [7]had been affected before the simpler ones. If, unusually, the illness strikes a patient under 65, it [8]is termed 'early onset dementia'. Another minority of patients have what [9]is know as 'mixed dementia'.

**E** Put the words in the correct order to complete the text about environmental laws.

1 been environmental has legislation passed
2 as being environmental imposed legislation on them
3 expected is know of them what
4 are member obliged pursue states this to
5 business factory having insulated its

<sup>1</sup>_____ in Brussels and Strasbourg on such diverse matters as climate change, air quality, waste, agriculture, chemicals, and building. 2009 saw the implementation of the EU Directive on Energy Performance of Buildings, which requires member states to apply minimum requirements to the energy performance of new and existing buildings. Some businesses may see <sup>2</sup>_____, but others see it as an opportunity. Once industry leaders <sup>3</sup>_____, they can adapt their businesses accordingly. For example, the EU Climate and Energy objectives are a reduction of 20% of carbon by 2020 and a 20% energy savings by 2020 (known as 20:20:20). <sup>4</sup>_____ as a policy, and governments need business on their side. A micro example of this would be a small <sup>5</sup>_____.

**F** Complete the text about protests against 'big business' with the correct passive form of the verb in brackets. Add the three agents in the box in the correct places.

by mining   by the state   by the poor

Protests against 'big business' tend to focus on companies which cause environmental problems or which operate in the area of financial services. For example, a lot of environmental degradation <sup>1</sup>_____ (cause). When the desired commodity <sup>2</sup>_____ (extract), and it is no longer economically feasible to continue, the mine <sup>3</sup>_____ (abandon), leaving, in the worst case scenario, a ruined landscape behind, suitable for nothing.

There are also protests against companies, especially banks, which <sup>4</sup>_____ (perceive, avoid, pay) their share of taxes. Some of these <sup>5</sup>_____ (bail out) when they were in trouble as a result of the banking crisis, and yet their senior managers managed to escape public responsibility. The ramifications of their poor economic decisions <sup>6</sup>_____ (continue, feel), and paradoxically, the main burden <sup>7</sup>_____ (bear). Until multinational companies become more aware of their impact on society, they <sup>8</sup>_____ (target) by anti-capitalist and environmentalist protestors.

# AWL GLOSSARY

**pursue** to do something or try to achieve something over a period of time

**diverse** very different from each other and of various kinds

**implementation** the act of making something that has been officially decided start to happen or be used

**requirement** something that you must have in order to do something else

# AWL GLOSSARY

**environmental** connected with the natural conditions in which people, animals, and plants live

**extract** to remove or obtain a substance from something, for example by using an industrial or a chemical process

**economically** in a way connected with the trade, industry, and development of wealth of a country, an area, or a society

**scenario** a description of how things might happen in the future

**aware** knowing or realizing something

**impact** the powerful effect that something has on something

**target** to aim an attack or a criticism at somebody

**G** A form of the verb *be* (e.g. *been*, *was*) has been omitted from seven of the nine sentences in the text about the material graphene. Complete the text with the missing words.

¹Graphene has called the latest miracle material. ²It is said to be the thinnest material in the world, and possibly the hardest and the strongest as well. ³Graphene is a form of carbon in which the atoms packed into a lattice structure which is so flat that it can considered two-dimensional. ⁴It described in the 1980s, but it took until 2004 before it was isolated and manipulated. ⁵The physicists whose experiments led to this increased understanding, Konstantin Novoselov and Andre Geim, awarded the Nobel Prize in 2010. ⁶They have been cautious in their claims for the practical implications of their discoveries, but other commentators, particularly media popularizers, have made grand claims about graphene. ⁷It has already made into a touchscreen, and the possibilities are enormous if the material can, as its supporters suggest, replace silicon. ⁸A great deal of industrial money and research time are currently invested in its future. ⁹Within a decade, either the promise of graphene will have fulfilled, or investors and scientists will have walked away.

**H** Write 100–200 words about a set of safety procedures, for example, what to do in case of fire at work or school. Use as many passive structures as possible.

## Introduction

There are a number of different ways of setting out an argument in academic English, but at some point you are likely to have to describe the following.

**1** The scope of your case (the elements you think it appropriate to include).

**2** Your thesis statement (your central point of view or main claim).

**3** A series of points that support your claim.

**4** A number of counter-arguments (significant views that are different from yours, on which you need to comment).

**5** The conclusions you have reached (and perhaps some recommendations arising from your conclusions).

This unit presents a range of words, phrases and structures to help you with these stages, and also looks at the ways of expressing advantages and disadvantages that you might need in a more discussion-based text.

> Read the two extracts, and write out the five phrases the writer uses to introduce arguments, both her own, and those of other authors. How is her use of the views of other writers different in the two extracts?

It seems obvious that, when the wealthier countries of the world are presented with evidence of extreme poverty in the developing world, there is a moral imperative to take action through reputable agencies such as Oxfam. As Seiber argues, one of the indicators of the success of a western democracy is its willingness to offer assistance beyond the confines of its own borders (2007).

According to Norman and Martinsen, all international aid, however well-intentioned, tends to be counter-productive in that it helps to create 'a self-perpetuating dependency culture in the recipient nation' (2008: 42). While it is clear that such a culture has taken root in some parts of the world, there are interesting examples of projects which, it might be argued, have had the opposite effect.

Suggested answers: see page 201

| Unit contents |
| --- |

Other units that deal with language that is useful for arguing include unit *6 Stating facts and opinions*, unit *7 Connectors*, unit *8 Being emphatic*, unit *12 Cause and effect*, and unit *14 Hedging*.

# 10.1 Scope

## 10.1 study

Stating the scope of an essay may involve analysis verbs, and sequencing and focusing language.

### 1 Analysis verbs

Verbs such as *analyse, consider, describe, define, examine, explain, evaluate,* and *introduce* can be used in the future tense with *will* or in the present simple to describe the purpose of the whole or parts of your essay.

- *This essay **will examine/examines** to what extent full political participation is realized in three mature democracies.*
- *In the third part of the essay, I **will consider** how the National Health Service could change over the next ten years.*

**TIP** For extra impact, we can use a continuous tense with verbs such as *suggest, argue,* and *discuss.*

- *In the final part of this report, I **will be arguing** that new legislation is required to control copyright abuse.*

### 2 Sequencing language

You can use the following verbs, words and phrases to describe the sequence of your essay.

**a** Verbs such as *start, begin, move on to, follow, finish,* and *conclude.*

**b** Words and phrases such as *firstly, first of all, in the second part, next, then, finally, lastly,* and *in conclusion.*

- *Our team was asked to recommend the next step for JavaBrew, a successful start-up. This report will **start by giving** some background on the company. It will **then move on to** the factors we took into consideration, namely PEST and SWOT analyses, a survey of competitors, and the needs of the owner-founders. We will **follow this with** an examination of possible alternative business models, and explain why some of them are not good fits for JavaBrew. **Finally**, we will **make** one concrete recommendation.*

Note above how, after these verbs (apart from *move on to*), you can use *by + -ing* form to add another verb (*start **by giving***) and *with* to add a noun (*follow this **with** an examination*).

**TIP** The sequencing language described above is also useful for presentations, where it is normal to begin with a description of the main parts of your talk.

- 💬 *I will start my presentation by defining the term globalization. Then I will examine two companies that seem to exemplify the concept…*

### 3 Focusing language

You may sometimes need to limit the scope of your work and explain what it does and doesn't cover. Verbs and phrases that describe the focus of your essay include *focus on* and *refer to* (sometimes with the adverbs *only* and *exclusively*), *for the purposes of, beyond/outside the scope of,* and *with reference to.*

- ***For the purposes of*** *this essay, I will take the example of the Hundertwasser Apartments in Vienna, and, **with reference to** the arguments that were put forward against the initial plans, comment on the reviews published shortly after completion. Issues concerning the pricing of the apartments are **beyond the scope of** this essay, which will **focus** exclusively **on** the technology and design.*

Note that you could rewrite the last sentence using a negative form of one of the verbs *cover, deal with,* or *touch on*: *This essay **will not cover** the pricing of apartments, but will focus exclusively on the technology and design.*

---

## 10.1 test yourself

**Complete the paragraph, using one or two of the words in the box in each space.**

> with the to of for on all lastly
> next will refer conclude identify

Evelyn Bestmeiler argues that businesses have three competing strategies for expansion beyond their country of origin: globalization, internationalization, and what he calls 'worldification'. First [1]_____, this essay [2]_____ define these models. Then it will [3]_____ examples of each of these in the strategies of well-known companies. [4]_____, it will move [5]_____ an evaluation of the value added by each model. [6]_____, the essay will [7]_____ an account of how a fictional company might go about choosing one of these three, and the likely consequences of this choice. Although these strategies can be employed by companies originating in any country, [8]_____ purposes of this essay I will [9]_____ only to British and American-based businesses.

## 10.2 Thesis statement

### 10.2 study

A thesis statement, normally found near the beginning of an essay, summarizes the position you will take in an argumentative essay. Generally speaking, such statements are optional, but you may wish to consult your department for advice.

If you do include a thesis statement, you need to make your opinion clear, though you can vary the strength from tentative to emphatic.

- *My contention is that our current prison system **tends to** render reoffending more rather than less likely.*
- *I will argue that **it is vital for** governments to introduce measures that will actively discourage the use of private cars in city centres.*

The modal verbs *can, should, will,* and *must* are all used in thesis statements, sometimes with connectors expressing cause and effect or results.

- *If they are cultivated in a properly regulated way, genetically modified crops **can**, in my view, offer powerful assistance in the fight against hunger and malnutrition.*
- *Supermarkets **should** be encouraged to support the fair trade movement because, as this essay will suggest, it has already proved its worth in terms of grass roots economic progress in developing countries.*
- *The promotion of national security **must** not, in other words, become an excuse for the erosion of civil liberties.*

To show that you are aware of a main counter-argument, you may wish to include a subordinate clause within the statement, introduced by a connector expressing contrast such as *however, although,* or *despite*.

- *I will demonstrate that the presence of oil, **despite holding out the hope of wealth for one of the world's poorest countries**, is likely to foster security difficulties, as new militia groups emerge.*

### 10.2 test yourself

Complete the sentences, using one of the words in the box in each space. One word is not needed.

> despite  although  if  because  however
> can  must  defend  argue

1. Stem cell research _____ be allowed to continue _____ of the medical benefits it will bring.
2. _____ degrading some song lyrics seem to be, this essay will argue that censorship is not the way forward.
3. _____ a law can be appropriately framed, assisted suicide should be permitted.
4. Homeschooling _____ benefit some families, as I will _____ in this essay.
5. This essay will _____ the 'first past the post' electoral system in the UK as being the fairest option.
6. _____ manned space exploration is no longer necessary from a purely scientific point of view, I will suggest that it is still a valuable component of national space programmes.

## 10.3 Presenting and supporting your arguments

### 10.3 study

You can begin your arguments with simple factual statements.

- *There are several clear differences between the financial crash of 2008 and that of 1929.*

Quite often, however, you will want to signpost your arguments with an introductory phrase, based around the words *argument* and *point*, or by using impersonal structures beginning with *there* or *it*.

*The main/principal argument for/against ... is (that) ...*
*One of the main/principal arguments for/against ... is (that) ...*
*The first point to be considered/made is (that) ...*
*There is no doubt that ...*
*It seems clear that ...*
*It is obvious that ...*

- ***One of the main arguments against** car ownership is the sheer cost of purchasing, insuring, and maintaining a vehicle.*
- ***It is obvious that** even if we improve methods of conserving energy, our overall energy costs will rise.*

You can introduce further arguments with expressions such as *secondly, thirdly* and *finally,* and connecting words that express additional information such as *furthermore, ...* and *as well as ...*

To support your points, you can use:

**1** verbs such as *show, demonstrate, exemplify, argue,* and *maintain*
*This is shown/exemplified by/in ...*
*As Thompson has argued/maintained ...*

**2** the nouns *example* and *case*
*An example of this is ...*
*For example, ...*
*A case in point is ...*

**3** the nouns *statistics, research,* and *studies.*
*Statistics indicate that ...*
*Research demonstrates that ...*
*Studies have shown that ...*

* *The process of internationalization does not guarantee a uniform service.* **A case in point is/An example of this is** *Google, where governments have been able to reach individual agreements with the company.*
* *In addition, it is clear that the level of the problem is frequently underestimated.* **Statistics indicate/ Research demonstrates***, for example,* **that** *one in five Americans experience a period of depression in any given year (Stevens, 2007).*

**TIP** You may find it useful in your conclusion to support your arguments with conditional sentences that describe positive or negative results.
* *The UK could gain an important competitive edge in manufacturing if the government and business leaders were to work together to bring new life to apprenticeship schemes.*

## 10.3 test yourself

**Correct each sentence by adding *is*.**

**1** Not all products should be advertised; a case in point tobacco, where discouraging young people from smoking should have priority over free market principles.
**2** Legislation can become more complex than it needs to be; this exemplified in planning law.
**3** There no doubt that, unless supply systems are improved, a crisis point is imminent.
**4** The main argument for prison its deterrent effect on criminal activity.
**5** The first point to be considered that the shortage of water in this region is severe.

## 10.4 Presenting counter-arguments

### 10.4 study

In making your case, you will need to introduce, comment on, and evaluate counter-arguments.

**1 Introducing counter-arguments**

To bring in the views of others you can use:

**a** verbs such as *argue, claim, point out,* and *state* (normally in the present perfect or present simple tense) or *believe, maintain,* and *contend* (normally in the present simple)
*Clarkson argues/has argued that ...*
*Clarkson believes/maintains/contends that ...*

**b** phrases that may include *view* or *opinion.*
*In the view/opinion of Clarkson, ...*
*In Clarkson's view/opinion, ...*
*According to Clarkson, ...*
*Some people believe/think that ...*

(See page 58 of unit *6 Stating facts and opinions* for introducing quotes, and unit *16 Paraphrasing* for ways of restating others' views.)

**2 Commenting on counter-arguments**

To comment on counter-arguments you can use connectors that express contrast such as *although, but, despite, however,* and *while,* and the kind of tentative or emphatic language that is appropriate to your meaning.
* *Jefferson maintains that significant scientific breakthroughs can only occur within a context of the regular use of animals in laboratories.* **While** *it* **may** *be difficult to disagree that animal-based experiments have advanced our understanding of medicine, it is also* **quite** *clear that a culture has developed where alternative methods of research have not been fully explored.*
* *It might be said that in the pressured environment of decision-making there is little time to evaluate fully the ethics of certain courses of action. Recent events,* **however,** *have proved that without a proper ethical framework, financial risk-taking* **can** *result in behaviour that citizens outside the world of commercial banking might describe as somewhat disturbing.*

### 3 Evaluating counter-arguments

To evaluate counter-arguments it is often useful:

**a** to explore their effects, using nouns such as *result, effect, consequence*, and verbs such as *cause, lead to*.
- One **consequence** of following Pearson's arguments for the control of immigration would be a costly and complex nationwide system of ID cards.
- The programme of public education suggested by the report on attitudes to global warming will **lead to** a level of expenditure that governments are unlikely to be able to afford.

**b** to make comparisons.
- Rogers advocates a system of proportional representation which would give parties, rather than the voters, much more power to control the final composition of the House of Commons.
- Foster's arguments are similar to those put forward by Mitchell in that they may underestimate the growing need for low-cost rental accommodation.

(See unit *2 Comparing and contrasting* for more information on making comparisons.)

---

## 10.4 test yourself

**Complete each sentence with one word.**

1 Dobie and Klein have _____ out that the ownership of a car is an important aspect of personal autonomy.
2 _____ to EMI, online copyright infringements will only be taken more seriously if there are a series of high-profile prosecutions.
3 Barrett argues that the study of a writer's life does not contribute in any significant way to the appreciation of their work. I would argue, _____, that biographical information has offered major insights into a number of 19th and 20th century novels.
4 Nuclear power is sometimes described as a clean form of energy. _____ it does not pollute in the same constant manner as, for example, the burning of coal, there are major concerns over the potential for radiation leaks.
5 Curfews imposed during riots may actually _____ a counter-productive level of resentment.
6 Abolishing the minimum wage would make economic recovery _____ likely by reducing the spending power of the lowest paid workers.

---

## 10.5 Expressing advantages and disadvantages

### 10.5 study

In some seminar discussions, or in essays where you are invited to discuss a topic, you may need to consider the advantages and disadvantages of a concept.

#### 1 Sentence patterns

Two sentence patterns that you will find useful are:

*an advantage of/a disadvantage of* + noun/*-ing* form + *is (that)* ...
*an advantage of/a disadvantage of* + noun/*-ing* form + *is* + noun phrase
- **An advantage of** cycling **is that** you can keep fit as well as completing a necessary journey.
- **A disadvantage of** toll systems on roads **is the** high cost of administration.

#### 2 *Advantage/disadvantage* synonyms

Useful synonyms include:

**advantage of**: *benefit of, positive aspect of, point in favour of*
**disadvantage of**: *negative feature of, drawback to/of, objection to*

#### 3 Collocations

Useful collocations include:

for **advantage** and **benefit**: *obvious, significant, major, minor*
for **disadvantage**, **drawback**, and **objection**: *serious, minor*

Note that instead of **an** *advantage*, **a** *disadvantage*, etc. you can say *one/a further/another/a second*, etc. *advantage/disadvantage*.

## 10.5 test yourself

Complete the sentences, using one of the words in the box in each space.

> of   to   advantage   drawback   serious
> second   favour

1 One further _____ to the creation of virtual galleries is that they cannot convey the physical properties of works of art.
2 A point in _____ of 'green chemistry' is that it encourages manufacturers to seek innovative ways of producing goods.
3 Another _____ objection _____ genetic testing is the impact it is likely to have on the cost of life insurance policies.
4 A _____ significant benefit _____ consulting a focus group is that it may produce ideas that advertisers will not have considered.
5 A major _____ of regular staff meetings is the sense of cohesion that they can produce.

## 10.6 Conclusions and recommendations

### 10.6 study

#### 1 Introducing conclusions

Useful ways include using a fixed expression or a phrase ending in *that ...* followed by your concluding remarks.

**a Fixed expressions**

> *To conclude, ...*      *To summarize, ...*
> *In conclusion, ...*    *In summary, ...*
> *To sum up, ...*        *As we have seen, ...*

**b Phrases ending in *that ...***

> *To conclude etc., we can/may say that ...*
> *To conclude etc., it can/may be said that ...*
> *Thus,/On the basis of these arguments, we can/may conclude that ...*
> *Thus,/On the basis of these arguments, it can/may be concluded that ...*

- *On the basis of these arguments, it can be concluded that if aid projects are constructed in such a way that their sustainability lies in the hands of the local population, a dependency culture such as Norman and Martinsen describe need not follow. As we have seen, this will depend on three key factors: firstly, ... , etc.*

#### 2 Making recommendations

You can use introductory phrases before your recommendation(s), or passive forms after them.

**a Introductory phrases**

> *It is therefore recommended that ...*
> *On the basis of this discussion, it would be advisable (for someone/something) to + verb ...*
> *On the basis of this discussion, it would be advisable for + noun ...*
> *It follows that there is a need (for someone/ something) to + verb ...*
> *It follows that there is a need for + noun ...*

- *It follows that there is an urgent need for states to reconsider the way in which they model the various scenarios that may follow any act of humanitarian intervention.*

Adjectives that collocate with *need* include *continuing, growing, immediate, pressing, urgent.*

**b Endings using the passive form**

> *... should/must be done/carried out/put in place.*
> *... is (therefore) recommended/needed.*
> *... could/should be considered.*

- *It is clear from these arguments that measures against cyber-bullying, agreed by the providers of social network sites, **should be put in place**.*

### 10.6 test yourself

Correct each sentence by amending or replacing one word only.

1 There follows that there is an urgent need to find strategies for preventing iron deficiency anaemia in infants.
2 Thus, it can be conclude that emotional intelligence is an important factor in the success of teamwork.
3 On conclusion, it is clear that many of the pollution problems have been resolved.
4 An approach that prioritizes community needs is therefore recommend.
5 On the basis of this evidence, it would be advised to ensure that electroconvulsive therapy is only used for the short-term treatment of patients with severe symptoms.
6 To conclude, we may be said that the bail-out package offered to Portugal holds out a reasonable prospect of recovery.

# 10 Challenge yourself

**A** Complete the paragraph from a text about organizational models, using the words in the box.

> argued   considers   describe   examine   firstly   introduces   lastly   next

Handy [1]___ his theory of organizational models in *The Gods of Management* (1978). He [2]___ the university an exemplar of the Dionysian model, and this essay will [3]___ to what extent that analysis is accurate. Certainly, one phrase used to [4]___ managing academics is 'like herding cats', as, typically, each academic attempts to pursue his or her own agenda. However, it can be [5]___ that universities demonstrate elements of each of the other models as well. [6]___ we will consider the club culture of Zeus, which can be seen in some academic departments, if they happen to have a strong chair who prefers to operate in that way. [7]___, we will show how the task-driven ethos of Athena comes to the fore in the setting up of working groups or projects. [8]___ and most importantly, we will evaluate the under-appreciated influence of the role culture of Apollo.

**B** First match the beginning of each sentence with the correct ending. Then put the sentences in the correct order to make a single paragraph about the banking crisis.

**1** The second difference is ...
**2** At the same time, ...
**3** The most obvious of these is size: ...
**4** This is demonstrated by ...
**5** The most conspicuous example of this was ...
**6** It seems clear ...

**a** the high proportion of GDP which relied on financial services at the beginning of the 21st century.
**b** that the under-regulated financial sector was engaging in very poor practices.
**c** that there are several differences between the 2008 banking crash and the one of 1929.
**d** that many millions of people had been persuaded to purchase houses for the first time, when their financial position made this an unwise decision.
**e** the financial industry had grown exponentially through the developed world, and especially in the UK and the US.
**f** other sectors such as agriculture and manufacturing had declined.

**C** Put the words in the correct order to complete the introduction to an essay about car ownership.

**1** a although are benefits car many owning to there
**2** both evaluate I of these will
**3** are beyond essay of the this scope
**4** consequences environmental focus instead, it on the will
**5** argue for I is it that vital will

In many countries, owning a car is a necessity for each household and sometimes for each adult. [1]_____, there are also disbenefits, on the one hand for the individual, and on the other hand for society. [2]_____. The geo-political ramifications of the world's dependence on oil [3]_____. [4]_____, understood in the widest sense, at the city or regional level. [5]_____ legislators to take account of the negative effects of cities designed around the private motor vehicle.

**AWL GLOSSARY**

**element** a necessary or typical part of something

**project** a planned piece of work that is designed to find information about something, to produce something new, or to improve something

**evaluate** to form an opinion of something after thinking about it carefully

**AWL GLOSSARY**

**proportion** a part or share of a whole

**rely** to need or depend on something

**purchase** to buy something

**AWL GLOSSARY**

**benefit** an advantage that something gives you; a useful effect that something has

**legislator** a member of a group of people that has the power to make laws

**design** to decide how something will look, work, etc., especially by drawing plans or making models

**D** Complete the extracts on a variety of topics, using the words and phrases in the box.

> will argue   contention   exemplifies   for the purposes
> of this discussion   in summary   it therefore follows
> on the other hand   studies have shown   then move on
> to conclude   will begin   will consider

Hyperson (2011) asserts that Google [1]_____ internationalization. Is this accurate? I [2]_____ that such an analysis represents an unhelpful oversimplification. Of course, it is true that Google is available in almost all countries. [3]_____ not all of the services remain the same to users around the world.

My [4]_____ is that there is no substitute for a thorough grasp of more than one language. [5]_____ that children who grow up multilingual exhibit a higher level of mental flexibility. [6]_____ that there is an immediate need for better education on the subject.

[7]_____, we have looked at the causes of spiraling personal debt, the role of companies offering short-term loans, and what the government is doing about the situation. [8]_____, new legislation is urgently needed.

In this essay I [9]_____ some of the world's most overlooked countries, the so-called micronations. [10]_____, the term refers to groups of people claiming territorial sovereignty, but whose claims are not recognized by any major international organization. Examples include Sealand and Seborga. (Micronations are to be distinguished from microstates such as Singapore and Vatican City.) I [11]_____ by looking at the impact of their formation on a macro level, and [12]_____ to examine their impact on the lives of individuals.

**E** Write the introductory paragraph (150–250 words) to an essay on one of the following subjects. Make sure you state clearly what you intend to argue in the essay, and how you intend to prove your case.

1 The (banking, newspaper, higher education, food, etc.) industry has proved that it cannot govern itself, and so needs tighter regulation.
2 Healthcare should be provided by the state.

## Introduction

> **Read the text and underline the six modal verbs.**
>
> City authorities should consider the advantages to be gained from creating cycle-friendly road systems. As the proportion of cyclists to motorists increases, the level of pollution will fall, for example, and traffic will flow more quickly during the rush hours. But, apart from the benefits that an increased level of cycling can bring to the city as a whole, we must also think of the gains to the health of its citizens; a daily cycle to and from work can easily satisfy a person's weekly requirement for exercise.
>
> **Of the four different modal verbs you have underlined (two of the six are repeated), which one means:**
>
> 1 it's necessary? _____
> 2 it's possible? _____
> 3 it's a good idea? _____
> 4 it's likely to? _____
>
> Suggested answers: see page 202

There are nine modal verbs: *can, could, may, might, must, shall, should, will,* and *would.* Although different in meaning, they all share the following grammatical features.

**1** Their form doesn't change.

**2** They are all followed by the infinitive without *to.*

**3** They all come before *not* in negatives, and before the subject in *yes/no* questions.
- *First of all,* **I will discuss** *the effects of overfishing in the waters around the UK.*
- *Plans to separate retail banking from more speculative types of investment* **may not** *succeed.*
- 💬 (in a seminar) **Could you** *please explain exactly how you define 'congestion'?*

In addition there is a small group of 'semi-modal' verbs, which have a similar function to modal verbs: *ought to, need, have to, have got to, had better,* and *be supposed to* (all covered in this unit); and *be going to* and *used to* (covered in unit *1 Tense review*). Occasionally, modal and semi-modal verbs are used together.
- *If Plan A for the economy failed, the government* **might need** *to have a Plan B.*

Modal verbs are a key tool for expressing a writer's attitude or point of view in academic English. In this unit, they are divided into groups that express similar types of meaning, finishing with a section on the use of modals in spoken academic situations such as meetings with tutors, seminars, and presentations.

Other units that deal with modal verbs are unit *1 Tense review*, unit *8 Being emphatic*, unit *14 Hedging*, and unit *17 Conditionals*.

# 11.1 Ability (can, could, be able to)

## 11.1 study

### 1 Can

Can expresses present ability (often very similar in meaning to possibility).
- *Scientists **can** observe images of atoms by using an instrument known as an electron microscope.*
- *It is both a strength and weakness of Wikipedia that anyone **can** update its pages.*

Note that be able to has the same meaning: *Scientists **are able to** observe ...*

Sometimes, because of the way you want to start a sentence, you will need to use a passive form of can (can + be + past participle).
- *A parallel **can be drawn** between a country's reaction to a natural disaster and a company's response to recession.* (instead of *We can draw a parallel ...*)

### 2 Could

Could expresses general ability in the past.
- *When mass share ownership was at its height, small investors believed they **could** 'play' the stock market alongside corporate stockbrokers.*

But remember that for specific actions (often achievements), you can't normally use could. Instead of could you can use was/were able to. You can also use succeeded in + -ing form of verb or managed + infinitive with to.
- *After lengthy talks, the British and Irish governments ~~could~~ **were able to** sign the Good Friday Agreement on 11 April 1998.*
- *African-American athlete Jesse Owens ~~could win~~ **succeeded in winning/managed to win** four gold medals at the Berlin Olympics of 1936.*

Note that this rule does not apply to could not, or to could only, could hardly, and could before the verbs see, hear, taste, and smell, which can all be used for general or specific ability in the past.
- *The team **could not** find a way of isolating the chemical they wanted to work with.*
- *The two climbers **could only** get to the summit with computer-based logistical support.*
- *When she woke the next morning, naturalist Jo Bailey **could hear** a group of gorillas close to her tent.*

Could have + past participle can be used for things that people or organizations had the ability to do, but didn't actually do.
- *Wentworth Holdings plc **could have offered** their customers refunds as a goodwill gesture, but declined to do so.*

### 3 Be able to

To write about ability in the future, or describe a situation where a present perfect or infinitive form of a verb would be appropriate, you need to use a form of be able to.
- *If the building contractors start work on the refurbishment of the theatre in May, the owners **will be able to** reopen it for performances in October.*
- *Researchers **have not yet been able to** formulate a model of the human brain that everyone can agree with.*
- *The NHS hopes **to be able to** open six new cancer clinics in the next five years.*

## 11.1 test yourself

**Correct the verb forms. Sometimes more than one answer is possible. Some sentences are already correct.**

1 Fortunately rescue ships could remove the crew safely from the sinking tanker.
2 The government may have bailed out the failing steelworks, but decided not to take this course of action.
3 The company claims to be able to produce an effective recyclable plastic bag.
4 Investigators could immediately see what had caused the accident.
5 No one can ever be able to prove so far that Goldman's Conjecture works for every even number.
6 In May 2011 scientists from IBM Zurich could produce images of electrons using a scanning microscope.
7 The duties of an absent member of staff can sometimes be share out among colleagues.
8 According to scientists at the University of Geneva, we will soon be able to produce short bursts of rainfall safely through the use of lasers.

## 11.2 Possibility (*may, could, might*)

### 11.2 study

**1** *May (not)*, *might (not)*, and *could* (but not *could not*) are used to say that something is possible (or not possible) in the present or future.

- *In any situation where redundancies are planned, there **may/could/might** be tension between those who are staying, and those who are losing their jobs.*
- *Indeed, the government **may not/might not**/~~could not~~ find a solution to the housing problem in the foreseeable future.*

The meaning of the three verbs is similar in the first example above, although *could* is slightly weaker than *may*, and *might* is sometimes considered to be the weakest.

**2** *May/might/could* + *have* + past participle is used to talk about possibility in the past.

- *The demonstrators **may/might/could have weakened** their case by allowing some of their supporters to cause criminal damage.*

But note that *could not have* has a different meaning from *may/might not have*.

- *The climbing team **may/might not have reached** the summit without helicopter assistance.* (= they possibly would not have reached the summit ...)
- *The climbing team **could not have reached** the summit without helicopter assistance.* (= they definitely would not have reached the summit ...)

**3** You will find *might/could* (sometimes in passive form) useful in discussion-based writing. Starting a sentence with *It might/could be argued that ...* is a way of being cautious, for example (see page 128 in unit *14 Hedging* for more information), and *could* is also useful for discussing what it is and isn't possible to achieve.

- *It would be a mistake to think that the model of British supermarkets, which is so successful in their home market, **could be rolled out** across the world.*

(see page 128 in unit *14 Hedging* for more information)

### 11.2 test yourself

Complete each sentence with one of the phrases in the box. One phrase is not needed.

> might have    may not    could not
> may focus    could soon    may explain
> might be

**1** It _____ suggested that the team's research methods were less than perfect.

**2** In anti-capitalist demonstrations, protestors _____ on specific companies.

**3** A personal computer device _____ be developed with the sole purpose of detecting medical conditions.

**4** Foll argues that the geological team _____ overlooked some of the evidence at the site of the volcano.

**5** Genetic research at the Harvard Medical School _____ why women suffer more from migraines than men.

**6** Proponents of 'intelligent design' assert that evolution _____ possibly have produced certain biological structures.

## 11.3 Obligation and necessity (*must, should, ought to, have to*)

### 11.3 study

**1 Obligation**

*Must, should, ought to*, and *have to* are all used to express obligation (things that people or organizations have a responsibility to do). *Must* and *have to* both express strong obligation, but *have to* is more common in conversation than in academic English. *Should* and *ought to* are not as strong, and *ought to* is less common in all forms of English.

- *We **must** begin by looking at the effects on the country of colonial rule.*
- *Judges **should not** assume that juries will understand the reasons for giving shorter prison sentences.*

💬 The negative form of *ought to* is normally *oughtn't to* in spoken English and *ought not to* in written English.

- *Law firms **ought not to** encourage the notion that whenever a member of the public suffers an accident, he or she should seek personal injury compensation.*

**TIP** *Must not* means 'it is not permitted' (*You must not arrive late for an exam*), whereas *do not have to* means 'you are not obliged to' (*You do not have to stay for the last half hour of the exam if you have finished*).

The past form of both *must* and *have to* is *had to*. (For the meaning of *must have* + past participle, see **2** below.) The past forms of *should* and *ought to* are *should have* + past participle and *ought to have* + past participle.

• *In a speech in 2007, President Bush controversially seemed to suggest that Americans troops* **should have stayed** *longer in Vietnam.*

**2 Logical necessity**

*Must, should, ought to,* and occasionally *have to,* are also used to express logical necessity (often referred to as 'deduction') either in the present or past. Again, the meaning of *should/ought to* is weaker.

• *The results* **should** *be reliable, given that the drug was extensively tested over a period of five years.*
• *If he reached the summit, Mallory's final ascent without modern equipment* **must have been** *very difficult.*

Note that in this meaning we do not use *must* or *must have* + past participle in the negative. We use a form of *can* instead.

• *Gilway argues that the government's calculation of expenditure* **cannot** ~~must not~~ *be right in this instance.*
• *When the law was passed, the government* **could not/ cannot have known** *how quickly the business power of the internet would increase.*

**3 Passive forms**

Passive forms of these verbs are useful when the agent (person or organization doing the action) is unknown, unimportant, or difficult to specify.

**a Obligation**
• *Measures to counter global warming* **must be put** *in place over the next ten years.* (= put in place by governments, international agencies, multinational corporations, etc.)

**b Logical necessity**
• *Records* **must have been destroyed** *before the police arrived.* (= agent unknown)

**11.3 test yourself**

**Circle the correct option.**

1 Defence counsel claimed that the case against their client must not/could not be proved because the evidence had been contaminated.
2 If they ask, unsuccessful candidates must/ had to be given reasons for their failure to be included in shortlists.
3 The charity ought/should to have been aware that some of the funds were being spent in the wrong way.
4 During a tour of the factory, health and safety inspectors declared that the company had to stop/must have stopped production until a series of tests were carried out.
5 British citizens must not/do not have to show a form of identification when they vote, except in Northern Ireland.
6 The report stated that the hospital should/must have ensured that its records were stored safely.

## 11.4 Forms of *need*

**11.4 study**

There are several ways of using *need*. It can be used as an ordinary verb or as a semi-modal verb. These are the main structures with *need* that we use in academic English.

**1 *Need* + noun phrase** (ordinary verb)

• *Some of California's cities already* **need** *much more water than their local supplies can provide.*

**2 *Need* + infinitive with *to*** (ordinary verb, similar meaning to *must/have to* for obligation)

• *Tony Blair realized that the Labour Party* **needed to** (= had to) *appeal to the voters of 'middle England' if it were to be elected to government.*

**3 *Needn't/need not* + infinitive without *to*** (semi-modal verb)

This semi-modal form is normally used in spoken academic English, but in writing, we tend to use the negative form of the ordinary verb instead.

• 💬 *We* **needn't examine** *every single study to realize that there is a link between the presence of the virus in the cells, and the onset of the disease.*
• ~~We needn't examine~~ *We* **do not need to** *examine every ...*

**4** *Need not/needn't* + *have* + past participle

This semi-modal form, used in writing (as *need not* rather than *needn't*) and speech, describes unnecessary actions that people/organizations have taken.

• *Frank Whittle, inventor of the jet engine, argued that Britain* **need not have fought** *the Battle of Britain at all if the government had funded his research at an earlier stage.*

This semi-modal form cannot be replaced by *did not need to*, because the past negative form of the ordinary verb means something different – actions that people didn't take because they were unnecessary.

• *In the end, the USA* **did not need to** *look further than its own backyard for the new source of energy called 'shale gas'.*

---

**11.4 test yourself**

**Circle the correct or more appropriate option. If both are correct, circle both.**

**1** The experiment needed/had to be repeated after faults were discovered in the procedure.
**2** This report does not need to/needn't address the situation in Nigeria because it has already been resolved.
**3** Victor plc did not need to go/need not have gone bankrupt if they had limited their business to the UK.
**4** If local farms are to survive, water resources must/need to be better protected.
**5** We needn't/don't need to spend too much time in this talk on the work of Everson because it has been largely discredited.
**6** Money was saved because the company need not have built/did not need to build an extension to the dam.

---

## 11.5 *Will, would, shall*

**11.5 study**

**1** *Will*

*Will* is used for:

**a** describing the future (*The Prime Minister will spend two days in Moscow.*)

**b** first conditional sentences (*If temperatures rise, forest fires will break out again.*)

**c** describing the scope of an essay (*This essay will consider three types of bacteria.*).

**2** *Would*

*Would* is used:

**a** as the past tense of *will* in reported speech and to describe the 'future in the past'
• *The government denied that its budget cuts* **would harm** *education.*
• *Few of James Joyce's relatives, during those early years in Dublin, realized that the aspiring writer* **would become** *one of the 20th century's major literary figures.*

**b** in second and third conditional sentences (*If we paid in dollars, would we get a discount?*)

**c** for habitual actions in the past (*In those days, coal would be transported by barge on canals.*)

**d** in tentative phrases (*It would seem that ... Many people would argue that ...*)

**e** in polite phrases (*Would you mind lending me your dictionary?*).

(See section **11.6** for more examples.)

**3** *Shall*

*Shall* is quite rare in academic English and sounds very formal. You can occasionally use it instead of *will* (but only with *I* or *we*) to say what you plan to do in an essay or presentation.

For its use in offers and suggestions, see section **11.6**.

---

**11.5 test yourself**

**Complete each sentence with *will* or *would*.**

**1** There _____ appear to be three main objections to the proposed site for a new airport.
**2** Marie Stopes's work in family planning _____ influence the birth control movement throughout the 20th century.
**3** This case study _____ describe the ways in which two companies have made significant cutbacks in costs.
**4** Some of the competitors' innovative schemes _____ probably be adopted commercially.
**5** It _____ have a huge economic impact if the UK left the European Union.
**6** Further progress _____ not be achieved if the funding for inner city projects is reduced.

## 11.6 Spoken modal use

### 11.6 study

💬 Modal verbs are regularly used in tutorials, seminars, group work, and presentations. This section covers the semi-modals *have got to* and *be supposed to*, and the language of permission, requests, offers, suggestion, and advice.

#### 1 *Have got to, be supposed to*

*Have got to* means the same as *have to*, and in its positive form is more common in spoken English.
- *I've got to finish two essays by tomorrow.*

In negatives and question forms, however, *have to* is often preferred.
- *You don't have to attend every lecture, you know.* (= You haven't got to attend every lecture.)

*Be supposed to* is used to talk about expectations.
- *Are we supposed to take notes?*
- *Angie was supposed to join our group.*

The continuous form often implies criticism.
- *You're supposed to be working, aren't you?* (= You should be working but you clearly aren't.)

#### 2 Permission and requests

To ask for permission to do things, or to request other people to do things, we use *can* or the more polite *could/would* (including *would you mind + -ing*), sometimes adding *please* or *possibly*.
- (to tutor) *Would it be possible for me to have a short extension on my essay?*
- (to classmate) *Can I borrow your dictionary for a moment, please?*
- (to librarian) *Could we possibly leave our bags here for half an hour?*
- (to classmate) *Would you mind giving out the handouts while I'm starting the presentation?*

#### 3 Offers

To make offers, we use *Shall I ...?*, *can/could* and sometimes *Would you like me to ...?*
- (to classmate) *Shall I take some notes for you if you can't attend the lecture?*
- (to tutor) *Would you like me to tell the rest of the group that we'll be in the computer lab?*
- (to classmates in group) *I could do the introduction to the presentation, if you like.*

#### 4 Suggestions and advice

To make suggestions, we use *can/could* and *Shall I/we ...?*.
- (to classmate) *We can do some revision while we're waiting.*
- (to classmate) *You could try switching the photocopier off and on again.*
- (to classmates in group) *Shall we prepare some kind of questionnaire?*

To give advice or make suggestions, we use *can, could, should,* and *had better. Should* is stronger than *can/could*, and *had better* is the strongest, suggesting that something negative could happen if we don't act. Notice how we use *think* and negative question forms to 'soften' suggestions.
- (to classmate) *Couldn't/Can't you just take your laptop with you?*
- (to classmate rehearsing a presentation) *I think you should show those figures on a graph.*
- (to classmate) *Don't you think you should talk to your personal tutor?*
- (to classmates in group) *We'd better look at the last case study now, or we'll run out of time.*

*Had better* has a negative form, and the question form is usually negative too.
- *You'd better not work all night if you've got an exam tomorrow.*
- *Hadn't we better leave some time at the end for questions?*

### 11.6 test yourself

**Correct each sentence by adding one of the words in the box.**

| possible | could | better | supposed |
|---|---|---|---|
| has | to | we | I |

1 Shall start the presentation by introducing us all?
2 I contact one or two local companies and see if we can do some staff interviews.
3 I believe that society got to take a more pragmatic attitude to the use of drugs.
4 Don't you think we'd look at some non-UK companies too?
5 We're supposed include a bibliography, aren't we?
6 Would it be for me to do my presentation at the end of next week?
7 I thought that the UN forces were to be preventing those sorts of incidents.
8 Could present our work as a poster display?

# 11 Challenge yourself

**A** Rewrite the phrases in italics, using the correct form of the word in brackets, to complete the text about logistics.

[1]*It is possible to* illustrate *the science of logistics* (can) using the sport of climbing. [2]*It is necessary for anyone planning a serious expedition to be aware* (need) of the importance of transporting, storing, and securing their equipment. A brief survey of mountaineering trips that have failed will reveal how, more often than not, it is a logistical error that has led to defeat. [3]*It is possible for modern climbers to use* (can) logistics software on their laptops or mobile devices; climbers in pre-computer days [4]*were obliged to do* (have) their calculations with pen and paper.

A recent unsuccessful attempt on K2 [5]*should serve* (ought) as an example. [6]*It was not necessary for Niles Brangwen and his team to fail* (need) if they had allowed time for a second supply of provisions to be transported to the camp below the summit. With extra supplies, [7]*it was possible for the two lead climbers to have waited* (could) until the weather improved to make their move to the top. After a few days, they [8]*succeeded in descending* (manage) safely, but [9]*there can be little doubt that they regretted* (must) this gap in their planning as they made their way homewards.

**B** Circle the correct verb form in the introduction to an essay about retrials. If both are correct, circle both.

For an appeal to be upheld in a court of law, there is a requirement that new evidence [1]*could/should* be presented. Scientific advances in areas such as DNA testing, however, mean that there is now a growing trend for cases that [2]*might/must* have remained closed to be considered for retrial. Berenger (2012) cites the case of Maxwell Jordan, who believes he [3]*will be able to/could* prove his innocence through a report that his lawyers have commissioned from scientists who study the behaviour of bullets.

Jordan's team will argue that he [4]*could/must* not have fired the gun twice within the period of time described by the prosecuting counsel at his trial. If this new evidence is accepted, it [5]*can/should* prove persuasive enough to put Jordan's conviction in doubt. This essay [6]*might/will* explore Jordan's case in more detail.

**C** Circle the correct verb forms in the text about infrastructure projects. If both are correct, circle both.

The location of a new rail system or airport [1]*needs to/should* take into account the conflicting interests of a number of different groups of people. Politicians in power [2]*must/may* not benefit immediately from an infrastructure project, but they [3]*could/might* gain credit in the medium term for a boost in employment when construction work begins. It [4]*would/shall* seem, on the surface, that the business community in general [5]*will/needs to* benefit when a major transport project is initiated, but, as in sport, where there are winners there [6]*might/must* always be losers.

Amongst the public, commentators [7]*would/should* argue that there are two groups: the general population who [8]*must/will* often be supportive of modernizing programmes, and those directly affected, the ones whose houses [9]*need/ought* to be demolished or whose quality of life [10]*will/could* be reduced by the endless departure and arrival of long-haul jets. Bryson (2009) suggests that thirty or forty years ago, the complaints of this latter group [11]*can/would* regularly be ignored, whereas these days, a protest movement [12]*can/needs to* be established and attract public attention within days of a project being announced.

**AWL GLOSSARY**

**illustrate** to make the meaning of something clearer by using examples, pictures, etc.

**transport** to take something from one place to another in a vehicle

**secure** to protect something so that it is safe and difficult to attack or damage

**error** a mistake, especially one that causes problems or affects the result of something

**AWL GLOSSARY**

**conflict** if two ideas, beliefs, stories, etc. conflict, it is not possible for them to exist together or for them both to be true

**benefit** to be in a better position because of something

**credit** praise or approval because you are responsible for something good that has happened

**medium** in the middle between two sizes, amounts, lengths, temperatures, etc.

**D** Correct the mistakes in the extract from a text about the work of smaller charities.

[1]Although the charity FoodExpress had only been in operation for two years, most commentators agreed that its senior staff ought have aware that the funding allocated to relief projects in the region was not being effectively monitored. [2]What FoodExpress should not have predicted, however, was the outbreak of fighting that followed the regional elections. [3]Fearing that the conflict will lead to civil war, the charity could withdraw its aid workers, but could not at the same time ensure that money provided for the improvement of infrastructure was prevented from falling into the hand of local warlords. [4]Managers at FoodExpress cannot blame for the ultimate use to which their funds were put, but it could argued that some of the smaller charities working in the developing world lack the hard-won experience of larger and longer-established organizations such as Oxfam and UNICEF.

[5]Grice (2009), on the other hand, takes a slightly different point of view. She suggests that the bigger charities could do more to share the local knowledge they have accumulated, and that they ought to not overlook that it is only by working with smaller charities that all of a region's needs can satisfy. [6]She commends the work of the Kitchen Tables Charities Trust, which promotes the work of smaller charities, and highlights in her article a series of outcomes that must not have been achieved without their interventions.

**E** ⬤ Complete the conversation about a group presentation on economic forecasting. More than one answer may be correct.

---

A   We've got all the material we need. It's just a case of organizing it.
[1]_____ I begin by introducing us all?

B   Sure. Perhaps you [2]_____ also outline the whole presentation as normal? And we're [3]_____ to let people know at the beginning when they can ask questions, aren't we?

C   [4]_____ we let them ask questions whenever they like?

A   I like that idea. If the questions begin to take up too much time, we [5]_____ always ask people to wait until the end.

D   Would you all [6]_____ if I did my piece next, where I look at some of the forecasting disasters? I'll get really nervous if I have to wait until the end.

A   I think that's fine, Mike. It'll grab people's attention. After that, though, we'd [7]_____ look at the statistics. Are you OK with that, Joanne?

B   Yes, that's no problem. But I've [8]_____ to check my figures with you all. There are a couple of stats that seem to contradict each other.

A   OK. We'll do that later. After your piece on statistics, I [9]_____ do mine on the way companies use forecasting, if you like.

C   I'm not sure, Ann. Don't you [10]_____ you should finish things off, since you introduced it all?

A   All right. That's fine with me. That means you would go after Joanne. OK, is there anything we haven't covered?

D   Yes, aren't we [11]_____ to give handouts?

A   Well, we don't [12]_____ to, but I think it's recommended. Would you like me to draft something?

---

**F** Write 100–200 words about a city or region that has changed significantly in the last fifty years. Consider what the place might now be like without those changes. Discuss what may happen over the next few years. Use as many modal verbs as you can.

# Introduction

The relationship between cause and effect is central to a great deal of academic writing, and may be expressed in a number of different ways. In this unit the language of cause and effect is divided into three types: verbs such as *produce*, connectors such as *therefore*, and nouns such as *consequence*. Effect clauses are highlighted in blue.

Note the following.

**1** Either causes or effects may be expressed first in a sentence. The order you choose may depend on which aspect you see as more important, or on the way you decide to arrange your ideas within a paragraph.
* *If we destroy forests, we lose the insects that pollinate food plants*. (cause → effect)
* *Brown Brothers of Ontario were able to expand their network of bookshops as a result of a sophisticated campaign of niche marketing.* (effect → cause)

**2** You can also vary the strength of the link between cause and effect. You could express a weak link by using hedging language such as *may* or *possibly*, and a strong link by using emphatic language such as *clearly* or *obviously*.
* *Public confidence in European politicians has been eroded over the last thirty years. This **may in part be** a consequence of the rising power of the media.*
* *High levels of taxation in the 1970s were **clearly** the reason for a number of business people and successful entertainers to seek tax exile outside the UK.*

---

Look at the essay questions (1–5). What do they all have in common? What is the difference in emphasis between question 2 and question 3?

1 Why did the USA enter the Second World War? What were the immediate results?

2 What have been the social consequences of the post-war rise in house ownership in England?

3 Discuss the reasons that led to the development of mass tourism in the UK in the 1960s.

4 What went wrong with the Japanese economy in the 1990s, and how did the country survive as an economic force in the world?

5 Explain how nanomaterials pose a threat to human health.

Suggested answers: see page 203

Other units that deal with cause and effect language are unit *7 Connectors*, and unit *17 Conditionals*.

## 12.1 Verbs, cause → effect

### 12.1 study

1 The verbs *cause*, *produce*, *lead to*, and *result in* all have the same meaning, and are used in the middle of sentences to express cause → effect.

- *The digital revolution in TV (cause) has caused/produced/led to/resulted in* far greater consumer choice. (effect)
- *A rise in global oil prices will inevitably cause/produce/lead to/result in* higher prices in the shops.

Using the *-ing* form of these verbs is particularly useful for describing the next step in processes (one step causes or leads to the next step). The following structures are possible.

**a** *Causing something; causing something/someone to do or become something*

**b** *Leading to/resulting in something; leading to/resulting in something happening or someone doing something*

**c** *Producing something*

- *The liquid is heated, **producing** a vapour which is trapped inside a glass cover. The temperature inside the cover is then reduced, **causing** the vapour to solidify.*
- *Waves strike a cliff face, **leading to** cracks and splintering. As time passes, the cracks may grow, ultimately **resulting in** caves forming where the cliff meets the sea.*

2 The verbs *create*, *bring about*, and *give rise to* also express cause → effect, but are slightly less common.
- *Mapping the human genome may eventually **create/bring about/give rise to** advances in medical treatment.*

**TIP** *Bring about* is a phrasal verb; it's possible to say *bring something about* as well as *bring about something* (see page 133 in unit *15 Phrasal and prepositional verbs*).

3 The verb *be* is also used for cause → effect in the phrase *be responsible for*.
- *Poor street lighting could **be responsible for** an increase in traffic accidents at night.*

(See section **12.5** for the use of *be* + nouns.)

Note that you can use the adverbs *ultimately*, *eventually*, and *inevitably* (see examples above) before all these verbs, and also between the verb and the preposition in *lead to*, *result in*, and *give rise to* (e.g. *resulting ultimately in*).

### 12.1 test yourself

Complete each sentence with the correct form of the verb(s) in brackets. Add a preposition if necessary.

1 The closure of the coal mines in the 1980s inevitably _____ (lead) a severe rise in regional unemployment.
2 Investment in small-scale technology such as mobile phones can _____ (produce) growth in developing countries.
3 People left the countryside to find work in factories, ultimately _____ (result) whole villages being abandoned, and _____ (create) pressure on urban housing.
4 A slight rise in the temperature of the sea can _____ (bring) an increased level of water in the air.
5 The new arts centre revived the fortunes of the town centre, _____ (cause) investors _____ (return).
6 Air pollution may be _____ (responsible) an increase in cases of asthma.

## 12.2 Verbs, effect → cause

### 12.2 study

1 To express effect → cause, you can use *result from* or *stem from*.
- *Some forms of abstract art (effect) **resulted/stemmed from** early experiments in cubism by the artists Picasso and Braque (cause).*
- *A career in a particular field may ultimately **result/stem from** the approach taken to the subject by an inspiring teacher at primary level.*

Note that the adverbs *ultimately* (in the example above), *eventually*, and *inevitably* can precede both of these verbs, or be placed between the verb and the preposition (e.g. *result ultimately from*).

2 When there is a simple, factual link between effect and cause, the passive form of the verbs *cause*, *produce* or *bring about* are often used.
- *Landslides **are** sometimes **caused by/produced by/brought about by** mild earth tremors.*

3 You can use the passive form of the verb *trigger* (from the part of a gun that you pull to make it fire) to suggest an automatic effect or response.
- *Mills argues that a number of riots **have been triggered** by the arrest of a member of the local community.*

## 12.2 test yourself

Complete each sentence with the correct form of the verb in brackets. Add a preposition if necessary.

1 Symptoms that may _____ (produce) trauma include flashbacks, sleeplessness and periods of intense anger.
2 According to a recent study, most accidents _____ (result) carelessness around the house.
3 Lyme disease _____ (cause) the bite of a tick, which passes bacteria into the bloodstream.
4 An inability to think clearly can _____ (stem) a lack of sleep.
5 A period of depression may _____ (trigger) a single short event.
6 Hypothermia _____ (bring) prolonged exposure to extremely low temperatures.

## 12.3 Connectors (*as*, *since*, etc.)

### 12.3 study

As well as linking ideas within and across sentences, connectors are used to show cause and effect. There are a number of different connectors, which are covered in this section and in section **12.4**.

**1 *As, since, so, such***

*As* and *since* are normally used at the beginning of a sentence to express cause → effect.
• *As/Since Britain was still recovering from the war,* (cause) *some food products were in short supply.* (effect)

**2 *So ... that, such ... that***

*So* and *such* are useful in expressing cause → effect. *So* is used before adverbs, adjectives, and quantifiers such as *much* and *few*.
• *The rate of reoffending is so high* (cause) *that some politicians are questioning the usefulness of prison sentences for all but the most serious crimes.* (effect)

*Such* is used before nouns, or adjectives + nouns.
• *Until now there has been such a consistent outcry against genetic testing by insurance companies that no companies have wished to be seen arguing for a change in current practice.*

**3 *As a result, consequently, therefore***

These words and phrases are used between two complete sentences or ideas to express cause → effect.
• *Student feedback criticized the size of seminar groups, saying that there were few opportunities to ask questions.* (cause) *As a result,/Consequently,/ Therefore, the course leader decided to set a maximum of fifteen participants.* (effect)

Note that in the example above you could use a semicolon (;) or *and* rather than a full stop after the word *questions. Therefore* and *consequently* can be placed later in the second sentence (*... to ask questions. The course leader therefore/consequently decided to ...*)

TIP *So* can be used to express cause → effect, but it has a weaker effect and tends to occur in spoken English.
• 💬 *The conflict spread across the country and caused great damage to the infrastructure, as you can see from this slide. But it ended after about six months, so local people were able to return to their villages and start repairing things.*

**4 *Which***

If you want to express a cause → effect link more emphatically, you can use the pattern *which + means that/is why/explains why.*
• *Arts subsidies were reduced significantly in the 1990s, which is why less popular operas were performed more rarely.* (You could also say *which **was** why,* because you are dealing with a past situation.)

*This* can be used instead of *which*, but you need to use a semi-colon or full stop rather than a comma.
• *Many voters are dissatisfied with the British 'first past the post' electoral system. This means that there are always calls for reform.*

## 12.3 test yourself

**Complete each sentence with one word.**
**Sometimes there is more than one correct answer.**

1 Vietnamese fighters were able to move with _____ speed through the jungle that US commanders were forced to request additional air support.

2 It is difficult to measure a leader's success without taking into account the state of the business at the time of his or her appointment. Benton _____ created a points system for assessing a company's position at a given time.

3 _____ the new drug had unexpected side effects, it was withdrawn from general use.

4 The Chernobyl nuclear plant did not have a confinement shell, which _____ that radiation escaped into the atmosphere.

5 Computers with internet access are now a common feature in most households; _____ a result, there has been a steady decline in the sale of printed reference books such as encyclopedias.

6 There are _____ many ecological problems facing the Aral Sea that it is unlikely to survive in its present form.

## 12.4 Connectors (*due to*, etc.)

### 12.4 study

This section gives more examples of connectors that are used to show cause and effect. See also the previous section (**12.3**).

**1 *Due to, as a result of***

You can use these phrases (followed by a noun or *-ing* form of a verb) to express cause → effect if you place them first in sentence (with a comma afterwards), or to express effect → cause if placed in the middle.

• *Due to/As a result of overcultivation,* (cause) *the soil no longer contains enough nutrients*. (effect)
= *The soil no longer contains enough nutrients* (effect) *due to/as a result of overcultivation.* (cause)

Note that *owing to, as a consequence of,* and *on account of* can all be used in the same way.

**2 *If***

You can also express cause → effect and effect → cause with *if*.

• *If managers are allowed to control their budgets,* (cause) *their motivation levels will inevitably rise*. (effect)
= *Managers' motivation levels will inevitably rise* (effect) *if they are allowed to control their budgets.* (cause)

(See unit *17 Conditionals* for more information on the use of *if*.)

**3 *Because of, because***

*Because of* (followed by a noun or the *-ing* form of a verb) can be used in the middle of a sentence, where it has the same meaning as *due to* and *as a result of*, to express effect → cause.

• *A series of important discoveries were made at the end of the century* (effect) *because of a number of laboratory accidents,* (cause) *rather than any carefully organized progress.*

*Because* (before clauses) is normally used in the middle of a sentence to express effect → cause.

• *Residents have tended to leave these inner city areas because crime rates have risen.*

*Due to/owing to/on account of + the fact that* means the same as *because*, but highlights the effect → cause relationship more emphatically.

• *Investors began to sell their shares due to the fact that fighting had broken out in several of the company's key mining regions.*

## 12.4 test yourself

**Correct each sentence by adding one word.**

1 Diseases such as cholera are now likely in the refugee camps because a lack of sanitation.

2 A number of mistakes were made account of the fact that no trained medical staff were present.

3 An employee remains in a particularly stressful post for a prolonged period, 'burnout' can occur.

4 'Technostress' is the term used by some medical practitioners to describe symptoms such as headaches and anxiety which occur in adolescents as a result playing and frequently losing computer games.

5 During the Great Depression farmers moved to California they had been told there were jobs there.

6 Due a lack of exercise and poor diet, childhood obesity is now common in the developed world.

## 12.5 Nouns

### 12.5 study

Academic English often prefers sentences based around nouns. (See **4.1** on page 039 in unit *4 Being formal and informal* for more information.) There are a number of nouns, including *cause* and *effect* themselves, that are useful for talking about causes and effects, usually with the verb *be*. Note the prepositions used after each noun.

**1 Nouns like *cause***

*cause of, reason for, source of*
- One obvious **reason for** the high level of unemployment in the town is the recent closure of an electronics company with a workforce of around 800.

Another useful noun is *factor*, which can be used with *contribute to, lead to, give rise to,* and *result in*.
- Bank failures and the stock market crash of 1929 are two of the key **factors that contributed to** the Great Depression in the USA.

Useful adjectives that collocate with *cause, reason, source,* and *factor* are *fundamental, key, main, obvious, possible,* and *underlying*.

**2 Nouns like *effect***

*effect of, result of, consequence of, outcome of*
- One likely **effect of** the search for better regulatory control of banks **will be** a clear split between the high-street function, sometimes called 'retail banking', and the risk-taking element that has caused so much of the recent controversy.
- Environmental damage to some of the last wildernesses of the Earth, such as Alaska and the Antarctic, is a possible **consequence of** the endless search for new sources of oil.

Useful adjectives that collocate with *effect, result, consequence,* and *outcome* are *beneficial, desirable, inevitable, likely, possible, probable,* and *unfortunate*.

### 12.5 test yourself

Correct each sentence by adding a preposition.

1 High blood pressure is a possible result an excessive intake of salt in the diet.
2 The main reason the female leopard's behaviour may have been the proximity of her newly-born cubs.
3 There are several consequences people living longer, one of which is the raising of the age of retirement.
4 It is not always possible to establish the underlying cause mental illness.
5 Factors that contribute poor performance at interviews include inadequate communication skills and an inability to demonstrate skills through the use of appropriate examples.
6 One inevitable outcome the growth of internet fraud is the creation of companies selling security software.

# Summary of cause and effect language

| cause → effect | effect → cause |
|---|---|
| **verbs (12.1)**<br>*cause*<br>*produce*<br>*lead to*<br>*result in*<br>*create*<br>*bring about*<br>*give rise to* | **verbs (12.2)**<br>*result from*<br>*stem from*<br>*be brought about by*<br>*be caused by*<br>*be produced by*<br>*be triggered by* |
| **connectors (12.3 and 12.4)**<br>*As ...*<br>*Since ...*<br>*so/such ... that ...*<br>*As a result, ...*<br>*Consequently, ...*<br>*Therefore, ...*<br>*which/this means that ...*<br>*which/this is why ...*<br>*which/this explains why ...*<br>*Due to ...*<br>*As a result of ...*<br>*Owing to ...*<br>*As a consequence of ...*<br>*On account of ...*<br>*If ...,* | **connectors (12.4)**<br>*... because of*<br>*because ...*<br><br><br><br><br><br><br><br><br>*... due to ...*<br>*... as a result of ...*<br>*... due to/owing to/on account of + the fact that ...*<br>*... if ...* |
| **'effect' nouns (12.5)**<br>*effect of*<br>*result of*<br>*consequence of*<br>*outcome of* | **'cause' nouns (12.5)**<br>*cause of*<br>*reason for*<br>*source of* |

# 12 Challenge yourself

**A** Rewrite the sentences, following the instructions in brackets.

1 Continuous evaluation of any new training course enables the organizers to measure its success in detail. (start with *If a new training course ...*)
2 War and the resulting political turmoil are causing an acute shortage of food. (start with *One consequence ...*)
3 Stein (2007) argues that due to the lack of print archives in modern governmental department offices, there has been a kind of institutional memory loss. (use the verb *result*)
4 The reunification of the two Koreas would lead to a surge southwards of economic migrants from the (former) communist state, according to Masefield (2010). (use *triggered by*)
5 The hiring of professional negotiators was partly responsible for the successful conclusion of the deal. (start with *One factor ...* and use the verb *contribute*)
6 The cause of high fish mortality was a dioxin spill further up the river. (use the verb *lead*)
7 The experiment with advertising methods brought about a noticeable change in the demographics of Centra's customers. (start with *One outcome ...*)
8 Tax cuts, in the view of Conway (2009), may be a source of medium-term economic growth. (use the verb *stem*)

### AWL GLOSSARY

**evaluation** the process of forming an opinion of something after thinking about it carefully

**migrant** a person who moves from one place to another

**professional** having a job which needs special training and a high level of education

**method** a particular way of doing something

**source** a place, person, or thing that you get something from

**B** Complete the text by adding the number of words in brackets. Pay attention to the punctuation. There may be more than one correct answer. If you need help, refer to the box following the text.

There is no doubt that the special export zones (SEZs) set up in developing countries [1]_____ (three words) new jobs. Essentially, what happens is that the host government establishes a miniature tax 'island' [2]_____ (one word) such havens tend to attract foreign companies wishing to contract out their manufacturing. Klein (2005), however, is critical of some SEZs which, [3]_____ (two words) of the strict rules imposed on their employees, operate in a similar way, she argues, to the slave plantations of early America.

For example, any laws permitting unionization are in effect suspended and, [4]_____, (three words), employees have little or no protection. In some of these factories, the safety record is [5]_____ (one word) bad [6]_____ (one word) no experienced workers will stay for long. [7]_____ (two words) that the workforce continues to be underskilled.

It is a classic example of the chicken and egg paradigm: inexperienced employees have more accidents, [8]_____ (one word) better workers to stay away; and [9]_____ (one word) the situation never improves. Nonetheless, SEZs remain popular with the governments of many developing countries, [10]_____ (one word) of the industry and employment they attract.

> this means   that   give rise to   on account   consequently   because *(x2)*
> as a result   so   causing

### AWL GLOSSARY

**export** the selling and transporting of goods to another country

**suspend** to officially stop something for a time; to prevent something from being active, used, etc. for a time

**classic** with all the features you would expect to find; very typical

**C** Link the ideas, following the instructions in brackets. You may need to change the order of the ideas. There may be more than one correct answer.

1 a rising level of childhood asthma/the pollution generated by road vehicles (start with *One probable result …*)
2 Very little rain fell in the early part of the year/the government banned people from using domestic hosepipes (use *explains*)
3 pedestrians are unable to reach their destinations/some new urban roads are built without pavements (start with *Since …*)
4 the huge size of the United States/the disparate attitudes of the American people (use *caused* and the hedging verb *may*)
5 There has been public anger over tax avoidance schemes/parliament has tightened the appropriate financial regulations. (use *such*)
6 The marketing department was forced to make three account managers redundant/it overspent its budget. (start with *As a consequence …*)
7 an economic collapse finally followed /under-regulation allowed some banks to make risky loans/there was uncertainty in the financial markets when the loans were not repaid (use *producing* and then *causing*)
8 people have less disposable income/charities may suffer during a recession (use *due* and *fact* in the middle of your sentence)

**D** Write a short text describing the causes of Japan's 'lost decade' in the 1990s. Use the notes, which show causes → effects, and language from unit 12 (e.g. *bring about, lead to, produce, cause something to happen, as a result of*).

- falls in real estate value and bad bank loans (late 1980s) → rapid drop in prices; period of economic stagnation
- continuing deflation → the government reduced interest rates to zero (early 1990s) → but no revival in the country's economic fortunes (which continued to decline throughout the 1990s)
- the global slowdown in the closing year of the millennium → signs of improvement in the Japanese economy (towards the end of the 1990s) were short-lived.

**E** Write a short text describing the effects of hypothermia. Use the notes, which show effects → causes in chronological order, and language from unit 12 (e.g. *be caused by, result from, consequence of, outcome of*).

1 violent shivering → the body's need to produce heat
2 mild confusion → a decrease in blood pressure and heart rate
3 lips, ears, fingers, and toes may become blue → the body's attempt to draw warm blood back towards the vital organs
3 victims will find it almost impossible to walk or use their hands → the closing down of the body's metabolic systems

**F** Write 150–250 words about an organization in trouble, the reasons for its difficulties, and the consequences of its actions. You may want to think of a business that went (or nearly went) bankrupt, or a political defeat. Use cause and effect linking language at least five times. (There is a useful summary on page 113.)

**AWL GLOSSARY**

**domestic** used in the home; connected with the home or family

**attitude** the way that you think and feel about something; the way that you behave towards something that shows how you think and feel

**scheme** a plan for getting money or some other advantage for yourself, especially one that involves cheating other people

**appropriate** suitable, acceptable, or correct for the particular circumstances

**regulation** an official rule made by a government or some other authority

**disposable income** the money that somebody is free to spend after paying taxes, etc.

## Introduction

Read the text and then complete the table showing the grammatical patterns that follow the verbs in bold as they are used in the text.

| Verb + infinitive with *to* | start |
|---|---|
| Verb + infinitive without *to* | |
| Verb + *-ing* form | |
| Verbs + *that* | |
| Verb + *wh-* (i.e. a question word, e.g. *what*): | |

Farmers' markets have **started** to appear in many UK towns and cities. The local people who frequent them apparently **enjoy** buying produce that might not be available in supermarkets. Advocates of such markets **argue** that smaller farmers **can** maximize their profits by selling directly to shoppers, and provide answers for consumers who **are** increasingly **asking** where their food originates. Critics **contend** that, without regulation, some of these markets **enable** unscrupulous vendors to 'mislabel' their goods as organic or local, and that the anti-supermarket ethos **justifies** selling produce at inflated prices. This essay will attempt to **explain** how these markets first established themselves, and where the trend **may** lead.

Suggested answers: see page 204

A verb can be followed by one of four major types of clause.

**1** infinitive with or without *to* clause
- *Managers **must trust** their staff, or they will **fail to get** the best out of them.*

**2** *-ing* clause
- *Edward Kennedy **delayed reporting** the car crash that led to the death of Mary Jo Kopechne.*

**3** *that* clause
- *Some bankers **believe that** their profession is frequently misrepresented in the press.*

**4** *wh-* clause (*wh-* = *what, when, where, which, who, why* or *how*)
- *Critics cannot always **explain why** some films seem to strike a chord with the public.*

This unit gives examples of common verbs that are used in the four patterns described above. Some verbs are frequently used in more than one pattern, and these will be listed more than once. Other verbs may be used frequently in one pattern and less frequently in others. These will only be listed according to the pattern in which they are most frequently used. Note that sometimes the meaning of the verb changes when it is used in a different pattern.

Verbs are generally listed alphabetically, although words which are closely related in meaning are grouped together at the beginning of each list.

Other units that deal with verbs are unit *11 Modal verbs*, and unit *15 Phrasal and prepositional verbs*.

# 13.1 Verb + infinitive with *to* or *-ing* form

## 13.1 study

Verbs in this section can be followed by an infinitive with *to* or an *-ing* form.

### 1 No change in meaning

| | |
|---|---|
| begin | like |
| start | love |
| continue | prefer |
| | hate |

These verbs can be followed by the infinitive with *to*, or the *-ing* form, with no change in meaning.

- *As the recession of the early 1990s began **biting/to bite**, companies looked for immediate savings in their daily costs.*
- *Most office workers hate **to feel/feeling** that their contribution to the overall success of the company is being overlooked.*

Note that *would* + *like, love, prefer,* or *hate* always takes the infinitive with *to*.

- *However much a successful research scientist **would prefer to claim** all the credit for a new discovery, the likelihood is that it has resulted from a team effort.*

**TIP** Two *-ing* forms are not used together.
- *Davo plc was **beginning** ~~enjoying~~ **to enjoy** some success when the UK entered a period of sustained recession.*

### 2 Different meaning

| | | |
|---|---|---|
| remember | stop | try |
| forget | go on | mean |

Whether you use the infinitive with *to*, or the *-ing* form after these verbs depends on the meaning. The pairs of examples below show the difference.

- *Small businesses should **remember to seek** guidance before placing job advertisements in order to ensure that they do not contravene the existing legislation on discrimination. (= not forget)*
- *Most tourist **remember staying** in a hotel that did not meet their expectations. The difference nowadays is that accommodation can be vetted in advance through the use of consumer-driven websites. (= have a memory)*

- *The difficulty arises when a junior doctor who has been on duty for eighteen hours **forgets to check that** a patient is, for example, allergic to penicillin. (= not remember)*
- *Most people will never **forget buying** their first car. The challenge to the trader is to replicate that excitement when consumers are selecting their tenth vehicle. (= not have a memory)*

- *If an employee cannot **stop to take** a reasonable lunch break, their work may suffer in the afternoon. (= stop doing one thing in order to do another)*
- *GlaxoWellcome plc **stopped trading** under that name in 2000, when it merged with SmithKline Beecham plc to become GlaxoSmithKline. (= finish doing something)*

- *Madeleine Albright spent four years as US Ambassador to the United Nations. She then **went on to become** the first female US Secretary of State in 1997. (= do one thing after another)*
- 💬 *(in a presentation) I could **go on talking** about the various interpretations of Kafka's The Trial for several hours, but I want to leave some time for questions, so I'll finish there. (= continue doing something)*

- *BP has **tried to repair** some of the damage done to its reputation in the USA following its response to the Deepwater Horizon oil spill. (= attempt)*
- *A group of families in Maine **tried living** without their computers or mobile phones for a month. (= experiment)*

- *Cadbury's claimed that they did not **mean to insult** the model Naomi Campbell in an advertisement that seemed to compare her to a bar of chocolate. (= intend)*
- *Going global in a real sense **means understanding** how business works across cultural boundaries. (= that is the consequence).*

## 13.1 test yourself

Circle the correct option. If both are correct, circle both.

1 If patients stopped to take/taking this drug, it would put them at risk of a heart attack.
2 The legislation was meant discouraging/to discourage traders from buying illegally-acquired copper.
3 The 'Hayflick limit' is the point at which cells no longer continue to divide/dividing.
4 None of the witnesses remembered seeing/to see the helicopter drop before it exploded.
5 Many business people travel because they prefer doing/to do business face-to-face.
6 Despite early setbacks, Lowton plc went on winning/to win the UK's largest defence contract of 2009.
7 The research team noted the exact moment when the subject would start to hesitate/hesitating before replying.
8 Some householders have tried lowering/to lower their heating thermostats by two degrees to save energy.

## 13.2 Verb + infinitive with *to*

## 13.2 study

In this section, the verbs listed are normally followed by the infinitive with *to*, with or without an object.

**1 Usually without an object**

| | | |
|---|---|---|
| appear | agree | plan |
| seem | promise | prepare |
| tend | refuse | |

| | | |
|---|---|---|
| (can) afford | demand | need |
| aim | deserve | offer |
| arrange | fail | pretend |
| attempt | hope | threaten |
| choose | learn | wait |
| claim | manage | wish |
| decide | | |

The verbs in this group can be followed by an infinitive with *to*, and do not normally take an object.

• *No prime minister **can afford to ignore** the mistakes made by his or her predecessors.*
• *We **need to consider** first of all the various types of protest that a modern government can face in Europe.*

• *The BBC's foreign correspondent **pretended to be touring** the sites, when she was actually interviewing local inhabitants of the region.*
• *At several points during the night, both sides in the negotiations **threatened to walk out**.*
• *The O2 development **appears to have succeeded**, where the Millennium Experience – the original purpose of the dome – failed commercially and in the public mind.*

Note the use of the perfect infinitive (the past form) in the last example, and the continuous infinitive in the example about the BBC foreign correspondent.

**2 Usually with an object**

| | | |
|---|---|---|
| allow | advise | persuade |
| permit | enable | remind |
| | encourage | teach |
| | force | tell |
| | invite | warn |
| | order | |

These verbs are normally followed by an object and an infinitive with *to*.

• *Although the police **persuaded the protestors to leave** Parliament Square quite quickly, the march had a significant effect on public opinion.*
• *Some commentators **warned Marks and Spencer not to expand** into the USA in the late 1980s.*
• *American soldiers **allowed photographers to enter** some parts of Helmand, but advised them to hire security guards from one of the local agencies.*
• *A sophisticated computer model **enables the likely deterioration pattern of a new building to be examined**.*

Note the use of the passive infinitive in the example above, and the negative infinitive in the Marks and Spencer example.

**3 Sometimes with an object**

| | |
|---|---|
| ask | help |
| beg | intend |
| expect | want |

These verbs sometimes have an object.

• *Universities **expect most academics to have** a research interest and to publish articles or books in that area.*
• *The British company Dyson Ltd **expected to attract** criticism when they moved production overseas.*

## 13.2 test yourself

**Complete each sentence, using the past form of one of the verbs in the box.**

> help   manage   invite   refuse
> remind   agree

1 Professor Curnick _____ her team not to talk to journalists from the medical press during the drug trial.
2 Selco only _____ to survive the recession by selling its assets in Spain.
3 When Muhammad Ali _____ to serve in the US Army during the Vietnam War, his boxing licence was immediately revoked.
4 When he finally _____ to be interviewed by the BBC, Tony Hayward, former chief executive of BP, admitted that he had made mistakes in his handling of the oil spill in the Gulf.
5 In 1993 Louis Herman _____ Adam Pack to join him in establishing the Dolphin Institute.
6 Cyclist Gino Bartali was honoured by Israel because he had _____ Jews to avoid deportation to concentration camps during the Second World War.

## 13.3 Verb + infinitive without *to*

### 13.3 study

Three small groups of verbs are followed by the infinitive without *to*.

1 **Modal verbs** (*can, could, may, might, must, ought to, shall, should, will, would*)

- *Some politicians have argued that print media **should fall** under the same kind of regulatory control as broadcast media.*

(See also unit *11 Modal verbs*.)

2 *Let, make, had better, would rather*

- (in a presentation) *If we **let** sixteen-year-olds **vote**, they may develop a long-lasting interest in politics.*
- *Recent opinion polls show that most Americans **would rather** their government **cut** spending than enter into any new programme of stimulus investment.*
- (in a seminar) ***We'd better move** the discussion on to unemployment statistics, or we'll run out of time.*
- *The assumption that water metering **would make** the public **save** water is difficult to argue against.*

Note that *had better* is normally used in spoken rather than written academic English.

Note that when the passive form of *make* is used, *to* is required.
- *The argument of the 'tiger mother' movement is that children will benefit from a parenting style through which they **are made to achieve** their potential by disciplined practice.*

3 *Feel, hear, notice, see, watch*

With this small group, we tend to use the infinitive without *to* to focus on a completed action. The *-ing* form can be used to focus on an action in progress.
- *Investors in Broadman Enterprises **saw** the value of their shares **fall** by 45% in the first quarter of the year.*
- *When junior members of the government **saw** the public **turning against** the poll tax, they began to realize that it would make sense in terms of their careers to distance themselves from the Prime Minister, Margaret Thatcher.*

### 13.3 test yourself

**Complete each sentence, using one of the words in the box.**

> would   let   made   must   will   watch

1 Chemicals can be _____ to react through the input of an energy source such as heat.
2 I _____ rather take all questions at the end of the presentation, if you don't mind.
3 This essay _____ explore the organizational differences between Apple Inc. and Microsoft Corporation.
4 Observers at the aquarium are able to _____ octopuses feeding on crab.
5 There were reports that the hospital had _____ patients lie unattended in corridors for up to eight hours.
6 Foreign companies _____ float at least 50% of their shares if they wish to be considered for the FTSE's UK indices.

## 13.4 Verb + *-ing* form

### 13.4 study

These verbs can all be followed by *-ing* forms.

| | | |
|---|---|---|
| acknowledge admit deny | carry on keep (on) | detest dislike resent |

| | | |
|---|---|---|
| enjoy feel like | end up finish give up | delay postpone put off |

| | | |
|---|---|---|
| anticipate appreciate avoid consider describe discuss | imagine involve justify mention (not) mind miss | practise propose resist risk suggest |

- *Staff induction normally **involves meeting** colleagues, touring the premises, and receiving an ID card.*
- *Officials at Alder Hey Children's Hospital in Liverpool **admitted storing** the organs of children who had died at the hospital between 1988 and 1995 without the permission of parents.*
- *Restaurant customers may **resent being presented** with a service charge option when paying by credit card if service has already been included in the bill.*
- *In his autobiographical book* What Mad Pursuit, *Francis Crick **describes leaving** the field of molecular biology for neuroscience.*

Note the passive form in the restaurant example, and note also that all of these verbs could be followed by a noun instead of an *-ing* form (*Francis Crick **describes the change** in his research focus from molecular biology to neuroscience*).

Correct each sentence by adding one of the words in the box.

> not   offering   on   being   losing   delayed

1 Fundraisers fear that if the arts centre carries making a loss, it will be closed by the end of the year.
2 Zantec plc launching their new smartphone when rumours circulated that it had a serious design fault.
3 Most new companies must anticipate money in their first year of business.
4 Some local authorities acknowledge having the funding capacity to offer hostel space to the majority of the homeless people in their area.
5 Companies which do not innovate risk overtaken by their competitors.
6 Dyson has proposed research and development tax credits to technology start-ups.

## 13.5 Verb + *that* or *wh-*

### 13.5 study

Many verbs connected with speaking and thinking can be followed by *that* or *wh-* clauses (clauses beginning with *what, when, where, whether, which, who, why,* or *how*). These verbs offer useful ways of reporting what people have written or said. With *that* and *wh-* clauses, you can change the subject or use a modal verb (which you cannot do with infinitive and *-ing* forms).

- *The prime minister at the time denied offering honours to business associates in an inappropriate manner.* (*-ing* form; no change of subject possible)
- *The prime minister at the time denied that his secretary had offered honours to business associates in an inappropriate manner.* (*that* clause; change of subject)

1 Verbs that can be followed by *that* and *wh-* clauses include:

| | | |
|---|---|---|
| consider think | discover find out | explain reveal show tell |

| | | |
|---|---|---|
| forget remember | imagine know realize understand | note notice observe see |

| say | accept | guess |
|-----|--------|-------|
| state | believe | hear |
| suggest | confirm | learn |
| | decide | mean |
| | deny | mention |
| | estimate | predict |
| | find | regret |

- Wanafeller **notes that** small-scale or peasant agriculture still feeds a majority of the population in countries such as Vietnam.
- Commentators **considered what** the news of the CEO's arrest would mean for the company's share price.
- Several recent studies **have shown why** good mental health is facilitated by regular exercise.
- Some office managers **may decide that** the best way of sharing information is to write everything down.
- Liechtenstein's size **means that** it always runs the risk of being overlooked by its more powerful neighbours.
- In this essay, I will try to **explain how** one or more of the business models suggested by Handy can fit together in the same organization.

**2** Verbs followed by *that* clauses, but not normally by *wh-* clauses include:

| admit | appear | argue |
|-------|--------|-------|
| deny | seem | contend |

| assert | insist | assume |
|--------|--------|--------|
| claim | maintain | suppose |

| agree | expect | recommend |
|-------|--------|-----------|
| be | feel | remind |
| complain | hope | reply |
| conclude | imply | suspect |
| demand | pretend | threaten |
| doubt | promise | warn |
| ensure | | |

- Warrander **asserts that** most of London's hospitality industry should be classed as part of the UK's invisible exports.
- The predominant model of health insurance **assumes that** at least one member of the household is in employment.
- Klein's trenchant observation **is that** companies based in Europe and the US now put all of their energies into marketing and branding their goods, rather than manufacturing them.

**TIP** It is grammatically possible to omit the word *that* in most verb + *that* clauses, but it is more common to do so in informal than in academic English.

**3** Verbs followed by *wh-* clauses, but not normally by *that* clauses:

| ask | mind |
|-----|------|
| depend (on) | wonder |
| discuss | |

- 💬 (in a presentation) We need to **ask where** waste of this type can be safely dumped.
- The success of the CERN project may **depend on which** questions the research team decide to ask.
- 💬 (in group work) We'll have to **discuss how** we present the information we've discovered.
- A realistic conclusion may be that the general public does not **mind** very much **who** represents them in parliament, as long as he or she is prepared to stand up for the serious concerns of local people.
- The American public was left **wondering when** BP would accept full responsibility for the oil leak.

## 13.5 test yourself

**Circle the correct option.**

1 Recent research has revealed that/when the tomb was built.
2 Sawyer implies that/what the tower block was badly designed in the first place.
3 Commentators wondered whether/that entrepreneur Barbara Fisher would recover from her losses.
4 In his documentary, Michaels explains that/what he discovered in the deepest of the caves in the system.
5 Two layers of lead ensured which/that no broadcast signals could affect the results of the experiment.
6 The advisory panel recommended that/what Bournemouth Airport should be closed for two days.
7 The board spent two days discussing that/who would take ultimate control of the companies during the merger.
8 The auditors realized why/that the bankrupt company had failed when they inspected the accounts.
9 Despite finding the aircraft's black box, investigators could not discover that/how the accident had happened.
10 News reports at the time suggested what/that £6m had been lost in the company's first year of trading.

# 13 Challenge yourself

**A** Complete the text about the setting up of small art galleries, using the infinitive or -*ing* form of the verb in brackets.

Browne (2008) describes [1]_____ (set up) a small art gallery in an unfashionable part of Birmingham in 2003. She acknowledges [2]_____ (spend) much more than the business earned in the first few years, but explains how it was managing [3]_____ (make) a modest profit by the end of 2006. Her account and that of Bannister and Ives (2009) appear [4]_____ (suggest) that two key factors need to be borne in mind if the new gallery owner wishes to avoid [5]_____ (make) what could be a very costly mistake.

For anyone planning [6]_____ (open) a small gallery, the first factor is financing. Browne warns the would-be owner [7]_____ (allow) enough capital for at least two years of trading before any significant income is generated. The second factor is location. Bannister and Ives considered [8]_____ (establish) their gallery in London's trendy Brick Lane before realizing that there would be too much competition. They carried on [9]_____ (look) elsewhere in London until colleagues in Wales encouraged them [10]_____ (acquire) empty retail premises at much lower cost in Newport. Now, with a National Lottery regeneration grant, they anticipate [11]_____ (expand) their gallery into neighbouring premises.

**B** Circle the correct option to complete the text about embedded journalists.

One of the Pentagon's successes during the initial stages of the war in Iraq was to [1]*argue/persuade/demand* news organizations to accept the concept of the 'embedded' journalist, who would [2]*operating/to operate/operate* under the protection of a battlefield unit. Newspapers and TV networks could not afford [3]*to turn/that they turn/turning* down this opportunity to witness the conflict at close hand, but many reporters [4]*discussed/wondered/suspected* that the challenge of remaining independent and impartial might prove insurmountable.

Dillow (2005) remembers [5]*spending/to spend/spend* his first three days as an 'embed' on his stomach, as his unit defended itself against heavy enemy fire. On more frequent occasions, however, when soldiers who [6]*prefer/would rather/want* see action have nothing to do except polish their rifles and maintain their vehicles, Dillow [7]*confirms/reminds/discusses* that an embedded reporter gains a fascinating insight into the daily life of men and women at war.

**C** Correct the mistakes in the text about websites based on consumer reviews. Some sentences have more than one mistake.

[1]Some websites enable that consumers post reviews of services or products in such a way that they can be easily searched and read by the general public. [2]This normally means to accept all the reviews that are submitted, except for those that a website manager decides to block on the grounds of their obviously abusive nature. [3]Cannon (2009) contends this phenomenon to produce, particularly in the area of hotel and restaurant reviewing, a new breed of consumer who appears spending his or her life touring the country as an amateur critic. [4]Such consumers may explain that they are doing in terms of public service, but they may well risk undermining the original purpose of this type of website. [5]Cann goes on discussing the recent difficulties experienced by TripAdvisor, where hotel owners have threatened that they take legal action against the site for not screening out this new type of full-time amateur critic.

**D** 💬 Complete the discussion about bargaining between four students, using the words in the box. Two of the words are not needed.

when   why   which   better   rather   watch   wait   might   expect
contend   enjoy   accept   let

A   Bargaining, or haggling, is something that British consumers just aren't used to.

B   I know what you mean, but it depends on ¹_____ sector you're talking about, doesn't it? For example, people ²_____ to bargain when they're buying a house, don't they?

C   That's true, and if you go into an antiques shop, the owner will usually ³_____ you make an offer.

A   OK, I ⁴_____ that there are a limited number of contexts where you can try to lower a price, but it's not nearly as common in the UK as it is in places like Indonesia.

B   And that helps to explain ⁵_____ British tourists find it so difficult in markets abroad!

D   That's true, but if they understood the culture of haggling they ⁶_____ find it easier.

C   What do you mean?

D   Well, if you ⁷_____ a trader selling something, you'll notice that the first step is to establish a relationship with the customer and then 'create value' around the product.

B   Whereas the tourist would ⁸_____ hear a starting price immediately!

D   Exactly. They need to relax, and then they might actually ⁹_____ haggling.

A   And if they can't, they'd ¹⁰_____ find a fixed price shop, hadn't they?

D   Sure. But even there, the owners often don't mind ¹¹_____ you put in an offer.

**E** Circle the correct option to complete the text about the legal aspects of international projects. If both are correct, circle both.

Sito and Mayer (2011) show ¹*how/that* a lack of legal preparation can lead international companies into difficulty, and a close reading of their study may explain ²*what/why* Ronson Capital Enterprises (RCE) was forced ³*suspending/to suspend* construction for nine months at the Sunshine leisure complex in the Nha Trang region of Vietnam.

When RCE began ⁴*to build/building* the Sunshine complex in 2007, they assumed their lawyers ⁵*had/to have* completed the necessary land purchases. Later in the year, however, two local farmers refused ⁶*allowing/to allow* bulldozers to enter a strip of land south of the river, claiming ⁷*that/why* they had never agreed to sell their property.

As the legal dispute unfolded, it appeared that RCE accepted as early as 2009 ⁸*when/that* they would not be able to open on schedule in 2012. Gallo (2012) discusses in detail ⁹*what/that* went wrong, and suggests ¹⁰*that/how* developers planning similar projects in Southeast Asia can learn lessons for the future. His recommendations can be found in the conclusion to this report.

**F** Write 150–250 words about a well-known person who has recovered from a serious setback in their professional or personal life. Use some of the verbs you have studied in this unit.

## Introduction

In academic writing you need to make it clear when you are expressing a claim or opinion as opposed to a fact. The best way of doing this is to distance yourself to some extent from the claim by 'hedging' (i.e. using less direct language in order to make your views more measured and cautious).

In this unit, the following hedging techniques are covered.

**1** The use of hedging verbs such as *appear* and *tend*.
- British shoppers **do not appear to care** where their food comes from as long as it is cheap.

**2** The use of hedging adverbs such as *arguably* and *fairly*.
- Internet Protocol Television is **arguably** the most interesting new media development.

**3** Using *that* clauses to hedge.
- **It is widely accepted that** the Athenians of Ancient Greece formed the world's first democracy.

**4** The use of the language of probability.
- We **may** require a different model of social mobility if we are to establish a truly egalitarian society.

**5** The use of hedging expressions.
- **On balance**, patients require years of support before they can overcome post-traumatic stress disorders.

Note that another way of hedging is to make your claim less personal by referring to other authorities (*Samson believes that …*). The use of direct quotation is covered in unit *6 Stating facts and opinions*, and the use of paraphrasing is covered in unit *16 Paraphrasing*.

> **Read the text. What do the underlined words and phrases have in common? Why does the writer use them?**
>
> The latest research <u>appears</u> to confirm that buildings are responsible for <u>approximately</u> 40% of energy consumption and 35% of EU carbon emissions. <u>It has been suggested that</u> companies should take a lead in adopting policies to reduce these emissions. Such policies <u>might</u> include retrofitting and energy reduction. <u>As a rule</u>, most factories and offices can make these kinds of changes without it affecting their efficiency.
>
> **Suggested answers: see page 205**

## 14.1 Hedging verbs

### 14.1 study

#### 1 *Appear, seem, look*

By placing the emphasis on appearance, these verbs introduce an element of doubt.

- *There **appears to be** a connection between adolescent vegetarianism and eating disorders.*
(The use of *appears to be* rather than *is* implies that the connection has not definitely been proven.)

*Appear* and *seem* can both be used with the infinitive with *to* or *It + that* ….

- *People **appear/seem to enjoy** the autonomy of arranging their own holidays.* (Or ***It appears/seems that** people enjoy …*)

All three verbs can be used with *It + as if/though.*

- ***It looks/appears/seems as if** an agreement between the two sides will be reached at the summit in November.*

#### 2 *Tend*

As a hedging device, *tend* is used with the infinitive with *to* to introduce the idea that this is the way in which people or things normally (but not always) behave.

- *Supporters of the* Encyclopædia Britannica ***tend to claim** that the quality of its trained staff ensures a higher standard of research than that of Wikipedia.*
(This is allowing for more flexibility in behaviour than saying *Supporters of the* Encyclopædia Britannica *claim that the quality …*)
- *Destructive divisions within political parties **tend to emerge** when they have been in power for more than ten years.*

**TIP** The noun *tendency* can be used instead of the verb (*There is a tendency for destructive divisions to emerge …* or *Destructive divisions have a tendency to emerge …*).

#### 3 *Suggest, indicate, estimate*

All three of these verbs are weaker in meaning than verbs such as *conclude, state, confirm, prove,* or *demonstrate,* and can therefore be useful in hedging.

- *A 2005 study by the journal* Nature*, however, **suggested/indicated** that although the structure of some of the scientific material in Wikipedia was poor, its accuracy was similar to that of the* Encyclopædia Britannica.

*Estimate* tends to be used for numbers, statistics, etc.

- *Historians have **estimated** that up to 90% of the indigenous population died from the diseases introduced by European invaders and then settlers.*

#### 4 *Contribute, help*

The verb phrases *contribute to* + noun or *-ing* form and *help* + infinitive with *to* can be useful in hedging, because they suggest that the subject is probably not the only factor involved. Note that *help* tends to be used where there are positive outcomes.

- *Most commentators agree that deregulation **contributed to** the banking crisis of 2008.*
(Deregulation was not the only cause, but it was one of the causes.)
- *For a small organization with limited resources, electronic storage **helps to** reduce costs.*

### 14.1 test yourself

**Rewrite these sentences as hedged statements, using the words in brackets and making any other changes necessary.**

1 It has been stated that 25% of homeless adults suffer from some form of mental illness. (estimated)
2 The practice of short selling brought about the collapse of Lehman Brothers. (contributed)
3 Drought is the major problem in some parts of Sub-Saharan Africa. (appears)
4 Wasps with a greater number of black spots on their heads are more aggressive, according to research. (tend)
5 The report concludes that in some parts of the country bipolar disorder is being overdiagnosed. (indicates)
6 Smaller electronics companies are doing better than their larger rivals. (looks)

## 14.2 Hedging adverbs

### 14.2 study

The adverbs in this section can all be used to reduce the certainty of your statement or make your meaning less extreme.

**1 *Apparently*, *arguably*, etc.**

Here is a selection of adverbs that you can use to express a degree of doubt.

> *apparently* = it appears that, it is apparent that
> *approximately* = not completely accurate; also *roughly*
> *arguably* = it could be argued that
> *reasonably* = fairly, to some extent
> *relatively* = fairly, when compared to other similar
>   things or situations
> *reportedly* = it is reported that
> *supposedly* = it is supposed that, people suppose
>   that, it is generally believed that
> *typically* = normally, usually
> *not necessarily* = not always

- *The fact that a word is **apparently untranslatable** does not necessarily mean that it should be left in the original language.*
- *It seems **reasonably certain** that greater regulation of banking practice will follow what was **arguably** the biggest financial crisis since the depression of the 1930s.*
- *Bolivia's mountains have rendered it **relatively safe** from invasion.*

**2 *Slightly, fairly, quite, rather***

These adverbs are typically used to make adjectives weaker. *Slightly* is the weakest. *Rather* is the least weak, and normally expresses surprise or a negative opinion. *Slightly* and *rather* can be used with comparative adjectives and adverbs, unlike *fairly* and *quite*. Note that *quite* comes before *a/an*.

- *American and Canadian footballs may look the same, but the sizes are **slightly different**.*
- *It is, however, **rather more difficult** to understand why, on an objective level, some convicted murderers are kept far longer in prison than others.* (rather + comparative adjective, not ~~fairly more difficult~~ or ~~quite more difficult~~)
- *The two leaders had a **rather tense** meeting.* (negative opinion)
- *Politicians sometimes argue that it is **quite an easy/a fairly easy** step from soft to hard drug use.*

**TIP** It is important to remember that although *quite* + a gradable adjective (such as *easy* above) means *fairly*, its meaning changes to *completely* with ungradable adjectives such as *sure/certain, right/wrong, clear/obvious, true, different*, and *impossible*.

**3 *Sometimes, normally, usually*, etc.**

Adverbs of frequency can be useful in making a statement more cautious.

- *A specification for a new post is **usually written** by the new employee's line manager.*

### 14.2 test yourself

**Circle the most appropriate option. In two sentences, two options are appropriate.**

1. The US economy grew fairly/slightly/approximately faster in the first quarter than was expected.
2. Mature students do not reasonably/rather/necessarily manage their deadlines better than younger colleagues.
3. The transition from prison life to ordinary society is fairly/quite/relatively a difficult one.
4. Although it works faster than other treatments, the new drug is relatively/approximately/reportedly expensive to produce.
5. Smaller shops quite/normally/reasonably suffer a decline in trade when a supermarket opens nearby.
6. Physical exercise relatively/supposedly/roughly reduces the symptoms of mild depression.
7. Third-year undergraduate courses typically/fairly/usually cover less ground in greater depth than the first two years.
8. Groundnut oil is similar in character but approximately/quite/rather more expensive than grapeseed oil.
9. There are approximately/reasonably/relatively 100 billion neurons in the human brain.
10. In pollution control, it is apparently/quite/sometimes impossible to establish a firm link between a specific event, such as a leak of chemicals, and harm to the local population.

## 14.3 Using *that* clauses

### 14.3 study

You can use several types of impersonal *that* clause to distance yourself from an argument or point of view. Note that the phrases below are only 'semi-fixed' in that you can, for example, change a verb such as *suggest* to *show* or *indicate*.

**1** *It … that …*

Using *It …* (sometimes called the 'empty' or 'preparatory' subject) allows you to avoid phrases such as *I would argue that …* Here are some examples of ways to open your sentences.

> It is widely accepted
> It has been argued
> It is possible to argue } *that …*
> It has been suggested
> It seems fair to say

- **It has been argued that** the reunification of the two Koreas would eventually be of benefit to both.
- **It seems fair to point out that** most of these new jobs have been created in the low-paid, part-time sector.

(See unit *9 Passives* for passive forms of reporting verbs such as *It is believed …* and *… is reported to …*)

**2 Reference to studies, etc.**

> The latest research appears to show/indicate
> Studies show/have shown
> The evidence suggests } *that …*
> Statistics demonstrate/have demonstrated
> Published sources indicate

- **Studies have demonstrated that** good mental health is facilitated by physical exercise.
- **The evidence suggests that** low prices and convenience continue to drive the food industry in the main.

**3 Reference to other people**

> Most people agree
> Some people say
> Many taxpayers feel } *that …*
> Most economists argue

- **Most people agree that** there are certain freedoms that all democracies should possess.
- **Most economists argue that** 'boom and bust' cycles are the most damaging features of the post-war years.

**TIP** *Would* is sometimes used as an additional hedging device with verbs such as *appear, argue, assume, say, seem,* and *suggest.*
- *Some nutritionists **would** suggest that food labelling still hides as much from the consumer as it reveals.*

Note that with all these expressions you may need to support the ideas expressed with reference to actual statistics, published works, etc.

### 14.3 test yourself

**A Correct each sentence by adding one of the words or phrases in the box.**

> been    to argue    demonstrated    would
> would say    appears to

**1** The latest research indicate that the picture was painted by Michelangelo.
**2** Most people that it is normally wrong to lie.
**3** It is possible that economic sanctions rarely achieve their primary purpose.
**4** Statistics have that the life expectancy gap between men and women is shortening in Canada.
**5** It has suggested that schizophrenia should be regarded as a collection of disorders.
**6** It seem that the inspectors' advice on fire safety was ignored by several of the company's senior managers.

**B Correct the mistakes in the sentences. Note that some sentences may be correct.**

**1** It seems fair conclude that private finance initiatives (PFIs) in the public health sector have suffered in some instances from poor project management.
**2** The evidences would suggest that stricter regulation of online loan companies is required.
**3** It has been argue that the process of globalization should ultimately reduce global inequalities.
**4** Published sources indicate that 43 journalists were imprisoned during the regime's first year in power.
**5** Many medical practitioners would argue that assisted suicide is never justified.
**6** It has widely accepted that a good reputation is one of the most important assets that a company possesses.

## 14.4 Expressing probability

### 14.4 study

Using the language of probability rather than certainty allows you to be cautious about the past, present, and future.

**1 *Can, may, might,* and *could***

These modal verbs can all be used to say that something is possible rather than definite. *Can, may, might,* and *could* can all be used to talk about the present. *Could* and *might* are more cautious than *can* and *may.*

- *There **can** be a number of reasons why a particular group of people resist new scientific theories.* (This is more cautious than *There are a number of reasons ...*)

*May, could,* and *might* can also be used to talk about the future and past.

- *We **might** see a significant rise in the repossession of houses as mortgage holders become unable to make their monthly repayments.* (This is more cautious than *We will see ...*)
- *The patients **could have** recovered more quickly if they had been given counselling as well as medication.* (This is more cautious than *The patients would have recovered ...*)

[TIP] *Possible* (adj.), *possibly* (adv.), *perhaps* (adv.) can be used to express a similar meaning to *can, may, might,* and *could.*

- *It is possible to drive for hours through the Australian Outback without seeing another car or house.* (= *Drivers can travel for hours ...*)

**2 *Should, likely, unlikely***

These words allow you to be cautious, but express a stronger probability that something will or will not happen. Note the grammatical patterns for *(un)likely.*

**a** Something *is (un)likely to happen* (present tense with future meaning)
- *People who take no exercise and eat a great deal of 'junk food' **are likely to** become obese.* (This is more cautious than *will become obese*, but less cautious than *could become obese.*)

Note that *should* in this context is only used to talk about positive outcomes, so it couldn't be used in the first example above about obesity.

- *The clean-up of the rice fields contaminated by salt during the tsunami **should** be completed soon.*

**b** Something *is (un)likely to have happened* (past)
- *The very small quantity of oil that escaped from the tanker is **unlikely to have harmed** local marine life.* (This is more cautious than *did not harm*, but less cautious than *may not have harmed.*)

[TIP] *Probably* (adv.) can be used to express a similar meaning to *should, likely,* and *unlikely.*
- *Scientists at NASA argue that the asteroid Apophis will **probably** pass close to the Earth but avoid hitting it.* (= *Apophis is likely to pass close to ...*)

### 14.4 test yourself

**Rewrite the sentences, using the words in brackets and making any other changes necessary.**

1 These new studies into brain function help us to understand cases of slow development in some children. (can)
2 High-speed rail travel in Europe will take more market share from short-haul flights. (possible)
3 Scientists have found a way of changing the immune system to prevent food allergies. (may)
4 Medical research will not determine the cause of autism. (unlikely)
5 There is likely to be a worldwide shortage of rare earth metals in the near future. (probably)
6 Sparks from electric power lines caused some of the forest fires in the region. (likely)
7 Space debris will damage key communications satellites. (could)
8 The amount of cybercrime in the USA and Europe will decrease as security software improves. (should)
9 Recent government campaigns did not have any long-lasting impact on levels of adult obesity. (unlikely)
10 The latest fall in unemployment will improve consumer confidence in the economy. (might)
11 A horse that is deprived of sensory stimulation will stop eating. (possibly)
12 Changes in the chemical composition of the material occurred as a result of careless handling in the laboratory. (could)

## 14.5 Hedging expressions

### 14.5 study

There are a number of fixed expressions that you can use to hedge a statement. Many of them are prepositional phrases. They include the following:

*on balance*
*as a rule/in principle*
*to some extent/up to a point*
*in some/many respects*
*in a/one sense*
*for all practical purposes*
*more or less*

- *The great advantage of promoting educational courses on the internet rather than by brochures is that web pages can be updated **more or less** instantly.*
- *There are **for all practical purposes** only two solutions in situations where individuals fear that their mental health is at risk: either they must adapt to the situation, or they must remove themselves from it.*
- ***In many respects** football should be regarded as a business rather than a sport, at least as far as the major clubs are concerned.*

All of these expressions have become clichés, and while they can be helpful, should not be overused.

There are also three fixed expressions with a hedging effect that are used as connectors to link two clauses in a sentence:

*insofar as/to the extent that*
*in the sense that*

- *The proposed reforms will be useful **insofar as/to the extent that** they address the needs of the local community.* (These two expressions have a slightly more cautious effect than *if*.)
- *The proposal by Wilhelm plc is more cost-effective **in the sense that** it does not require any additional factories.* (This expression has a slightly more cautious effect than *because*.)

### 14.5 test yourself

**Correct each sentence by adding a preposition.**

1 The new antibiotic has principle better long-term prospects.
2 The situation in the region has improved the extent that tourists are now beginning to return.
3 The new CEO Jackie Dell has one sense little left to prove after twenty years of top-flight management.
4 There are balance several advantages to leasing rather than owning a car.
5 The advertising campaign worked the sense that people became aware of the risks of passive smoking.
6 The new law will some extent reduce the opportunities for tax evasion.

# 14 Challenge yourself

**A** Make the text about homelessness more academic by using hedging techniques. Rewrite or add to the phrases in italics, using the words in brackets. You may need to change the form of the verbs.

Given the nature of their lifestyle, statistics on the number of homeless people [1]*are difficult to obtain* (can). Despite this, [2]*the latest research shows* (appear) that in London the number of people who find themselves in this situation is rising. [3]*The figure now stands at 4,500* (estimate, approximately). [4]*The recession is responsible* (likely) to some extent for this increase. [5]*Unemployment causes relationships to break down* (may), leading to one member of the household being forced to leave. According to Bowcott, [6]*economic stress increases levels of alcohol abuse* (tendency), which can put at risk an individual's ability to maintain a job and a tenancy.

## Homelessness

### OFFICIAL GOVERNMENT STATISTICS

[7]*The situation has been made worse* (seem to) by the presence among the newly unemployed of economic migrants, who are not necessarily familiar with UK support systems. Simpson (2010) [8]*notes the high proportion of young people* (relatively) from the Eastern European accession countries among the homeless population. [9]*Apart from their obvious economic problems* (possible), such people find it psychologically difficult to return home.

**B** Complete the text about stem cell research, using the words in the box. Two of the words are not needed.

> arguably   balance   extent   principle   reasonably   respects   rule
> slightly   typically   widely

Stem cell research is [1]_____ the most important area of medical research for a generation. Scientists in this field are [2]_____ confident that major breakthroughs can be achieved within the next ten years. Reports on past successes [3]_____ draw attention to improvements in the treatment of leukemia; as for the future, it is [4]_____ accepted that progress in the fight against cancer, multiple sclerosis and Parkinson's disease can be made.

On [5]_____, most people would agree that stem cell research is a medical success story. However, as Miller (2011) points out, it is rare to find a scientific advance that does not, to some [6]_____, cause concern amongst the general public. In this case, it is the use of embryonic stem cells, which are, as a [7]_____, essential to the experiments currently being carried out in some of the key research centres. In some [8]_____, the two positions taken on this issue can be represented by China, which is relatively permissive of this type of research, and Iran, where an outright ban has been imposed.

**C** Hedge the phrases in italics in the text about sanctions by rewriting or adding to them, using the words in brackets. Do not change the words in italics.

[1]*Economic sanctions against a country are preferable to war* (agree). Indeed, [2]*a properly calibrated system of sanctions should be* implemented *in full* (argued, normally) before the application of military force is considered. However, [3]*the situation on the ground, where sanctions are actually experienced, is more complicated* (the evidence, rather).

Holler (2007) maintains that economic sanctions, when they are first applied, [4]*unify the people affected* (tend) against the institution or country imposing the measures, [5]*and thus strengthen the* regime *in power* (help). [6]*This was the case* (seems as), at least in the early stages, in North Korea, where international sanctions were applied after the Korean War. Holler continues by explaining that [7]*sanctions are not effective unless the blame for their effects* (only, insofar) can be transferred to the country's governing class.

**D** Read the information in brackets and hedge the sentences if necessary.

**1** According to Harper and Maxwell (2009), one third of Londoners believe that the roads in their city are unsafe for cyclists. (This is an estimate.)
**2** Support for Scottish home rule will increase, the longer a referendum on independence is delayed. (This is not a certainty.)
**3** Laboratory tests have revealed that a package sent to the Foreign Secretary on 13 March last year contained traces of a poisonous substance. (This is a fact.)
**4** It is unusual for salts to melt at low temperatures. (Make the first adjective weaker.)
**5** The supply of new money, known as quantative easing, stimulates medium-term growth in the economy. (This generally happens.)
**6** New insights into the causes of dementia will emerge from a doubling of government research funding. (There is a very good chance of these insights emerging, but we cannot be certain.)
**7** Research has demonstrated that people at risk of type 2 diabetes will reduce the risk of developing the condition by losing weight. (This has been proved.)
**8** There is an increase in the level of crime in poorly-maintained city centres. (Make the verb *be* weaker.)

**E** Hedge the phrases in italics in the text, using any of the language from unit 14.

Obesity, the medical condition where an excess of body fat *causes* an adverse effect on health, is now the focus of a great deal of media attention. This interest *is explained* by research that *shows* that the incidence of obesity in higher income countries is now rising at its fastest ever rate. Stories in the press, however, *are* accompanied by photographs designed to shock rather than by statistics designed to educate.

The pictures that draw attention *are* those of children, and the background narrative concentrates on the diet of junk food that younger people *enjoy*. If space allows, there *is* also a reference to a lack of exercise, often with a graphic example, such as the children who are driven to schools that *are* within easy walking distance of their homes. *The* overall *result of this kind of coverage, however,* is a distortion rather than a clarification of the problem.

**AWL GLOSSARY**

**implement** to make something that has been officially decided start to happen or be used

**unify** to join people, things, parts of a country, etc. together so that they form a single unit

**regime** a government, especially one that has not been elected in a fair way

**AWL GLOSSARY**

**incidence** the extent to which something happens or has an effect

**accompany** to happen or appear with something else

**concentrate** to give all your attention to something

**distortion** the act or process of changing facts, ideas, etc. so they are no longer correct

**clarification** the act or process of making something clearer or easier to understand

## Introduction

Verbs can combine with 'particles' (adverbs or prepositions) to make two- or three-part phrasal or prepositional verbs. Some have meanings that are easy to understand (e.g. *slow down*) and others are more difficult to work out (e.g. *get on* = do well or succeed).

- *Production **slowed down** during the period of restructuring.*
- *Most interviewees admitted that for them **getting on** in life meant no more than finding a steady job, buying a flat or house, and eventually starting a family.*

Apart from a small group of phrasal verbs that are normally restricted to informal spoken English (e.g. *Get off!* or *Shut up!*), most phrasal and prepositional verbs are widely used in academic English, and while some have an exact one-word equivalent (*leave out* = omit), others do not (*to look up a word*, for example, means 'to seek the meaning of a word from a source of reference such as a dictionary'). Sometimes a phrasal verb, like an ordinary verb, can have more than one meaning, and may work differently grammatically, depending on the meaning.

Although meaning is the most important aspect of these verbs, it can be helpful to divide them into groups because different types of verbs work in different ways grammatically. For example, *call for* is a prepositional verb. *Call* cannot be separated from *for*. On the other hand, *set up* is a phrasal verb with an object and *up* can come before or after the object.

- *A small group of politicians is **calling for** a debate on the subject.* (We cannot say ~~calling a debate for~~ on the subject.)
- *The CEO of Bardworth plc may **set up** a new company by the end of the financial year.* (We can also say **set** a new company **up**.)

> **Read the text and note down six phrasal or prepositional verbs (e.g. *look up*, *benefit from*). Which ones take an object?**
>
> The reasons for saving animals and languages are quite different. Species tend to be on the brink of being wiped out because of hunting, legal or illegal, or because of habitat changes; languages, on the other hand, become extinct mainly because of domination by speakers of other languages and by cultural shifts. Fragile ecosystems which rely on particular species to carry out certain functions, for example, spreading seeds throughout the area, may be destroyed if the animal dies out, but if a language expires then a country or people will still carry on. They will adapt to another language.
>
> **Suggested answers: see page 132**

See also unit *13 Verb patterns*.

# 15.1 Phrasal verbs + object

## 15.1 study

Phrasal verbs that take an object (transitive phrasal verbs) consist of a verb and particle that can stay together before the object or that can separate before and after the object.

- *Fragile ecosystems rely on particular species to **carry out** certain functions/**carry** certain functions **out**, such as the spreading of seeds.* (carry out = perform)

But note that they always separate for a pronoun object.

- *It became clear that many Americans who had taken out home loans could not **pay** them **back**.* (not ~~pay back them~~)

They tend to stay together before long objects.

- *When reading in a foreign language, it does not necessarily make sense to **look up** all the words that are new to you.* (not ~~look all the words that are new to you up~~)

Here are some of the most useful transitive phrasal verbs, grouped by particles.

### + up

**blow up** explode: *blow up a bridge*; enlarge: *blow up a photograph*
**bring up** raise: *bring up children*; *bring up an item at a meeting*
**draw up** prepare in writing, normally through discussion: *draw up a contract*
**fill up** make full: *fill up a plane with fuel*
**firm up** confirm, make more definite: *firm up an arrangement, a meeting, the details*
**give up** stop doing something: *give up cigarettes; give up control of a company*
**hold up** delay: *a safety check held up the experiment*
**keep up** continue: *keep up the pressure/pace; keep up payments*
**look up** search for something in a reference source: *look up an event in an encyclopedia*
**make up** invent: *make up an excuse*
**pick up** collect, find: *a train picks up passengers; a microphone picks up a sound*
**point up** emphasize: *point up the cost of a project*
**set up** establish, make arrangements for: *set up a business or a meeting; set up equipment*
**take up** start: *to take up a new post; to take up an idea*
**weigh up** consider carefully: *the company needs to weigh up its options*
**write up** write formally/write from notes: *write up the experiment*

Note that:

**1 hold up** can also be used intransitively, see page 135

**2 keep up with** means 'know about the latest developments': *keep up with research in your field*. (See page 138 for more three-part prepositional verbs.)

**3 make up** can also mean 'to be a part of': *Young people make up a large part of the Turkish population*. In this meaning, a pronoun object is never used.

**4 take up** can also mean 'to fill space or time': *Research takes up most of Professor Bryant's working year*. In this meaning, a pronoun object is never used.

### + off

**call off** cancel: *call off a trip*
**finish off** complete: *finish off a report*
**lay off** make redundant: *losing the contract meant laying off half the workforce*
**put off** postpone: *put off a meeting*
**take off** remove: *take off clothes*
**tell off** speak angrily to: *tell off a child*

Note that *take off*, with the particle separated, can be used in *take a day/week*, etc. *off work* and *take the pressure off someone*. It also has an intransitive form, see page 135.

### + on

**put on** organize: *put on an exhibition*; also *put on clothes, a light, the radio*, etc.
**try on** put on clothes to see if they fit
**take on** assume: *take on responsibility, take on a task*; also employ: *take on an assistant*

**TIP** The phrasal verb *tell apart* (= distinguish between) always separates for a direct object, whether it is a pronoun or not.

- *Both roots and non-roots can contain taproot and hypocotyl tissue, making it difficult to **tell some types apart**.*

## + out

**bail out** rescue from financial difficulties: *several banks were bailed out by the government*

**carry out** perform: *carry out an investigation*

**check out** see if something is reliable: *a company should check out potential suppliers*

**cross out** delete wrong text: *to cross out a mistake in a report*

**find out** discover: *find out what has gone wrong*

**hand out** distribute: *hand out printed information at a talk*

**lay out** present something carefully: *lay out plans;* also *lay out tables*, etc. *in a room*

**leave out** omit accidentally or deliberately: *leave out an important detail*

**point out** show: *point out a mistake;* in her article, *Miller points out that ...*

**print out** produce a document from a printer; also *print off*

**read out** read aloud: *read out a paper at a conference*

**rub out** erase a pencil mark: *rub out a mistake*

**sort out** resolve: *sort out a problem;* also arrange: *sort out your notes for revision*

**take out** obtain: *take out a loan, mortgage, insurance;* withdraw: *take out money from your account*

**try out** test: *try out an idea*

**wipe out** destroy: *wipe out a disease*

**work out** calculate: *work out this year's profits*

Note that:

1 **set out** can be used in the same way as *lay out*, but is preferred for ideas, objections, strategy. *Set out* also has an intransitive meaning, see page 135.

2 **strike out** can have a similar meaning to *cross out*, but tends to be used in legal contexts: *strike out a law from the statute book.*

3 **take out**, with the particle separated, can be used in *take six months/a year*, etc. *out*, meaning 'take a break in your studies or career to do something different'.

⌐TIP *Hand over (to)* has a number of connected meanings, including 'give your position to someone else': *In 1994, Stefanie Gibbons handed the company over to her son;* 'give something/someone to someone in authority': *They had to hand the documents over to the police;* and, as an inseparable prepositional verb, 'give someone else a chance to speak': *now I'm going to hand over to Mike, who will talk about the results of the experiment.*

## 15.1 test yourself

**Complete each sentence with the correct form of the correct verb.**

1 I'll _____ my talk off by making two recommendations, and then take any questions you may have.

2 After the application closing date, the interviewing team will _____ up a shortlist of candidates to interview.

3 Employees need to be consulted before they are told to _____ on significant new responsibilities.

4 The idea for a new business came quickly to the partners, but it took them five years to _____ the company up.

5 The days when British governments would _____ out failing car manufacturers have passed.

6 Sometimes the attempt to define the terms of a debate can _____ up a great deal of time.

7 Employees have the right to contest and ultimately _____ out some of the clauses in their contract.

8 It appears that as soon as a child can talk, it begins to _____ up stories.

9 Digital TVs sometimes _____ up signals from the wrong transmitter.

10 A complete tier of middle managers were _____ off in an attempt to save costs.

## 15.2 Phrasal verbs without an object

### 15.2 study

Intransitive phrasal verbs are less common in academic English. Here is a list of those that are sometimes used.

**carry on/go on** continue: *the strike carried on/went on through the winter*

**bounce back** recover: *share prices bounced back*

**die out** disappear: *jobs for life are dying out;* become extinct: *the Beach Mouse died out in the 1950s*

**eat out** eat in a restaurant, café, etc.

**end up** find yourself in an unexpected, often negative, situation: *two of the directors ended up in prison*

**get back** move back: *the protestors were told to get back;* return home: *they got back at midnight*

**get on** do well: *get on at college/in your career;* have a good relationship: *he gets on (well) with his boss*

**go ahead** proceed: *the project went ahead despite the resignation of its director*

**go away** leave, disappear gradually: *suspicions of malpractice have not gone away*

**go back/date back:** *a custom which goes/dates back to the 16th century*

**go up** increase: *the retirement age for men will probably go up to 67* (also **go down** decrease)

**hold on** keep going in a difficult situation: *Boston Chemicals are holding on despite severe losses*

**hold up** remain strong: *critics have suggested that Menson's arguments do not hold up*

**join in** participate: *bullying can start in a playground activity when one child refuses to join in*

**move in/out** begin to live in a new house/area, etc. or to leave it: *richer people have moved out of the area*

**ring off** end a phone conversation: *sales staff need to engage potential clients before they ring off*

**set off** start a trip: *tourists setting off on their holidays will tolerate minor delays without complaint*

**slow down** to go at a slower speed: *the economy slowed down in the first two quarters of this year*

**speak out** say what you think publicly: *people in the region are no longer afraid to speak out*

**take off** begin to fly: *a plane takes off*; become successful: *an idea, a product, sales, etc. can take off*

**turn out** attend an event: *ten thousand people turned out for the march through London*

Note that:

**1 hold on to/onto** means 'keep'.
- *The Democrats are unlikely to **hold on to** their lead in the forthcoming elections.*

**2 set out** can replace *set off*, but *set out* can also suggest a much longer or figurative journey.
- *When the company **set out** in 1928, no one would have thought that it might become a multinational corporation.*

**3 set out to do something** means 'have as a long-term aim'.
- *Sally Bronwen **set out to** make MaxCo the UK's biggest retailer of garden furniture.*

**4 stand up** can mean 'hold up' but is usually followed by a prepositional phrase.
- *Critics have suggested that Menson's arguments do not **stand up under** close examination/**to** close scrutiny.*

**5 turn out** can also be used with an adverb such as *well* or *badly* to describe the way in which a situation developed.
- *The shareholder meeting did not **turn out well**.*

(See section **15.6** on page 138 for more three-part prepositional verbs.)

## 15.2 test yourself

Complete each sentence with the correct form of the correct verb.

1 Production _____ down while the factory installed new equipment.
2 Print on demand (POD) has refused to _____ off, despite more than a decade of effort by some publishers.
3 The share price dropped to £150 at the beginning of April, but _____ back later in the month.
4 If someone's job is at risk, they are unlikely to _____ out against their employer, whatever type of malpractice they may have witnessed.
5 Relief workers could not _____ on saving lives because of the severity of the flooding.
6 Those in favour of the 'big society' argue that community self-help has been _____ out in recent times, and should be revived.
7 In hard economic times, consumers continue to _____ out, but tend to spend less on their restaurant meals.
8 Householders are quite likely to _____ off when they hear the voice of a cold-caller.

## 15.3 Prepositional verbs 1

### 15.3 study

Prepositional verbs consist of verb + preposition + (prepositional) object.
- *Garufa is a village in eastern Kenya that regularly relies on food supplies from aid agencies.*

Unlike phrasal verbs, the object always follows the particle (adverb or preposition), even if it is a pronoun.
- (to a tutor) *An area of research that especially interests me is the mother-daughter relationship amongst primates. If it's possible, I'd like to **work on** it for my dissertation.* (not *work it on*)

Some common verbs can be followed by more than one preposition, depending on the meaning.

**1 agree** *I agree with you; the board of directors **agreed on** a way forward* (= made a joint decision); *the company **agreed to** the sale of some of its assets* (= agreed under pressure).

**2 apply** *apply for* a job, passport, etc. (but *apply to* a company *for* a job); also *this deadline applies to all coursework* (= concerns).

**3 argue** *argue about* something; *argue with* someone (*about something*).

**4 hear** most people have *heard about/of* the Terracotta Army (= know about); *have you heard about the strike* (= have you been told); *have you heard from your parents* (= received news); *at this point the jury had not heard from the defendant* (= had not got his/her view).

**5 think** most savers are currently *thinking about* which options are safest (= consider); *they were unable to think of* a viable solution (= imagine).

**6 work** *work for* a company (= be employed by); *they are working on* a new design (= are occupied with) also *work on* your computer skills (= practise).

Here is an alphabetical list of some of the most useful prepositional verbs, from *account for* to *draw on*. (See **Prepositional verbs 2** below for *engage in* to *worry about*.) Definitions are given where the meaning may not be clear from the main verb.

**account for** explain: *account for the success of a business*; record spending: *account for printing costs*

**adapt to**

**add to** increase: *an amendment has been added to the Bill*

**allow for** include in planning: *allow for delays*

**apologize for**

**approve of** agree with: *approve of a plan*

**believe in** think that something is valuable: *believe in subsidizing the arts*; also *believe in God*

**belong to**

**benefit from**

**break into** enter illegally: *break into a house*; enter with difficulty: *break into a new market*

**call for** make a public request/demand: *call for a strike*

**call on** request: *to call on the government for support*; *to call on the Bank of England to raise interest rates*

**care for**

**change into** put on other clothes: *change into a suit*

**check into** register at a hotel

**come from** originate from: *most of the raw materials come from Russia*

**complain about**

**comply with** act according to a rule/law: *comply with health and safety legislation*

**concentrate on** spend time on: *in this essay, I will concentrate on the manufacturing sector*

**consist of** be composed of: *the committee consists of experts in educational practice*

**contribute to** help to cause: *corrupt government has contributed to the country's decline*

**cooperate with** work together: *TV producers cooperate with health authorities not to glamorize smoking*

**crash/drive into** hit while driving: *the lorry crashed into a tree*

**deal with** handle: *deal with complaints/problems/difficult customers*; do business with: *Seltech is currently dealing with 25 suppliers*; be about: *Murakami's novel deals with urban alienation.*

**decide on** choose after careful thought: *the company has not yet decided on a launch date*

**depend/rely on**

**differ from**

**discriminate against/between**

**draw on** use resources: *draw on your experience to do something*; *draw on savings/reserves*

Note that:

**1 cope with** also means 'handle' (see *deal with*) but is less positive: *are you sure you can cope with this?*

**2 change/transform into** can also be a transitive phrasal verb: *drought changed/transformed the land into a desert.*

## 15.3 test yourself

**Complete each sentence with a preposition.**

**1** Chemtech are currently working _____ a series of new antibiotics.

**2** Dodsworths plc was fined for not complying _____ health and safety regulations.

**3** None of the candidates could think _____ an answer to the final exam question.

**4** Manucorps plc only deals _____ wholesalers.

**5** A number of staff members have applied _____ a transfer to another branch.

**6** In preparing their budget, the team did not allow _____ travel expenses.

**7** In recent years political parties have wanted greater numbers of young people to benefit _____ higher education.

**8** The union has agreed _____ an external arbitration process.

## 15.4 Prepositional verbs 2

### 15.4 study

**engage in** take part in: *engage in research*
**enquire about**
**escape from**
**focus on**
**get through** make phone contact: *to get through to the right person*; reach: *aid does not always get through*; survive: *get through the recession*; be officially approved: *the law may not get through*
**go into** start a career: *go into business, teaching* etc.; examine: *go into the details*
**go through** experience, often negative: *the company has been through some hard times*; check the details: *go through a contract*; do a number of actions: *go through the interview process*
**happen to**
**insist on**
**keep to** respect: *keep to an agreement/a schedule*; be relevant: *keep to the point/subject*
**laugh at**
**lead to** result in/cause: *recessions lead to unemployment*
**liaise with** communicate with in an official capacity: *protest march leaders are liaising with the police*
**live for** see something as important in your life: *live for your work*
**look at**
**look into** investigate: *look into a complaint*
**make for** move towards: *the soldiers were making for base when the attack occurred*
**object to**
**occur to** come to mind: *it occurred to the team that their calculations might be wrong*
**point to** indicate: *the evidence points to a link between stress at work and illness*
**protest against**
**qualify for** pass the entrance test: *she has qualified for the Olympics*
**recover from**
**refer to**
**resign from**
**respond to** take action as a result: *customers responded to the price increase by cutting back on orders*
**result in**
**run into** experience: *run into difficulties, opposition*, etc.; cost a great deal: *the final bill will run into billions of dollars*
**smile at**
**specialize in**

**stare at**
**succeed in**
**suffer from** have an illness or problem: *businesses may suffer from a lack of investment*
**vote for**
**worry about**

Note that:
**go through with** means 'complete something difficult'.
• *Going through with the merger will mean making a third of the staff redundant.*

(See section **15.6** on page 138 for more three-part prepositional verbs.)

---

### 15.4 test yourself

**Complete each sentence with the correct form of the correct verb.**

1 Metterlune _____ into the controversy around the Beckendale copyright case, and concluded that most of the evidence _____ to difficulties arising from the interpretation of the term 'original creation'.
2 When first interviewed by police, victims of crime may still be _____ from shock.
3 Trauma victims may _____ through a long period where they attempt to suppress memories of the original incidents that _____ to their present condition.
4 Some companies within the financial sector have been accused of _____ in very poor practices.
5 In order to _____ for funding, postgraduate students must already have registered for a PhD programme.

---

## 15.5 Prepositional verbs with two objects

### 15.5 study

The following is a small selection of verbs that can take a direct object as well as a prepositional object.

**accuse/suspect** someone **of** something
**blame** someone **for** something
**borrow** something **from** someone
**compare** something/someone **with** something/someone

congratulate someone **on** something
**download** something **from the internet/a website**
   (also **upload** something **to** ...)
**explain** something **to** someone
**fill** something **with** something
**invest** some **money/time in** something
**lend** something **to** someone
**obtain** something **from** someone
**prevent/stop** someone/something **from** something
**protect** someone/something **from** someone/something
**provide** someone **with** something
**remind** someone **of** something

## 15.5 test yourself

**Complete each sentence with the correct form of a verb and a preposition.**

1 Balance of trade figures are formed by _____ _____ the value of imports _____ the value of exports.
2 The City Leisure Group has _____ £10m _____ updating five restaurants in the borough of Westminster.
3 Poor hygiene practices in the canteen kitchen have been _____ _____ sixteen cases of food poisoning at the factory.
4 There is a growing market for TV documentaries that _____ complex scientific theory _____ the general public.
5 _____ a small company's buildings _____ fire is a priority that is sometimes overlooked in budgets.

## 15.6 Three-part prepositional verbs

### 15.6 study

A few three-part prepositional verbs (verb + adverb + preposition) are sometimes used in academic English. They always take an object, and the ones given below cannot be separated.

**catch up with** reach a higher standard/level: *catch up with competitors*
**catch up with/on** to bring yourself up to date: *catch up on your reading*
**come up against** encounter difficulties: *come up against opposition*
**come up with** think of an idea: *come up with an answer, solution, explanation*, etc.

**cut back/down on** reduce: *nutritionists advise the public to cut back/down on red meat*
**face up to** deal with a difficult situation: *face up to a problem, crisis*, etc.; *face up to responsibilities*
**get down to** give attention to: *get down to work, business*
**get out of** leave, escape from: *get out of a car; get out of the city; get out of an agreement*
**go along with** agree, often reluctantly: *they have no choice but to go along with the recommendations*
**live up to** be as good as expected: *the company failed to live up to its reputation for quality*
**run out of** finish the supply: *run out of food, money, time, patience*, etc.
**watch out for** be aware of: *consumers need to watch out for the small print in contracts*

## 15.6 test yourself

**Complete the sentences, using three of the words in brackets in the correct order.**

1 Soros argues that the USA must _____ _____ (come/up/to/of/face) the dangers of the global market in derivatives.
2 With these reforms, the government is likely to _____ (with/against/up/go/come) considerable public criticism.
3 There is a limit to the regular expenses that a small business can _____ (on/get/cut/of/back) in a recession.
4 A national helpline has been set up to help people to _____ (out/along/get/go/of) debt.
5 The Pacific island nation of Tuvalu runs the constant risk of _____ (coming/out/up/of/running) drinking water.
6 Brand agencies can help companies to _____ (up/get/down/with/come) a name for a new product or service.

## 15.7 Passive prepositional verbs

### 15.7 study

A number of prepositional verbs are often used in the passive form (*be* + past participle + preposition). Note that the regular meaning of the verb does not change through its preposition.

- *An advertisement can sometimes **be aimed at** a very small market in a cost effective way by being placed in, for example, a specialist magazine.*

Here is a list some of the most useful of these prepositional verbs, with explanations provided where the meaning may not be clear.

**be aimed at**

**be associated with**  be connected to: *violence is sometimes associated with alcohol abuse*

**be based on**

**be considered as/be regarded as/be seen as**

**be defined as**

**be derived from**  come/originate from: *some medicines are derived from plants*

**be divided into**

**be involved in**

**be known as**

**be prejudiced against**  have an irrational dislike of: *some people are prejudiced against gay men and women*

**be required for**

**be used in**

### 15.7 test yourself

**Complete each sentence with the passive form of one of the verbs in the box and a preposition.**

> base   prejudice   regard   associate   require

1 A painting can _____ subversive if it is seen to undermine moral values of the state.
2 Judges have to decide whether juries may _____ defendants as a result of media coverage of a case.
3 A focus group, rather than a questionnaire or street interview, may _____ some types of market research.
4 The shortlisting process _____ an assessment of how well the candidates meet the criteria in the job specification.
5 Vitamin D deficiency _____ various types of obesity.

# 15 Challenge yourself

**A** Complete the text about science programmes on television with the correct adverbs or prepositions.

TV programmes in which experts explain science [1]_____ the public date [2]_____ to the early years of television. According to Hopkins (2007), such programmes can be divided [3]_____ two types. The first of these is the illustrated lecture, where an eminent scientist essentially reads [4]_____ a simplified paper, and, depending on the occasion, members of the audience may join [5]_____ the event by taking part, for example, in a simple experiment. The second, more recent type, may be aimed [6]_____ a younger audience, and normally involves computer-generated images, voiceovers, and dramatic music.

Critics sometimes complain [7]_____ these programmes, arguing that they often leave [8]_____ some of the complexities of the scientific method in their attempt to put [9]_____ a good show. Hopkins, however, insists [10]_____ their usefulness, pointing [11]_____ the way in which they can contribute [12]_____ the popular understanding of difficult subjects, and allow viewers to catch up [13]_____ recent scientific discoveries. Whether commentators approve [14]_____ such programmes or not, it seems clear that they now occupy a small but significant part of the prime-time schedule.

**B** Complete the media studies text using the correct form of the words in the box.

> draw   about   as   know   object   set   up

Critics have argued [1]_____ the merits of Sergei Eisenstein's *Battleship Potemkin* since its release in 1925, but there can be little doubt that it is now regarded [2]_____ one of cinema's most influential films. [3]_____ on his own military experience, Eisenstein [4]_____ out to make a propaganda piece that would persuade the audience of the justice of the sailors' rebellion against their Tsarist officers. Though based on real events, the film-maker made [5]_____ some of the sequences, including the famous 'Odessa Steps' episode.

British censors, [6]_____ to the film's revolutionary message, banned the film until 1954, but, as Grice (2005) observes, contemporary critics acclaimed Eisenstein's innovative editing technique, which is [7]_____ as 'montage'.

**C** Complete the text about political strategy, using the correct form of the verbs in the box.

> define   account   point   provide   transform   vote

Political analysts at the time [1]_____ for the success of Barack Obama's presidential bid in 2008 by reference to the phenomenon of the 'Obama Republican'. What they meant was that a certain type of voter who had previously been [2]_____ as a Republican, was [3]_____ into a Democrat purely by the appeal of Obama's message. Obama Republicans, as Brandter (2011) [4]_____ out, were typically white working-class Americans who felt that mainstream Republican opinion had left them behind.

According to Fields (2010), a similar process [5]_____ Tony Blair with electoral success in the UK in the previous decade, as traditional Conservative supporters began to [6]_____ for his brand of middle-of-the-road politics.

**AWL GLOSSARY**

**complexity** the features of a problem or situation that are difficult to understand

**contribute** to increase, improve, or add to something

**occupy** to fill or use a space, an area, or an amount of time

**significant** large or important enough to have an effect

**schedule** the television programmes that are on a particular channel at a particular time

**AWL GLOSSARY**

**sequence** a part of a film that deals with one subject or topic or consists of one scene

**contemporary** belonging to the same time

**innovative** introducing or using new ideas, ways of doing something, etc.

**D** 💬 Correct one of the words in each phrasal or prepositional verb in italics in the discussion about the 'big society'.

| | |
|---|---|
| Annabel | In my view, one of the reasons why the idea of the 'big society' hasn't ¹*taken up* is that people don't really understand what it means. So can anyone here define it? |
| Benedict | It was ²*based* initially *of* the idea of giving power to local communities, wasn't it? |
| Annabel | Yes, and most people would ³*come along with* that, I guess, but what does it mean in policy terms? |
| Chihiro | Well, the Conservative manifesto ⁴*sets up* five key points. Point four, which is quite specific, talks about supporting co-ops, charities and social enterprises. |
| Benedict | That's why the Big Society Bank was ⁵*made up* in 2011, isn't it? |
| Annabel | And the idea was that the bank would ⁶*hand up* money to local groups? |
| Chihiro | Yes, but the launch has already been ⁷*switched off* several times. |
| Annabel | This is one of the reasons why people are ⁸*prejudiced with* the whole concept of the big society, isn't it? |
| Benedict | That's right. It seems to be a powerful idea, but it ⁹*stops up* being difficult to implement. |
| Chihiro | And the critics also argue that it's just a way for the government to ¹⁰*go back on* public expenditure. |

**E** Complete the introduction to a talk on the Chinese Terracotta Army, using the correct form of the verbs in the box. You will need to add an adverb or preposition to three of the verbs.

> add   agree   carry   come   concentrate   consist   differ   protect   specialize   use

The Terracotta Army, which ¹_____ at least 8,000 soldiers, dates back to the third century BCE. Excavation of the site in Xi'an has been ²_____ out for more than thirty years, but most experts ³_____ with the view that it is far from complete.

In this talk, I would like to ⁴_____ the construction of the figures themselves. It appears that the material used to make the soldiers ⁵_____ from Mount Li in the north-west of Xi'an. The researcher Duan Qingbo suggests that eight basic moulds were ⁶_____ in the creation of the faces. Apparently, the craftsmen who were employed to model the figures then ⁷_____ clay to the surface to provide individual facial features. This explains how one soldier can ⁸_____ another in appearance.

Duan Qingbo indicates that groups of craftsmen ⁹_____ in preparing the different parts of the body, and that the pieces were brought together in a kind of assembly line. The final figures were painted in bright colours, and ¹⁰_____ from decay by a lacquer finish. Although the colours have greatly faded, patches of blue, pink, brown, red, and green are still visible.

**F** Write 150–250 words about the steps that need to be taken before setting up a new restaurant in a town centre. You may want to discuss market research, appointing a head chef, and the creation of a menu. Try to use at least ten phrasal or prepositional verbs.

**AWL GLOSSARY**

**researcher** a person who studies something and tries to discover new facts about it

**creation** the act or process of making something that is new

**apparently** according to what you have heard or read; according to the way something appears

**individual** considered separately rather than as part of a group

**feature** a part of somebody's face such as their nose or eyes

**assembly** the process of putting together the parts of something such as a vehicle or piece of furniture

# 16 Paraphrasing

## Introduction

> The first text might have appeared in a book or journal. The second is a paraphrase of it that could be used in an essay. Find the phrases in the second text that paraphrase the underlined words or phrases in the first text. Then find four words or phrases that are in both texts, and say why this repetition is acceptable.

Humans have many [1]ways of genetically manipulating the life around us [2]in order to suit our needs. [3]For millennia we have engaged in selective breeding of plants and animals useful to us; in fact, [4]this is a large part of what traditional farming is about. In the [5]twentieth century [6]we developed ways of speeding up the process, such as mutagenesis by chemical agents or radiation. [7]Within the past generation, genetic engineering, or genetic modification, has begun to develop into a fully-fledged technology. (Davis, 2009: 93).

---

As Davis (2009) explains, there are many techniques for creating a living organism with the characteristics we want to see, and to ensure these changes are passed on to its offspring. The most basic of these is selective breeding, which for thousands of years was the way in which agriculture developed. In the last century scientists created more efficient techniques, as Davis demonstrates, using chemicals and radiation to trigger long-lasting change in the genetic structure. The latest form of these manipulations of life is genetic modification, also known as genetic engineering.

Suggested answers: see page 208

A paraphrase is an alternative to a direct quote. In rewriting an author's idea in your own words, you avoid plagiarism and show that you understand the original text. Paraphrases are normally a similar length to the original text, and always acknowledge the source. Although the style of writing should be your own, most paraphrases feature a combination of some the following techniques.

**1** A reference to the author with a reporting verb such as *indicate* or *claim*.
- *Stafford **concludes** that a golfer's familiarity with a course is not always a psychological advantage.*

**2** The use of synonyms such as *a business* instead of *a company* or *depend on* to replace *rely on*.

**3** A change in word form (i.e. part of speech, such as verb to noun).
- *The rate of crime **rises** (verb) in inverse proportion to the standard of living.*
  → *A **rise** (noun) in the level of crime follows a fall in living standards (Bridges, 2007).*

**4** A change in the structure of sentences.
- *In most extended droughts, farm animals begin to die of dehydration.*
  → *Dehydration causes the death of farm animals as droughts worsen, as Miller points out.*

This unit covers these techniques one by one; looks at some of the words and phrases you should repeat; and then shows the techniques working together. (Note that no one technique on its own will produce a paraphrase.)

## 16.1 Reporting verbs

### 16.1 study

A common way of referring to the original author in your paraphrase is to use his or her name with a reporting verb and sometimes with the word *as*.

**1** *Believe, consider, say, suggest, think*

The verbs in this first group all mean that the paraphrased writer is making a case.

- *First contact with a company in the service sector, as Willows has suggested, is crucial in terms of the image that the consumer will build. (or Willows suggests that first contact ...)*

**2** *Argue, assert, claim, conclude, confirm, contend, insist, maintain, state, warn*

The verbs in this second group have the same meaning but are a little more emphatic.

- *Selig maintains that within all group situations, leaders identify themselves first of all through body language.*

**3** *Demonstrate, explain, indicate, note, prove, reveal, show*

The verbs in this third group are all connected with the idea of showing.

- *As Hartner explains, we have to take into account in polling that the more personally-focused the questions are, the greater the likelihood that the respondent may not be telling the truth.*

Note that *demonstrate, indicate, prove, reveal*, and *show* are often associated with statistical or other firm evidence.

- *Figures released by the government in March show that unemployment is at its highest level for seven years.*

**4** *Accept, agree, deny, doubt*

In this fourth group, the paraphrased writer is normally commenting on someone else's work or opinions.

- *Howard, in her work on Shakespeare, doubts that the wide range of learning on display is an appropriate basis on which to question his authorship of the histories or tragedies.*

**5** *Blame, condemn, criticize*

In this fifth group the paraphrased author takes a negative or critical position.

- *Davidoff, in his article on Thatcher, condemns commentators for basing their analysis of some of her key decisions on her background as the daughter of a shopkeeper.*

⌈TIP⌉ The normal pattern for the verbs in this fifth group is *to blame/condemn/criticize someone* or *something for (doing) something.*

**6** *Characterize, classify, define, evaluate, identify, portray, present*

In this final group, the verbs are all connected with the idea of describing.

- *In his essays, Lawrence often seems to portray post-industrial society as a kind of destructive machine.*

⌈TIP⌉ The normal pattern for the verbs in this sixth group is *to characterize/classify*, etc. *someone* or *something as (doing) something.*

---

### 16.1 test yourself

**Circle the correct option.**

1 Milthorp doubts/criticizes the police for the length of time that protestors were contained in one place.
2 Markham has concluded/identified the poor performance of some schools as a key factor in youth unemployment.
3 The authors of the report demonstrate/evaluate that health and safety standards have risen on North Sea oil rigs.
4 As Rumisek states/classifies in the introduction to her book, the design of a hospital can have a positive effect on the health of its patients.
5 Barlow characterizes/contends Liverpool as a city where small regeneration projects have produced impressive returns on their initial costs.
6 Heller and Golding have believed/argued that the concept of the garden city as conceived by Sir Ebenezer Howard in the 19th century needs to be revisited.

## 16.2 Words or phrases that you don't change

### 16.2 study

There are two types of word or phrase that you should repeat in your paraphrase, even if synonyms exist, because you don't need to demonstrate that you know what they mean and using them won't leave you open to charges of plagiarism. Normally these words are single nouns, or nouns in pairs.

1 **Conventional words or phrases** (language that we all use for specific things) such as *passport, pension, house; annual holiday, residential area, processed foods.*
   - *The accepted tradition whereby junior doctors in hospitals may spend up to twelve hours a day on duty during a working week needs to be reconsidered as a matter of urgency.*
   → *According to Steele, we should question as a matter of priority the established practice of ~~young physicians~~ junior doctors working eighty-hour weeks in ~~medical facilities~~ hospitals.*

2 **Specialized words or phrases** within a particular subject area such as *barrister, plea bargain* (law); *asset, business plan* (business studies); *director, proscenium arch* (theatre studies).
   - *Small and medium enterprises can fail because they simply lack cash when it matters.*
   → *Carling warns that a shortage of ~~available money~~ cash at a critical time can undermine successful ~~medium-sized companies~~ small and medium enterprises.*

Note that in some cases, whether or not you can repeat a word will be a matter of personal judgment.

### 16.2 test yourself

Circle the words or phrases that you do not need to paraphrase.
1 High-speed trains are a prerequisite for a thriving modern economy.
2 The Asian tiger is under threat as a trophy for hunters on safari; as a source of parts for traditional medicine; and for its skin.
3 The share price dropped to an all-time low in January but bounced back at the end of the financial year.

4 Reaching agreement over copyright issues is the single most pressing issue that the music industry faces.
5 If they accomplish nothing else, water meters remind the consumer that this precious liquid is, ultimately, a limited resource.
6 Acting as a school governor allows a member of the public to put their specific expertise at the service of their local school.

## 16.3 Synonyms

### 16.3 study

An ordinary dictionary, a thesaurus, or a specialized dictionary of synonyms (sometimes with their opposites, antonyms) will provide you with synonyms, but you need to ensure that the synonym you choose represents the meaning of the original word in its particular context.
- Original text: *Incorrect versions of meetings were supplied to the committee on several occasions.*
   → Paraphrase: *Grierson argues that the committee was given ~~fake~~ false accounts of meetings a number of times.* (*Fake* might suggest that the meetings themselves were invented, or that true reports exist elsewhere.)

In this section, some examples of good synonyms are listed in brackets, with enough context to show you the meaning. Remember, however, that a single synonym in a sentence is only one element of a paraphrase; it will need to be combined with some of the other changes described in this unit. Note also that there are times, particularly when a writer uses an idiomatic expression, that you may need to provide a synonymous phrase to avoid repeating the idiom.
- *These days, very few investors **keep all their eggs in one basket.***
   → *As Burnstone concludes, investors nowadays rarely **place all their assets in a single financial institution.***

TIP Thesauruses are available in book form or online. All of them will offer you synonyms, but the important thing, once you have chosen one or two synonyms, is to check their meaning in context either in the thesaurus itself, if it provides that facility, or in a good English-English dictionary.

## 1 Noun synonyms

The **wealth** (affluence) *of the area was highlighted by the number of gated communities.*

*Rachel Stevens won the* **prize** (award) *seven times.*

*The theatre company had to look for a new* **sponsor** (backer).

*Laws exist to prevent a state of* **anarchy** (chaos).

*Fortunately, no* **harm** (damage) *was done to the nuclear reactor.*

*The chair of the enquiry asked for a full* **account** (explanation) *of the events.*

*A* **fine** (financial penalty) *was imposed on all three companies found guilty of polluting the river.*

*A degree of* **tolerance** (open-mindedness) *is required when people live in close proximity to each other.*

*There was an immediate* **backlash** (negative reaction) *against the law.*

## 2 Verb synonyms

**Mixing** (combining) *business with corporate entertainment can lead to poor decision-making.*

*A loss of confidence in corporate governance can* **reduce** (decrease) *a company's share value quite quickly.*

*Such problems will only* **go away** (disappear) *if they are tackled at source.*

*You can often* **find out** (discover) *the style of a holiday through knowing the destination.*

*There was a great deal of pressure to* **expand** (enlarge) *the scope of the enquiry.*

*The kingdom is* **ruled** (governed) *by the prince and a small council of elders.*

*This was an interesting attempt to* **explore** (investigate) *the effects of long-term isolation.*

*At this point the family* **controlled** (managed) *seven separate businesses.*

*A great deal can be learned simply by* **watching** (observing) *senior managers at work.*

## 3 Adjective synonyms

*But the* **juvenile** (childish) *behaviour of some disc jockeys does not help their case.*

*The severity of the cuts is likely to have a* **negative** (harmful) *effect on the economy.*

*At most they can be accused of a* **naive** (innocent) *trust in the good faith of their partners.*

**Fruitful** (productive) *talks do not always lead to* **sweeping** (extensive) *changes.*

*The company has shown a* **genuine** (real) *interest in* **charitable** (non-profit-making) *activities.*

*But this form of* **cursory** (superficial) *investigation is unlikely to lead to a* **fair** (just) *outcome.*

## 4 Adverb synonyms

*At that point there was* **practically** (almost) *nothing left in the budget.*

*Some of the prisoners at the camp were treated* **harshly** (cruelly).

*The proposed designs for the factory were* **wholeheartedly** (enthusiastically) *welcomed by the board.*

*It is an* **extraordinarily** (extremely) *difficult festival to organize.*

*The difficulties lie* **chiefly** (principally) *in the design.*

*The events surrounding the preparation of the contract were not handled* **properly** (professionally).

*Short-term goals that are* **recklessly** (rashly) *pursued are not likely to have successful outcomes.*

## 16.3 test yourself

**Replace the underlined words with a synonym. You may need to use a dictionary. There is usually more than one possible answer.**

1 The designers assured the board of directors that the heating ducts on the roof of the building would not be noticeable _____ from the ground.

2 A company may sometimes need to print _____ brochures for some of their clients, rather than simply referring them to a website.

3 The speech from an honoured guest can be the highlight _____ of a graduation ceremony.

4 Even the most astute investors were momentarily _____ blinded by the light of the dotcom boom.

5 The strain _____ produced by long-term debt may lead to forms of drug abuse, both legal and illegal.

6 Pacific salmon consistently _____ die within a few days of spawning.

7 Not all employees respond well to being complimented _____ .

8 The announcement of the acquisition produced an unenthusiastic _____ response from shareholders.

## 16.4 Changes in word forms

### 16.4 study

Many commonly-used academic words have several grammatical forms. Together these forms are called a 'word family'.

*analyse* (verb) → *analysis* (noun) or *analyst* (noun) → *analytical* (adjective) → *analytically* (adverb)

Changing the form of a word in a source text is useful in a paraphrase because it will necessitate a change in the grammar of your sentence, which in turn will help you in the process of creating a new sentence.

- A *requirement* for a comprehensive evaluation of the consequences of long-term unemployment would be a substantial quantity of data.
  → Peters explains that a thorough study of the effects of long-term unemployment would *require* a great deal of data.

For a useful source of word families, see the Academic Word List (AWL) developed by Dr Averil Coxhead at Victoria University of Wellington in New Zealand. (http://www.victoria.ac.nz/lals/resources/academicwordlist/)

This section provides some examples of word form transformations in sentence contexts.

### 1 Verb ↔ noun

- *Companies need to **distribute** their products in the most cost-effective way.*
  → *The cost-effective **distribution** of their products is vital to companies.*
- ***Competition** for quality jobs at postgraduate level is fierce at the moment.*
  → *Postgraduate students have to **compete** hard at the moment for quality jobs.*

### 2 Adjective ↔ adverb

- *Varying the height of the roofs in the complex was a **creative** response to the problem.*
  → *The architects responded **creatively** to the problem by varying the height of the roofs.*
- *The performance of the choir was **surprisingly** moving.*
  → *The performance of the choir moved the audience in a **surprising** way.*

### 3 Verb ↔ adjective

- *Consultants advised the company to **extend** the range of their products.*
  → *Consultants advised the company to make the range of their products more **extensive**.*
- *Whatever the virtues of its design, a restaurant has to be **functional**.*
  → *A restaurant must **function** well, whatever the virtues of its design.*

### 4 Adjective ↔ noun

- *A football stadium should be easily **accessible** by coach and foot, if not also by train and bus.*
  → *People should be able to gain easy **access** to a football stadium by coach and foot, if not also by train and bus.*
- ***Familiarity** with the policies of a prospective employer can be useful at an interview.*
  → *It can be useful at an interview to be **familiar** with the policies of a prospective employer.*

## 16.4 test yourself

**Rewrite each sentence, using the word in brackets.**

1 There is no direct link between how well a CEO is remunerated and the success of a company. (remuneration)
2 The mineral wealth of the Ural mountains has had a fundamental effect on the region's history. (fundamentally)
3 South Korea has the economic ability to buy its way out of any regional recession. (able)
4 It is beneficial for students to have undergraduates and postgraduates studying some of the same courses. (benefit – verb)
5 Markets can self-adjust to bring inflation under control. (self-adjustment)
6 Self-publishing ventures often owe their success to the power of the internet. (successful)
7 The ultimate effect of the rise of national pride in post-colonial countries is positive. (ultimately)
8 A thorough investigation of the different ways to collect payment is essential for the sole trader. (investigate)

# 16.5 Changes in structure

## 16.5 study

Changing the grammatical structure of a sentence can help you to make a paraphrase. In this section six areas where change is quite often possible are listed. For more information on these grammatical areas, page references are given. Note that these are not the only structural changes to be used; you will have to use your grammatical knowledge to make other transformations when you see the source text.

**1 Cause and effect** (see page 108 for more information)

*cause ↔ effect*
• *The spread of GM trials had led to* a series of protests.
  → A series of protests *has resulted from the spread of GM trials.*

*because ↔ as a result ↔ so ... that*
• *Medical services are coming under pressure **as a result of** people living longer.*
  → *Medical services are coming under pressure **because** people are living longer.*
  → *People are living **so** much longer **that** medical services are coming under pressure.*

**2 Comparison** (see page 016 for more information)

*than ↔ as ... as*
• *Sometimes paying a fine will be **cheaper than** going to court.*
  → *Sometimes paying a fine will not be **as expensive as** going to court.*

**3 Expressing contrast** (see page 064 for more information)

*although ↔ despite ↔ however*
• ***Although** Diana Fossey spent years studying gorillas, their behaviour would still surprise her.*
  → ***Despite** years spent studying gorillas, their behaviour would still surprise Diana Fossey.*
  → *Diana Fossey spent years studying gorillas; **however**, their behaviour would still surprise her.*

**4 Passives** (see page 082 for more information)

*active ↔ passive*
• *Carol Hardman **designed** the pioneering software.*
  → *The pioneering software **was designed by** Carol Hardman.*

**5 Participles** (see page 067 for more information)

*before, after, since + noun + verb → before, after, since + -ing form*
• ***After** Tom Azezi **left** the team, his inventions were all on a much smaller scale.*
  → ***After leaving** the team, Tom Azezi's inventions were all on a much smaller scale.*

**6 Modal verbs** (see page 100 for more information)

*can, could ↔ be able to*
• *In later years, Foubert plc **could not** match their earlier success.*
  → *In later years, Foubert plc **were unable to** match their earlier success.*

*may, might, could ↔ be possible*
• *A medical breakthrough in the field of cancer research **could** happen in the next ten years.*
  → *It **is possible that** a medical breakthrough in the field of cancer research **will** happen in the next ten years.*

*should ↔ be likely to*
• *We **should** see a reduction in the price of hybrid cars within five years.*
  → *We **are likely to** see a reduction in the price of hybrid cars within five years.*

## 16.6 Techniques working together

### 16.6 study

So far, to make things clear, the various techniques for creating a paraphrase have been examined separately. In this section and the 'Challenge yourself' exercises, you will see the techniques working together to create longer paraphrases, as in the example texts on genetic modification that opened the unit.

Note that in these longer paraphrases you can sometimes change the number and length of sentences (i.e. the techniques can work across sentence boundaries); for example, in the paraphrase of the text below, the first and second pairs of sentences are combined into one sentence each.

Note also that you will need to remind the reader later in your text that you are still paraphrasing, either by referring to the author once more by name (see below), or by using the Latin abbreviation (ibid.), which means 'from the same source' (see the paraphrase in **16.6 test yourself**).

### Source text

*The channels through which companies market their products have changed over the years. A hundred years ago commercial information could only be conveyed by 'small ads' in newspapers and large painted signs on the sides of buildings. Over the intervening years, the number of available media increased to include magazines, billboards, and television. Direct mail was another new approach. Although the advertisers did their best to target their spend, it was accepted that theirs was a broad-brush approach, with very little evidence that they were succeeding in the appropriate markets.* (Hill, 2010: 33)

### Paraphrase with notes

*Hill (2010) points out that* [reporting verb] *marketing methods* [verb *market* becomes adjective *marketing*] *are not the same as they were a century* [synonym for *a hundred years*] *ago, when 'small ads' in newspapers* [unchanged terms] *and signs painted on walls were the only way* [active structure replaces passive *could be conveyed*] *of transmitting the message* [synonyms for *conveying* and *commercial information*]. *The twentieth century saw the rise* [noun *rise* for verb *increase*] *of new ways to reach the consumer, from the billboard and the magazine, to television, and direct mail* [unchanged terms]. *Despite their efforts* [instead of *although* + verb phrase] *to advertise directly to the desired target* [noun *target* instead of verb *to target*], *advertisers were still aware, as Hill explains,* [second reference to the author] *that they were investing their money in a very wide audience* [synonymous phrase for *broad-brush approach*], *only some of whom were presumably interested.*

### Paraphrase without notes

*Hill (2010) points out that marketing methods are not the same as they were a century ago, when 'small ads' in newspapers and signs painted on walls were the only way of transmitting the message. The twentieth century saw the rise of new ways to reach the consumer, from the billboard and the magazine, to television, and direct mail. Despite their efforts to advertise directly to the desired target, advertisers were still aware, **as Hill explains**, that they were investing their money in a very wide audience, only some of whom were presumably interested.*

## 16.6 test yourself

Read the source text and the paraphrase, then complete the list of changes in the table.

### Source text

*Environmental sustainability in building design plays a significant role these days in the professional life of an architect. It is essential, if this demand is to be satisfied, that the plans begin by considering the manner in which the building materials were produced. The building's impact on the green or man-made environment that surrounds it also needs to be evaluated by the architect at this stage (Benn, 2007: 167).*

### Paraphrase

*According to Benn (2007), designing a building so that it is environmentally sustainable is now an important element in an architect's daily work. To meet this requirement, the plans must start by taking into account how the building materials were made. At the same time, the architect has to assess the effect of the structure on the surrounding natural or built environment (ibid.).*

| Source text | Paraphrase |
|---|---|
| **0** Environmental sustainability | so that it is environmentally sustainable |
| **1** Building design | |
| **2** plays a significant role these days | |
| **3** It is essential … that the plans | |
| **4** if this demand is to be satisfied | |
| **5** by considering the manner in which | |
| **6** The building's impact | |
| **7** green or man-made | |
| **8** needs to be evaluated by the architect | |

# 16 Challenge yourself

**A** Write paraphrases of the sentences.

**1** For a minor per capita cost, political parties could be publicly-funded, thus avoiding charges that government policy can be influenced by large private donations (Smith, 2010: 75).

**2** In attempting to attract the peak-time audience, the BBC depends too heavily on costume drama (Sutcliffe, 2011: 45).

**3** Arts funding in the UK, whether by the state or by private philanthropists, is undoubtedly London-centric, with the result that the requirements of the regions are rarely met (Alberge, 2010: 16).

**4** A system whereby parents put themselves in serious debt so as to purchase a house near a highly-ranked primary school is clearly absurd (Gardner, 2011: 26).

**5** The British painter Keith Vaughan has been overlooked by critics as a result of his depiction of the human form, during a period when his peers favoured the abstract in their art (Hamilton, 2009: 12).

**6** The failure of a business start-up is more often due to a lack of good guidance than a shortfall in its financing (Prosser, 2011: 67).

**B** Write paraphrases of the source texts.

## 1 The authorship of Shakespeare's plays

Doubts continue to surround Shakespeare's authorship of the plays currently attributed to him. No strong evidence, however, has been produced to defend any other candidate, and the concerns expressed appear to be based on nothing more substantial than a belief that the writer's humble origins seem incompatible with his poetic brilliance. Furthermore, all the extant documentary evidence, in terms of official records and the testimony of contemporaries, points to Shakespeare as author as firmly as any other accepted attributions of the period are made (Asher, 2006: 134).

## 2 Criticisms of farmed salmon

Salmon farming is not a particularly successful means of increasing the amount of fresh fish available to the modern consumer. To begin with, one must be aware that the salmon is a carnivorous fish with a heavy nutritional requirement. This means in reality that a farmed salmon does not produce as much fish as it eats. Vegetable proteins may prove to be an alternative, but as currently used, they reduce the amount of valuable omega-3 fatty acids in the product. Secondly, the use of open-net cages in the farming process allows disease and sea lice to spread from farmed salmon to local or transient stocks of wild salmon (Nye, 2006: 56).

### AWL GLOSSARY

**minor** not very large, important, or serious

**drama** plays or a genre for theatre, television, or radio

**whereby** by which; because of which

**abstract** a form of representation that does not depict people or things in a realistic way, but expresses the artist's ideas about them

### AWL GLOSSARY

**authorship** the identity of the person who wrote something

**attribute** to say or believe that somebody is responsible for doing something, especially for saying, writing, or painting something

**incompatible** two actions, ideas, etc. that are incompatible are not acceptable or possible together because of basic differences

**furthermore** in addition to what has just been stated

**contemporary** a person who lives or lived at the same time as somebody else

**alternative** a thing that you can choose to do or have out of two or more possibilities

### 3 The drawbacks of 'kettling'

'Kettling', the process through which protestors are contained by the police within a limited space for a number of hours, has three drawbacks. Firstly, it often leads to the detention of innocent bystanders who might have nothing to do with the demonstration. Secondly, it denies detainees access to food, water, and toilets. Thirdly, the atmosphere brought about within the 'kettle' might actually exacerbate the potential for disorder (May, 2010: 190).

### 4 The garden city experiment

The success of the garden city enterprise has not been properly gauged because the concept has never been realized as it was originally intended. The initiator of the garden city movement, Sir Ebenezer Howard, foresaw towns designed within quite specific parameters: the number of inhabitants limited to 32,000, for example, and sites spanning 6,000 acres. Despite this, his reliance on the investors in the company First Garden City Ltd meant that he was unable to hire the costly architects who would respect his designs (Patel, 2008: 276).

### 5 Problems with gated communities

Supporters of gated communities put forward arguments in their defense that do not bear much critical scrutiny. They maintain that by excluding strangers, the opportunity for criminal activity can be diminished. What they do not realize is that most of the strangers they mention have no criminal intentions, and that the presence of a number of passers-by might actually deter criminal activity. In fact, statistics indicate that in the United States there is no less crime among gated communities than there is in their non-gated neighbours (Martoff, 2007: 67).

### 6 The influence of Margaret Thatcher's childhood

All of the impulses that led to Margaret Thatcher's policy making of the 1980s can be traced back to her childhood in Lincolnshire. Her economic desire to balance the nation's budget is that of a grocer's daughter. Her sense of an individual taking responsibility for his or her own fate, rather than relying on the government, stems from her family's Methodist beliefs. Similarly, her commitment to civic duty derives from her father's example as an alderman and later mayor of Grantham (Weaver, 2009: 46).

**C** Select a short text in your own area of study or area of interest and write your own paraphrase.

## Introduction

Conditional sentences are a useful way of exploring the relationship between cause and effect, in all types of text, from factual writing to the development of arguments.

- *If you heat water to a high enough temperature, it boils.*
- *If diamonds had not been discovered in South Africa, the history of that region would have followed a less dramatic and probably more peaceful path.*

Conditional sentences always contain two parts: the *if* clause, which expresses the condition, and a clause expressing the result. The *if* clause can come first or second. When it comes first, you should put a comma after it.

- *If you invest in research and development, you will always get a good return on your money.*
- *You will always get a good return on your money if you invest in research and development.*

This unit looks at the two types of conditional sentence: 'real' (zero and first conditionals) as in the sentence above about boiling water, and 'unreal' or 'hypothetical' (second and third conditionals) as in the sentence about South Africa.

Look at sentences a to d below, spoken by a TV reporter at a scene of flooding. In which one does the reporter

1 form a theory about the past?

2 describe a situation that is always true?

3 make a prediction about the way someone will behave?

4 form a theory about the present?

a Whenever there is a period of heavy rainfall, there is a risk of flooding in the town of Flintchurch.

b If the flood barriers were higher, the houses on Weston Road would probably be secure from flooding.

c Water levels would have dropped to a safe level if the rain had stopped an hour ago.

d Unless the floodwater falls in the next half hour, the local authorities will begin to evacuate all buildings south of the river.

Suggested answers: see page 209

See also unit *12 Cause and effect* for more examples of conditional sentences.

# 17.1 Zero conditionals

## 17.1 study

Zero conditionals are 'real' conditionals, which means that they describe things that are true or are likely to happen. They normally have present tense verbs in both parts of the sentence and describe situations that always produce the same results. *When* or *whenever* (meaning 'every time that') can often replace *if*.

- *If/When/Whenever I **read** all day, I **get** a headache.*

They are common in a number of subject areas including science, business and law.

- *If/When/Whenever a small asteroid **hits** the Earth's atmosphere, it **burns up** immediately.*
- *We **are not able** to offer refunds if/when goods **are** returned without receipts.*
- *Completing an annual tax return **is** a legal requirement if/when you **are** self-employed.*

⌈TIP It's possible to use two past tenses together.
- *If/When scientists in those early days **made** discoveries that might offend religious authority, they sometimes **wrote** up their results in code. Some of these codes have been broken recently by computer programs.*

In a presentation, speakers occasionally use the form *What happens if ...?*
- 💬 *... and **what happens if** we apply this trend to the next decade? Well, you can immediately see from my next slide that ...*

---

### 17.1 test yourself

**Make complete sentences by adding *if*. Add commas and capital letters where necessary.**

1 local authorities are fined they do not recycle at least 25% of domestic rubbish.
2 you translate poetry into another language you lose some aspects of the original text.
3 phosphorus burns you expose it to air.
4 some travel companies guarantee to deliver your tickets within twenty four hours you pay online.
5 they overtrain athletes increase the risk of injury in competition.
6 transport costs are reduced most produce sold is grown locally.

---

# 17.2 First conditionals

## 17.2 study

### 1 Form and use

Like zero conditionals, first conditionals are 'real' conditionals. They typically use the present simple tense in the *if* clause, and the future with *will* in the result clause.

- *If temperatures **rise** again, there **will be** further outbreaks of fire in the forests of southern Greece.*

⌈TIP Remember that we don't use *will* in the *if* clause of first conditionals.
- *If it ~~will cut~~ **cuts** costs now, Mototron will survive the recession.*

First conditionals are often used for asking about or making predictions. Such predictions can be a way of giving a warning or of offering advice.
- *Many small companies **will lose** business if they **do not take advantage of** internet marketing.*
- *If you **submit** your essay after the deadline, it **will not be marked**.*
- *Who **will be** the winners in society if interest rates **rise** dramatically?*

They may also be used for offers and guarantees.
- *There is no fine print. If you **are not** completely satisfied with any item or service you buy from us, we **will refund** your money in full for up to one year after purchase.*

⌈TIP *Be going to* can be used in either parts of a first conditional sentence, particularly in spoken English. In this example, a student is giving a presentation.
- 💬 *No one is saying that there aren't conventional answers to social issues. But if **we're going to** find solutions to some of these urban problems, then we'll have to be willing to experiment.*

## 2 Verb variations

In the result clause, you can use a modal verb instead of *will*. *May*, *might*, and *could*, for example, express a less certain outcome.

- *We **may** see some improvement in the automatic translation of web pages if there is a greater investment in academic research in the area.*

*Should* can be used to mean 'it's the right thing to do' or, if the outcome is positive, 'will probably'.

- *If tourists visit sacred sites, they **should** ensure that they are familiar with the appropriate code of dress.*
- *A further outbreak of fighting **should** be avoided if both sides come to the negotiating table.*

*Be likely/unlikely to* + verb also expresses less certain results than *will/will not*.

- *Experiments have shown that if someone in uniform approaches members of the public and instructs them to do something, they **are likely to** obey.*

Note also that a present perfect form may be more appropriate in the *if* clause than the present simple.

- *If you **have tried** to get through to your bank by phone, you will be aware of the extent to which you are encouraged to resolve your problem online.*

### 17.2 test yourself

**A** Correct the sentences.

1 If you will not give people regular information about the progress of the hurricane, they will begin to panic.
2 The wealth of a country will diminish if banks will not perform their function successfully.
3 If you will ask managers about the general skills levels of trainees, many will say that they are insufficient.
4 You will not know if a new project is successful if you will not evaluate its outcomes.
5 These regional conflicts will only be resolved if the two sides will enter into dialogue with each other.

**B** Complete each sentence with one of the phrases in the box. One phrase is not needed.

> are likely to be    can increase
> are going to lose    should become
> may suffer    should suffer

1 Stress levels _____ amongst staff if management fails to communicate successfully.
2 If an important species dies out, the habitat that it lives in _____ as well.
3 South Korea _____ a major world economy if its present growth rate continues.
4 If a business uses raw materials to make products, there _____ significant delays between obtaining those materials, and acquiring income from the selling of the product.
5 Supermarkets _____ business if they do not respond to the growing consumer demand for 'ethical' products.

**C** Rewrite the sentences in **B** using *will* in the result clause.

## 17.3 *Provided (that), unless*, etc.

### 17.3 study

A number of words can be used in the *if* clause instead of *if*, particularly in first conditional sentences.

**1** *Provided (that)/as long as*

*Provided (that)*, *as long as*, and the slightly less formal *providing that* and *so long as* can be used to replace *if* when the meaning is 'but only with the expectation that'.

- *As long as/Provided that/If the public continues its love affair with the internal combustion engine, the demand for oil is unlikely to fall.*
- *~~As long as/Provided that/~~If you fail the exam, you will need to sit it again.*

## 2 Unless, otherwise

*Unless* means 'except if'.
- *Apprenticeship schemes will disappear altogether* **unless** *the government takes action.*
- **Unless** *an agreement is reached at the talks in Jakarta, these unfair trade practices are likely to continue.*

*Otherwise* means 'because if not'.
- *Local authorities need to ensure that urban areas have sufficient green spaces for public recreation.* **Otherwise**, *they can be accused of contributing to the build-up of urban stress.*

## 3 On condition that, in the event that

These phrases are formal alternatives to *if*. They tend to be used to describe rules, or to write about legal matters.
- **In the event that** *a candidate cannot produce ID, he or she will be unable to take the exam.*
- *Prisoners can sometimes be released early* **on condition that** *they agree to be electronically tagged.*

**TIP** *Even if* (which is also regularly used with second and third conditionals) means 'whether or not'.
- *The government is likely to press ahead with reforms to the House of Lords* **even if** *there are objections from its own backbenchers.*

### 17.3 test yourself

**Circle the correct option. In one sentence, both options are possible.**

1 An interview process can be defended as fair unless/provided that the successful candidate satisfies the criteria listed under 'person specifications'.
2 Commuters will not leave their cars at home. Otherwise,/home unless there is a real financial incentive.
3 Accommodation is offered at no charge on condition that/provided that it is not used for commercial gain.
4 As long as/If six more volunteers cannot be found, the experiment will have to be brought to an end.
5 There will need to be a cut in the scale of fishing even if/if new stocks of fish are found.
6 We should take action against global warming not only as countries but also as individuals unless/individuals; otherwise we simply won't produce the kind of momentum that we need.

## 17.4 Second conditionals

### 17.4 study

#### 1 Form and use

Second conditionals are 'unreal' conditionals. They are called 'unreal' because they can be used to imagine what might happen if circumstances were different. They can be an important way of exploring behaviour and testing theories.
- *If developing countries* **had** *a greater control of commodity prices, they* **would be able** *to plan their economies more efficiently.*
- *What do you think* **would happen** *in the UK if the law on self-defence* **were changed** *tomorrow?*

Second conditionals use a past tense in the *if* clause, and typically *would* + verb in the result clause.
- *If we* **paid** *in dollars instead of sterling,* **would** *we* **get** *a discount on a bulk purchase?*

As with first conditionals, *would* can be replaced with another modal verb.
- *Archaeologists* **might** *make important new discoveries if they were allowed long-term access to building sites in key areas of major cities. Instead, valuable discoveries are lost as bulldozers tear up the earth.*

**TIP** In formal writing, *were* is preferred in the *if* clause to the singular form *was*.
- *If fast broadband access* ~~was~~ **were** *introduced to remote areas of the peninsula, the local population might be able to sell of some their products on the internet.*

## 2 Changes to the *if* clause

The form *were to* **+ infinitive** can be used in the *if* clause instead of a past simple, where it tends to make the condition even less likely to be fulfilled.

- *If the business community **were to replace** international trade fairs entirely with online video conferences, it could lose that vital relationship when the sales team makes physical contact with retailers in the places where they live and work.*

You will also hear lecturers using this structure to evaluate options.

- 💬 *If we **were to incinerate** plastics on a large scale, what waste products would we produce?*

*If it were not for/Without* **+ noun phrase** can also be used.

- *If it were not for/Without easy access to solar energy, business costs in the region would be too high. (= If businesses did not have easy access to solar energy, their costs …)*

**TIP** In spoken English the words *suppose* (or *supposing*) can be used, meaning 'what if'.

- 💬 *Suppose/What if we applied that argument in every case? What would the result be?*

---

### 17.4 test yourself

**Correct the incorrect sentences. Some sentences are already correct.**

1 It would greatly benefit the regional economies if more business headquarters moved from London to cities such as Manchester.
2 If the UK would be committed to renewable forms of energy, it would benefit economically in the long-term.
3 Croker plc would benefit from the market in part-time workers if it has a more flexible recruitment policy.
4 If the government were introduced a 60% tax rate, more tax payers might use tax avoidance schemes.
5 If admission to the Vauxhall Art Gallery were cheaper, it might attract local office workers.
6 If there were not for its highly-skilled local workforce, car manufacturers could not operate in north-east England.

---

## 17.5 Third conditionals

### 17.5 study

#### 1 Form and use

Third conditionals are also 'unreal' conditionals. They use a past perfect tense in the *if* clause and typically *would have* + past participle in the result clause. We use them to talk about what would have happened if circumstances had been different in the past.

- *If the advertising campaign **had focused** on its target audience – young professionals with disposable income – it **would have produced** more impressive increases in sales.*

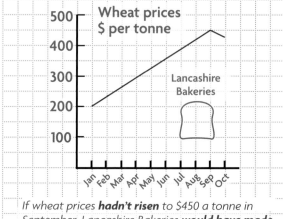

*If wheat prices **hadn't risen** to $450 a tonne in September, Lancashire Bakeries **would have made** a profit last year.*

As with other conditionals, another modal verb can replace *would*. In this example, the use of *should* expresses a critical attitude.

- *If there had been doubts about the funding of the project, an investigation **should have** followed immediately.* (An investigation didn't follow.)

Essay questions sometimes use third conditional questions.

- *What **would have happened** if von Stauffenberg's plot against Hitler **had succeeded**?*
- ***Would there have been** a depression if the government **had not bailed out** the banks?*

**TIP** 💬 In spoken English, it is quite common to use one clause only of the third conditional form. Look at this example from a seminar.

- A *It was clear to insiders that Northern Rock was having difficulties.*
  B *But no one warned the public. Why not?*
  C *Because (if people had been warned) the building society would have collapsed immediately!*

## 2 Changes to the *if* clause

Removing *if* and placing *had* at the front of the sentence makes the style slightly more formal.

- ***Had** the party changed its policy on inheritance tax, they might have won a greater share of the middle class vote. (= If the party had changed its policy ...)*

***If it had not been for/Without*** + noun phrase ... can also be used.

- ***If it had not been for/Without** the government's support, the private member's bill would never have been passed. (= If the government had not supported it, the private member's bill ...)*

[TIP] Sometimes you can mix the tenses that are typically used in second or third conditional sentences. In this example, a third conditional *if* clause is followed by a second conditional result clause because there is a present result.

- *If the factory **had invested** in new technology, it **would** still **be** in business today.*

### 17.5 test yourself

**Correct each sentence by adding one word only.**

1 Hamlin Brothers had attended the trade fair in Bologna, they might have won more orders.
2 If the office buildings in the centre of the city had better designed to withstand earthquakes, the number of deaths would have been much lower.
3 The school might not have failed the inspection if they produced a strategy for improving exam results.
4 Max Brod followed Kafka's instructions, he would have burned the writer's unpublished work after his death.
5 If the prosecutors had found the witness seen on the CCTV clip, they might won the case.
6 If it had been for the new computerized marking system, the college could never have processed the results in time.

# 17 Challenge yourself

**A** Complete the sentences with the correct form of the verb in brackets. What type of conditional is the sentence (zero, first, second, or third)?

1 Powerplay plc would have lost a significant share of the youth market if they _____ (increase) the price of their product.

2 I believe that I have the right attitude to revision. If I _____ (need) a break when I'm studying, I take one. It helps me to stay focused.

3 If there _____ (be) a regional centre for medical aid supplies, it would speed up the response time in emergency situations.

4 Practical skills are vital, but architects also need to maintain a sense of their initial inspiration, whatever problems they _____ (encounter) as the building work progresses.

5 We would not have been obliged to bail out the banks if we _____ (listen) to the quieter economic voices, who advised us against their riskier practices.

6 We _____ (not see) an improvement in the binge-drinking culture unless pubs and clubs begin to act more responsibly.

**B** Complete the text about 'green retailing', using the correct form of the verbs in the box. Use a negative form where necessary.

> wish   renew   act   present   label   place   be

Environmental considerations are often only a marketing strategy, and companies can easily be accused of 'greenwash'. Supermarkets, for example, are in the business of trying to anticipate demand. If new organic shops begin to open all over the city, then supermarkets [1]_____ new orders for organic produce, and [2]_____ it as ethical purchasing. But if consumer demand later dropped, they [3]_____ those orders.

Social enterprises, on the other hand, maintain environmental policies that are as important as their equal opportunities policies. They will have a sustainable procurement policy, for example, even if this [4]_____ just a preferred suppliers list. Furthermore, if their carbon footprint seemed excessive, they [5]_____ to reduce it, and if their suppliers or customers [6]_____ to learn about their decision mechanisms, they would be open to that in a way that is not common in the ordinary business community. As Carson (2010) points out, an enterprise such as Greenstock [7]_____ itself 'social' if it planned to be a conventional company.

**C** 💬 Complete the words in the group discussion on prisons.

A Some people think that prison is the best punishment for criminals, but [1]w_____ i_____ judges used community service more, instead of prison sentences?

B It depends on the type of crime, though, doesn't it?

C Exactly. [2]S_____ someone had been involved in violence, they would [3]n_____ to be kept apart from society.

B And how do you make sure that someone on community service doesn't just disappear?

A Well, [4]a_____ l_____ a_____ they're electronically tagged, the police [5]c_____ keep track of them.

D I think you've got a point about prison. All the statistics show that after they're released, ex-prisoners often reoffend anyway.

B   But if they ⁶im_____ the kind of education they get in prison, that situation is ⁷l_____ to change. Do you remember Prisoner B, for example, in last week's case study? With some job training, he ⁸m_____ n_____ h_____ reoffended.

C   Education requires additional funding, though, doesn't it? If you're really ⁹g_____ t_____ make a difference to the standards of literacy, and so on, you'll ¹⁰h_____ t_____ put a lot of money in.

A   But it's a good investment, isn't it? ¹¹U_____ an ex-prisoner has some qualifications, they ¹²w_____ be able to find work once they're back in society. That's when they start to think about crime again.

---

**D** Correct the text about the benefits of cycling by adding the words in the box. Some sentences are correct, and some sentences need more than one word.

| had   have   might   lead   switched   be   were   do |

¹If a substantial proportion of road users from cars to bicycles, this would an impact on the amount of road space and sheer wear and tear that the road network has to deal with. ²Even if there a switch of 10%, it would to a measurable reduction in the need for maintenance of the infrastructure. ³To take a very concrete example, there may be a weak spot in the road which the council knows needs to be refilled every year, or every time 100,000 cars have driven over it. ⁴Provided, over a year, that only 90,000 cars so, then the maintenance can postponed for a month. ⁵It is easy to see how this kind of 'stretching' can soon add up to significant budgetary savings. ⁶A spokesperson for one local borough in London admitted that if they invested £10,000 pounds more in their cycling campaign, they have saved half a million pounds in road maintenance costs.

**E** Circle the correct options in the text about staff recruitment.

A company ¹*had to/may have to* advertise a new job exclusively to internal candidates first, ²*if/unless/provided that* it is accepted practice to do so. At Benson plc HR Manager Phil Swales believes that if they ³*did advertise/had not advertised/had advertised* their new research post externally, it ⁴*might have/can have* produced a more interesting dynamic at the public presentation stage of the process.

When a company recruits for a post, externally or internally, an interview timetable is drawn up. If a satisfactory format ⁵*exists/will exist* already, this ⁶*has been/can be* used; ⁷*otherwise/unless*, a new format ⁸*needed/needs* to be devised.

**F** Write a short text (100–200 words) based on the following information, using conditional sentences as appropriate and following the instructions.

The catering company Eatwell has been doing badly for the last few years. Their senior staff have worked hard, and they have obtained some new contracts, but their 'brand identity' (the way in which the company wants to be seen by the customer) is not clear. Now they have appointed a new sales director to turn the company around. Write a short analysis of what went wrong, with some suggestions for the future. Begin your text, *If Eatwell had …*

**AWL GLOSSARY**

**exclusively** only to one particular person or group

**internal** involving or concerning only the people who are part of a particular organization rather than people from outside it

**externally** concerning or directed towards people from outside a place, an organization, your particular situation, etc.

**dynamic** a force that produces change, action, or effects

## Introduction

In an academic essay or report, it may be necessary to define a word or phrase, particularly if it occurs in the title itself. Definitions, which often occur at the beginning of a piece of writing, demonstrate that we understand key concepts, and they are sometimes important in order to clarify how a particular term is being used. They might be of the type that is found in a dictionary or be modified in some way to the context in which we are writing (as in the second and third examples below).

- *A retailer is a person who sells goods to the general public, normally from a fixed location such as a shop or by mail.*
- *A person in China is normally defined as 'obese' by medical authorities if their body mass index exceeds 28.*
- *For the purposes of this report, 'humanitarian intervention' will be restricted to the use of military force against a state with the publicly declared aim of preventing human rights violations.*

This unit begins by looking at short definitions and how to avoid common mistakes when defining. This is followed by a list of some of the key verbs used in defining, and a consideration of the ways in which we can extend definitions by giving examples and by making references to the history or to the typical characteristics of the things being defined.

**Read the essay title and the opening lines of the essay itself. What is the writer doing in the first sentence and why, in your opinion, might it be important?**

**What similarities and differences can you find in the episode of the South Sea Bubble of 1720, and the 'dotcom' crash of the late 1990s?**

The term 'South Sea Bubble' describes a period of financial speculation that saw share prices in the London-based South Sea Company rise tenfold in value during the year 1720, before collapsing and ruining thousands of individual investors. The speed at which share values rose and fell, and the lack of evidence to support the company's claims for potential growth, have given this episode its continuing resonance in economic study.

**Suggested answers: see page 210**

Other units in this book that deal with defining language are unit *3 Noun phrases*, unit *5 Relative clauses*, and unit *12 Cause and effect*.

# 18.1 Be + relative clause

## 18.1 study

### 1 Typical pattern

A defining sentence often follows this pattern: **term** (the thing being defined) + **be** + **class** (the wider group that the term belongs to) + **relative clause**.

* *A Special Economic Zone* (term) *is a geographical area* (class) *which is allowed greater economic freedom than other parts of the country* (relative clause).

⌐TIP Try to avoid repeating the term, or a different form of the term, in your definition.

* *A credit bureau is an agency that can provide information on whether individual consumers ~~are credit worthy~~ have shown that they are able to pay off loans and bills.*

⌐TIP Don't forget the class noun, or make it too general.

* *A white dwarf* ⟨is a small dense star that⟩ *can be located by the faint light that it emits.*
* *A dingo is a species of wild ~~animal~~ dog, which is normally found in the Australian Outback.*

### 2 Use of *a/an* and *the*

There is usually an indefinite article (*a/an*) before the term and before the class. However, there are times when you cannot use *a/an* in front of a term noun, such as when it is plural or uncountable.

* ***A** sociolect is **a** dialect which is associated with a particular social class.*
* ***Maize** is a cereal grain that originated in Mesoamerica.*

There are times when it is also inappropriate to use *a/an* in front of the class noun.

* *Lithium is **the lightest element** that is not a gas at room temperature.*

For more information on articles, see unit *3 Noun phrases*.

⌐TIP Make sure that your definition is not just an example.

* *An illuminated gospel is a ~~document such as The Book of Kells, held in Trinity College Library, Dublin.~~ representation of the New Testament in the calligraphic style known as 'Insular art', which is normally produced by monks. (Now you could continue: A good example of this is The Book of Kells, held in Trinity College Library, Dublin.)*

See section **18.4** for more ways of extending definitions.

⌐TIP Short definitions can sometimes be given in the middle or at the end of sentences, separated by brackets or commas.

* *Nomads carry extensive supplies of preserved food such as jerky (**dried strips of meat**).*
* *A cupola, **a small dome-like structure on the top of a building**, may actually serve a purpose, such as housing a light or lantern.*

---

## 18.1 test yourself

**Complete the definitions with a term and a class noun from the box and *is/are*.**

> the day of the year    a parasite
> a court order    a program    a carcinogen
> food products    an injunction
> the summer solstice    perishables
> a substance    a virus    an organism

1 _____ that can reproduce itself and be transmitted between computers.
2 _____ that will decay and become inedible over time.
3 _____ that lives on or inside another organism, feeding at the host's expense.
4 _____ which has the longest period of daylight.
5 _____ that is directly involved in causing cancer.
6 _____ which states that a person or organization must or must not do something.

---

# 18.2 By which, for

## 18.2 study

A number of class nouns are typically followed by *by which, whereby*, or *for + -ing* form.

### 1 By which, whereby

In definitions, class nouns such as *process, means, method, system*, and *technique* are often followed by a relative clause beginning with *by which* or *whereby*.

* *Criminal law is the means **by which/whereby** the government identifies behaviour considered wrong or damaging to individuals and society.*
* *'Scumbling' is a painting technique **by which/whereby** the artist applies a very thin coating of colour, allowing the paint underneath to show through.*
* *Remortgaging is the process **by which/whereby** the holder of a mortgage pays it off with the proceeds of a new mortgage, using the same property as security.*

## 2 *For* + *-ing* form

Class nouns such as *device, gadget, implement, instrument, machine, mechanism,* and *tool* are often followed by *for* + *-ing* form of the verb.
- *In genetics, a 'viral vector' is a **tool for delivering** genetic material into cells.*
- *A 'mute' is a **device for altering** the sound of a musical instrument.*
- *A Geiger counter is a **machine for measuring** levels of radiation.*

### 18.2 test yourself

**Correct the incorrect sentences. Some sentences are already correct.**

1 Electronic funds transfer is the system for money is moved between accounts by computer.
2 Privatization is the process by which an organization is transferred from public to private ownership.
3 A transmission electron microscope is an instrument whereby screening human tissue at high magnification.
4 Barter is a method which goods or services are exchanged without using money.
5 The Retail Prices Index is a mechanism for measuring the rate of inflation.
6 A harrow is an agricultural implement for break up and smooth the soil.

## 18.3 *Describe, be defined as*

### 18.3 study

There are a number of verbs, in addition to *be,* that are often used in definitions.

#### 1 *Describe, designate, mean, refer to, signify*

Definitions using these verbs sometimes begin with *The term ... , The word ... ,* or *The phrase ...*
- *The word democracy literally **means** 'people power' since 'demos' is Greek for 'of the people', and 'kratos' **designates** 'power'.*
- *The term 'lieutenant' normally **refers to** a person who is second in command.*
- *The suffix '-able' normally **signifies** a capability to perform specific actions.*
- *The phrase 'organic food' **describes** any foodstuff that is produced without the intervention of pesticides, chemical fertilizers, and genetically-modified organisms.*

We can use *What* + *mean/is meant by* + *be.*
- ***What I mean by** 'a cult' is any recent religious movement whose practices are generally considered to be strange or unconventional.*
(You could replace *I* with something like *social scientists.*)
- ***What is meant by** an isotonic solution **is** a liquid which has the same salt concentration as human cells and blood.*

We can also use *X means/refers to/signifies* + *-ing* form.
- *A 'short' sale **signifies selling** assets that have been borrowed rather than purchased from a third party.*

#### 2 *Defined as, known as*

The passive phrase *is/was defined as* is used to introduce direct quotations.
- *'Diplomacy' **is defined** in the* Oxford English Dictionary *as 'the profession or skill of managing international relations'.*

To give your own definition, use *may/might/can/could* + *be defined as.*
- *'Competence' at work **might be defined as** the ability to perform tasks to the required standard.*

When the definition comes before the term, you can use *is known as/is called.*
- *The ceasing of the circulation of the blood after the heart's failure to contract **is known as/is called** 'cardiac arrest'.*

### 18.3 test yourself

**Reorder the underlined words to make correct definitions. Add capital letters where necessary.**

1 In most dictionaries <u>as is defined literacy</u> the ability to read and write.
2 <u>an the alloy 'stainless steel' term describes</u> of steel and chromium that is resistant to corrosion.
3 An organism that can cause <u>a as is pathogen disease known</u>.
4 <u>as be the could defined 'people power' force</u> that resides in the general public to oppose the status quo.
5 <u>to the the moral 'ethics' principles word refers</u> that underpin a person's or an organisation's behaviour.
6 <u>alterations term statistical designates the</u> 'climate change' to the meteorological system over very long periods of time.

## 18.4 Extending definitions

### 18.4 study

In the examples below, definitions that you have already seen in this unit are extended in three different ways. Note the useful language in bold.

**1 Extending by examples**

- *The suffix '-able' normally signifies a capability to perform specific actions. 'Clickable', indicating a hyperlinked image or text area, **is an interesting recent example from** computing terminology.*
(You could also say: *... specific actions. 'Clickable', for example, indicates a hyperlinked image or text area in computing terminology.*)

- *'Scumbling' is a painting technique whereby the artist applies a very thin coating of colour, allowing the paint underneath to show through. This process **is exemplified in** (or **is exemplified by**) the work of the Dutch painter Jan van Eyck, where the scumbling is said to add depth and gradation to some of his work.*
- *A white dwarf is a small dense star that can be located by the faint light that it emits. Sirius B, monitored by the Hubble Space Telescope, **is an example of such a** star.*
(You could also say: *A white dwarf is a small dense star that can be located by the faint light that it emits, **such as** Sirius B, monitored by the Hubble Space Telescope.*)

**TIP** The phrase *Take, for example, ...* is sometimes used in spoken English: *Deciduous trees, plants and shrubs are those that lose their leaves for part of the year. **Take, for example**, beech and chestnut trees. By November, the branches of these two species of tree are normally bare.*

**2 Extending by reference to history**

- *In genetics, a 'viral vector' is a tool for delivering genetic material into cells. Paul Berg **was the first** molecular biologist **to use** the vector in the 1970s when he successfully infected monkey kidney cells.*

Apart from the words *first + use* as above, the following verbs can all be used to write about the person who 'invented' the term: *coin, create, devise, invent.*
- *James Watt **coined** the term 'horsepower' in order to compare the output of steam engines with the power of horses.*

*Describe, discover, identify, notice, observe,* and *recognize* are useful in writing about the history of terms used for natural and scientific phenomena.
- *The photovoltaic effect was first **observed** by Alexandre-Edmond Becquerel in 1839.*

**3 Extending by reference to characteristics or types**

- *The dingo is a species of wild dog, normally found in the Australian Outback. **There are three main types of dingo**: the alpine, the desert, and the tropical.*
- *A 'mute' is a device for altering the sound of a musical instrument. The 'straight mute', tipped with cork to hold it in place, **is the most common type** in brass instruments.*

### 18.4 test yourself

**Complete the sentences, using one of the words or phrases in the box in each space.**

| | | |
|---|---|---|
| was first recognized | | is an example |
| observed | coined | can be exemplified |
| are four main types | | |

1 A virus is a program that can reproduce itself and be transmitted between computers. According to his colleague, Fred Cohen (1984), the term 'virus' in connection with computers was first _____ by Leonard Adleman, now Professor of Computing Science at the University of Southern California.
2 A parasite is an organism that lives on or inside another organism, feeding at the host's expense. The parasitic worm, which lives inside its host, _____ of such an organism.
3 A carcinogen is a substance that is directly involved in causing cancer. There _____ of carcinogen, as classified by the International Agency for Research on Cancer (IARC).
4 The term 'stainless steel' describes an alloy of steel and chromium that is resistant to corrosion. This quality in alloys _____ by metallurgist Pierre Berthier, who _____ their resistance against attack by acids.
5 Privatization is the process by which an organization is transferred from public to private ownership. This process _____ in the UK by the transfer of British Telecom and British Gas into the private sector during the 1980s under the Thatcher administration.

# 18 Challenge yourself

**A** Complete the text, using the words in the box.

> coined   describes   examples   is   means   refer   which (x2)

Permaculture [1]_____ a system of ecological design [2]_____ bases itself around sustainable agriculture. Bill Mollison [3]_____ permaculture as 'a philosophy of working with, rather than against nature'. Franklin Hiram King [4]_____ the phrase 'permanent agriculture' in his 1911 book, *Farmers of Forty Centuries or Permanent Agriculture in China, Korea and Japan*. As he used it, the phrase [5]_____ types of farming methods and land management techniques [6]_____ can continue indefinitely. More recently, the two words, 'permanent agriculture', became one: 'permaculture'. This new term can also [7]_____ to 'permanent culture', that is, to a theory of development that includes social aspects as well as material production. [8]_____ of permaculture are agroforestry and rainwater harvesting.

**B** Put the words in the correct order to complete the text.

**1** a as be defined 'domestic violence' may of pattern term the
**2** as can forms, it many such take
**3** as by defined is it more narrowly *Oxford Dictionary of Law* the
**4** also can it mean
**5** all be can expressed in of of these types various violence ways
**6** a abuse abusive behaviour form is of verbal which

[1]_____ abusive behaviours by one partner against another in a marriage or marriage-like relationship. [2]_____ physical aggression or assault, sexual or emotional abuse, intimidation, or stalking. [3]_____ 'physical violence inflicted on a person by their husband, wife, or cohabitant'. Experts in the field, however, such as Smith (2007), agree that it is not limited to obvious physical violence; [4]_____ endangerment, criminal coercion, or kidnapping.

The phrase 'intimate partner violence' has become synonymous with domestic violence, superseding the terms 'wife abuse' and 'wife beating'. Family violence is more of an umbrella term, encompassing child abuse, elder abuse, and other intra-familial acts of violence. [5]_____: physically, psychologically, sexually, financially, and so on. [6]_____ involves the use of language. Verbal abuse may include actions such as swearing, ridicule, and disrespect.

**C** Correct the mistakes in the underlined phrases. Some phrases are correct.

Telemedicine [1]_____ <u>is defined as</u> the delivery of clinical health care remotely, that is, at a distance. The term [2]_____ <u>coined</u> to deal with the use of telecommunications to bridge the gap between doctor and patient. At first, this type of telemedicine [3]_____ <u>was exemplified</u> the use of VHF radios; now, video conversations (e.g. Skype) are the norm. Telemedicine is a system [4]_____ <u>to delivering</u> basic and continuing care, such as monitoring a chronic condition. The newest arm of the field is robotic surgery, [5]_____ <u>wherefore</u> a human surgeon in one place can direct a robot hand to operate on a patient in another location.

Telemedicine [6]_____ <u>is not referring to</u> the type of medical care in which a doctor or nurse travels to remote areas. The [7]_____ <u>first and best-known example of this</u> is the Royal Flying Doctor Service of Australia.

Telehealth [8]_____ is a broader term. It [9]_____ is referring to remote healthcare in a wider sense: not only the delivery of clinical services, but also administration and education accessed at a distance. Electronic health records are one example of the former, and training videos of the latter. A further development of telehealth are the gadgets for monitoring health conditions at home. Telehealth [10]_____ signifies the curative aspect of medicine, and also its preventative function.

**D** 💬 Circle the correct option (a–d) to complete the text.

Let me start my talk by defining my terms. When we speak colloquially of clones, we are usually [1]___ the science-fiction scenarios. You might have seen the film *Never Let Me Go*, about children created in order to serve as organ donors to the 'original' who commissioned them, or perhaps your thoughts turn to rows of identical figures, bred to serve society in exactly the same way, as in Aldous Huxley's *Brave New World*. That is not what scientists [2]___ cloning, and it is not what my talk is about today.

Biologists use the term cloning [3]___ any form of reproduction [4]___ ends up with genetically identical copies to the original. This occurs widely in nature. Take [5]___ bacteria. They simply divide and multiply; each daughter cell is the same as the mother. There are three types of cloning that I'd like to concentrate on: at the level of molecules, at the cell level, and at the level of the whole plant or animal.

Molecular cloning just [6]___ lots of copies of a given molecule. It is a technique for assembling DNA molecules. It has become very important in many branches of medicine and biology.

The term cellular cloning is more complicated. It [7]___ a cell from an adult organism, removing the DNA, and inserting that into an egg which has had its nucleus removed. The purpose of this is to create an embryo, which can then be used for stem cell research. This process is also [8]___ somatic cell nuclear transfer. 'Somatic' [9]___ of or about the body, because the cell can come from anywhere in the body. 'Nuclear' refers here to the nucleus of a cell, where the genetic material is stored.

So, the final type: whole organism cloning. Many plants are spread, in nature and by humans, in a way that makes each resulting plant a clone of the original. It's [10]___ vegetative propagation, and I can go into that in more detail if you'd like me to at the end.

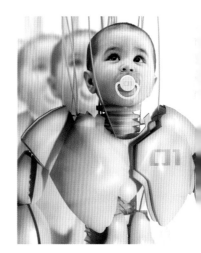

**AWL GLOSSARY**

**identical** similar in every detail

**occur** to exist or be found somewhere

**assemble** bring things together as a group

**insert** to put something into something else

**transfer** the act of moving somebody/ something from one place, group, or job to another; an occasion when this happens

| | | | | |
|---|---|---|---|---|
| **1** | a meaning | b referring to | c defined as | d signifies |
| **2** | a refer to | b describe by | c is meant by | d mean by |
| **3** | a as described | b to describe as | c to describe | d is defined as |
| **4** | a whereby | b as | c by which | d which |
| **5** | a for example | b as example | c in example | d by example |
| **6** | a means | b is defined by | c means making | d means for making |
| **7** | a refers to take | b refers to taking | c means to taking | d is known as taking |
| **8** | a known for | b known by | c known | d known as |
| **9** | a describes | b refers | c means | d is |
| **10** | a called | b is known | c is defined | d called as |

**E** Write extended definitions (50–100 words) of two or three of the following. Remember, you can extend by examples, by reference to history, or by reference to characteristics or types.

- a species of animal typical in your country
- a plant, flower, fruit, or vegetable
- a national holiday (e.g. President's Day)
- a branch of business (e.g. marketing or finance)

## Introduction

> Words that work naturally with each other and which are used together frequently, such as *heavy traffic*, are called 'collocations'. Complete the table with the six underlined collocations in the text.
>
> | 1 Noun + noun | |
> |---|---|
> | 2 Adjective + noun | |
> | 3 Verb + adverb | |
>
> The <u>latest figures</u> from the Office for National Statistics <u>establish conclusively</u> that we are seeing a <u>significant reduction</u> in the number of UK residents making visits abroad. The evidence that has been gathered by <u>government officials</u> shows a fall in 2010 of three million visits. <u>Travel disruptions</u>, the exchange rate, and <u>economic hardship</u> are likely to be responsible for this decline.
>
> Suggested answers: see page 211

Collocations are often defined as 'words that go together'. A knowledge of collocations is important because it allows you to speak and write more naturally. This means that you will be more easily understood by native speakers who will expect to hear particular combinations of words. In the text above, for example, you could say *a large reduction*, but the adjective *significant* collocates better. (*Significant* also collocates well with other nouns such as *impact* and *proportion*.) Similarly, *fiercely competitive* is more natural than *strongly competitive*; and native speakers say *a big mistake* but not *a big error*: instead, they use *serious* or *major* with *error*.

In this unit, a selection of useful collocations for academic English is divided into four grammatical categories.

**1** Adjective-noun collocations
- *There is a **widespread belief** that a life led close to nature is a more virtuous one than that of a city-dweller.*

**2** Adverb-adjective collocations
- *Texans are **justifiably proud** of Sam Houston, the first President of the Republic of Texas.*

**3** Verb + noun; verb + adverb
- *After **carrying out** an **assessment**, the NHS decides what services they can offer to support home carers.*
- *The local authority **responded favourably** to the museum's request for additional funding.*

**4** Noun + noun
- *A formula exists to produce films which will meet the important commercial criterion of '**family entertainment**'.*

> **Unit contents**

Note that collocations dictionaries, such as the *Oxford Collocations Dictionary for Students of English*, are available in bookshops and online.

See also unit *3 Noun phrases* for the grammar of noun + noun combinations, and unit *6 Stating facts and opinions* for verbs, nouns and adjectives that collocate with the words *data*, *evidence*, *fact(s)*, *information*, and *statistics*.

## 19.1 Adjective + noun

### 19.1 study

In this section, twelve key adjectives with their frequent noun collocations are listed in three groups.

**1 Adjectives of size and impact**

**considerable** + *amount, degree, difference(s), doubt(s), extent, impact, influence, interest, number, power, risk*

**important** + *aspect, contribution, decision(s), difference(s), point(s), question(s), reason(s)*

**major** + *change(s), concern(s), contribution, difference(s), factor(s), issue, problem(s), role, theme*

**significant** + *difference(s), effect, impact, increase, number, part, proportion, reduction*

**widespread** + *allegations, assumption, belief, destruction, opposition, practice, protests, support, use*

**2 Adjectives connected with areas of influence**

**economic** + *conditions, decline, difficulties, factor(s), hardship, policy/ies, prosperity, status, success*

**financial** + *burden, controls, crisis, data, implications, institutions, position, risk(s), security, support, world*

**political** + *agenda, factor(s), landscape, party, power, reform, rights, stability, system*

**social** + *class, factor(s), mobility, network(s), policy/ies, problems, relationships*

**3 Limiting adjectives**

**local** + *area, authorities, businesses, community/ies, economy, government, people*

**relevant** + *data, details, documents, example, factor(s), information, point*

**specific** + *case(s), characteristic(s), conditions, context, example, information, purpose, type(s)*

### 19.1 test yourself

**Circle the most appropriate option.**

1 Transport infrastructure is a major contribution/theme/power in business development seminars these days.
2 Could you give a specific purpose/example/point of acid rain causing serious damage?
3 Political stability/solidity/reliability is a pre-condition for most types of national wealth-creating plans.
4 Russia still has considerable emphasis/influence/weight on the independent states of Central Asia.

5 There is a widespread thought/point/belief that social mobility/movement/flow is dependent on educational opportunities.
6 Small businesses have a significant pressure/impact/force on a country's economic richness/rise/prosperity.

## 19.2 Adverb + adjective

### 19.2 study

In adverb + adjective collocations, the adverb either intensifies the adjective (*highly experienced*), or it adds meaning (*recently published*).

As with adjectives, adverb + adjective collocations can either stand on their own after the verbs *be*, *appear*, *become*, *look*, and *seem*, or precede a noun.

- *If a local workforce is to become **highly skilled**, education providers and businesses need to work together.*
- *The government has announced that it plans to create a new form of **privately-financed university**.*

**1 Intensifying adverbs**

In this group, the adverbs make the adjectives stronger.

*conspicuously **absent*** (= surprising that the person or thing is not present: *the CEO was conspicuously absent from the meeting with furious shareholders*)
*barely **adequate*** (= at an almost unacceptably low standard)
*generously **compensated***
*fiercely **competitive***
*strictly **confidential***
*seriously **delayed***
*severely **delayed***
*carefully **documented*** (*a carefully documented report is one that is based on a good and thorough use of evidence*)
*highly **experienced***
*heavily **fortified*** (often used in military contexts: *the rebel leader's heavily fortified headquarters*)
*critically **ill***
*deeply **offensive/offended***
*meticulously **planned***
*densely **populated***
*immensely **powerful***
*highly **qualified***
*strictly **regulated***
*extensively **reported***
*profoundly **sceptical*** (= very doubtful)
*highly **skilled***

## 2 Adverbs that add meaning

In many other adverb + adjective collocations, the adverb has a specific meaning rather than an intensifying effect.

Here are some examples:

*casually employed* (= not given a permanent contract of work)

*evenly matched* (used to describe the two sides in a contest, argument, etc.)

*falsely accused* (= incorrectly accused)

*justifiably proud* (= proud with good reason)

*largely justified* (= not completely justified)

*mainly theoretical* (= with very little practical application)

*newly appointed* (used to describe someone who has very recently been recruited to a post)

*privately financed, publicly financed* (often used to describe construction projects)

*recently published* (= published not long ago)

*wrongfully imprisoned* (= put in prison even though innocent)

**TIP** *Well* and *badly* collocate usefully with many adjectives, e.g. *well* or *badly designed* or *constructed*. *Badly worded* means 'poorly written'. Note that *badly advised* means 'given poor advice' but *well advised* is used in contexts such as:

• *Nolan plc would be well advised to pay compensation before their reputation suffers further.* (= it would be a good idea for Nolan plc to pay compensation)

### 19.2 test yourself

Complete each sentence with one of the adverbs in the box. Three adverbs are not needed.

> minimally   barely   deeply   incorrectly
> mainly   casually   informally   severely
> wrongfully

1 Most fruit pickers are ＿＿＿＿＿＿ employed, and are sometimes offered basic accommodation.
2 It was proved on appeal that all three men had been ＿＿＿＿＿＿ imprisoned.
3 Some critics attacked the TV programme, describing it as ＿＿＿＿＿＿ offensive.
4 Supplies to the villages were ＿＿＿＿＿＿ delayed by the collapse of two bridges, making the overall situation much worse.
5 Simpson (2009) suggests that facilities for the athletes were ＿＿＿＿＿＿ adequate.
6 The work carried out by Grigson on artificial intelligence was ＿＿＿＿＿＿ theoretical.

## 19.3 Verb + noun, and verb + adverb

### 19.3 study

The list below focuses on selected verbs, showing common noun and adverb collocations.

**analyse:** *the data, the evidence, the results*
**analyse:** *closely, in depth, in detail, systematically*

**carry out:** *an analysis, an assessment, an experiment, an investigation, a survey, a task*
**carry out:** *fully, systematically*

**consider:** *the evidence, the options*
**consider:** *carefully, seriously*

**deal with:** *an issue, a problem, the situation*
**deal with:** *effectively, swiftly*

**demonstrate:** *the importance (of), the need (for)*
**demonstrate:** *clearly, conclusively*

**deny:** *the accusation, the allegation*
**deny:** *categorically, strenuously*

**discuss:** *an idea, an issue, a problem, a question*
**discuss:** *at length, briefly, thoroughly*

**establish:** *the connection, the relationship (between)*
**establish:** *conclusively, firmly*

**examine:** *the evidence, the facts*
**examine:** *critically, thoroughly*

**identify:** *the causes (of), the factors (leading to)*
**identify:** *clearly, straightaway*

**raise:** *awareness, funds, morale, questions, standards*

**refer to:** *frequently, in passing, obliquely, specifically*

**respond to:** *an idea, a plan, a proposal*
**respond to:** *favourably, negatively, positively*

**result in:** *automatically, inevitably*

**resolve:** *an argument, a conflict, a dispute, an issue, a problem*
**resolve:** *eventually, speedily*

**study:** *conclusions, data, results, the situation*
**study:** *closely, in depth, in detail, thoroughly*

**suppress:** *evidence, personal freedom, protests,*
*a rebellion, social unrest*
**suppress:** *brutally, ruthlessly*

**write:** *authoritatively, convincingly, knowledgeably (on)*

## 19.3 test yourself

**Complete each sentence with the correct form of one of the verbs in the box.**

> consider   suppress   raise   deny
> resolve   demonstrate

1 Narrative structure normally involves some kind of conflict which is eventually _____ at the end of the story.
2 The purpose of the conference was to _____ awareness amongst doctors of the pressures on parents caring at home for children with disabilities.
3 Billings describes how the regime has brutally _____ all protests by opposition groups.
4 Dalston's research _____ conclusively that two of the local languages had no written form.
5 Senior managers at the company _____ categorically that they had encouraged a culture of bullying to develop in the workplace.
6 The enquiry panel _____ the evidence carefully over a period of six weeks in early 2009.

## 19.4 Noun + noun

### 19.4 study

Just as nouns are combined in everyday English (*table lamp, horse race*), so nouns collocate with each other in all types of writing and speaking. For an explanation of the grammar of noun + noun combinations, see page 032 in unit *3 Noun phrases*.

Listed below are seven of the most productive 'head nouns' (the nouns that come first in combinations) in general and academic writing, with some of their most frequent noun collocations. Note that some second nouns are regularly used in singular and plural forms, (*business trip(s)*); some are never used in plural forms because they are uncountable (*market growth*); some are normally used in plural form (*health cuts*); and some are normally used in singular form (*computer age*).

**business** + *community/ies, dealings, empire(s), environment, interests, objective(s), opportunity/ies, relationship(s), trip(s)*

**computer** + *age, animation, error(s), graphics, hardware, interface, model(s), problem(s), program(s), software, studies*

**family** + *background, business(es), car(s), doctor(s), entertainment, event(s), friend(s), photo(s), problem(s), wedding(s)*

**government** + *agency/ies, approval, bonds, control(s), decision(s), grant(s), minister(s), official(s), plan(s), policy/ies, regulation(s)*

**health** + *advice, centre(s), concern(s), cuts, hazard(s), industry/ies, issue(s), policy/ies, scare(s), service(s), treatment(s), worker(s)*

**market** + *crash(es), economy/ies, force(s), growth, penetration, potential, rate(s), research, saturation, segmentation*

**research** + *centre(s), data, evidence, findings, funding, grant(s), interests, methods, project(s), proposal(s), scientist(s), team(s)*

## 19.4 test yourself

**Circle the most appropriate option.**

1 Halliwells plc have maintained a solid performance in a very difficult business economy/environment/background.
2 The first film to take some advantage of computer studies/entertainment/animation was *Westworld* (1973).
3 Walter Scott's family background/issues/dealings, particularly his grandparents' home at Sandyknowe Farm, played a key role in the development of his romantic imagination.
4 The educational work of the charity Mindset has been put at risk by the loss of two substantial government revenues/incomes/grants.
5 Syms (2010) emphasizes that rural health workers/doctors/officers in developing countries are the stimulus behind regional progress in medicine.
6 With the withdrawal of central funding, many universities will now have to come to terms with working in the commercial world of market issues/forces/problems.

# 19 Challenge yourself

## A Complete the words in the text about a scientific hoax.

There has been [1]co_____ interest in the case of Piltdown Man, not for what it reveals about the evolution of mankind but for the way in which it demonstrates so [2]cl_____ the [3]im_____ powerful desire in humans to, as Carmichael (2004:2) describes it, 'believe against the facts'. When Charles Dawson announced in 1912 that fragments of an early human skull had been discovered at the Piltdown gravel pit, many of his colleagues in the scientific community were profoundly [4]sc_____, responding to his [5]pro_____ that the find might represent the 'missing link' between humans and apes with a strong measure of disbelief.

Despite these doubts and the publication of a [6]ca_____ documented article (Waterson, 1913) within a year of the discovery, arguing that Piltdown Man's jawbone was that of an ape rather than a human, some forty years were to pass before it was established [7]con_____ by Oakley and Clark (1953) that the skull was a forgery. This time lapse can be explained in part by the [8]fi_____ competitive atmosphere in which contemporary paleontologists operated. As Brooker (2001) suggests, there was a [9]wi_____ assumption that, after [10]imp_____ contributions to the science of evolution had been made by fossil discoveries in Germany and France, Britain's turn had come.

## B Complete the text about newspaper regulation, using the words in the box. Not all of the words are needed.

> **nouns:** detail   allegation   investigation   issue   need   policy   conflict
>
> **adverbs:** generously   closely   deeply   extensively   immensely   strenuously
>
> **adjectives and verbs:** adequate   possible   political   achieve   consider   raise

Government [1]_____ towards the regulation of newspapers has been analysed in [2]_____ over the last ten years. Carr (2008) points out that the ruling party's [3]_____ agenda at any given time seeks to balance two almost contradictory aims: a genuine aspiration to preserve the ancient freedoms of the country, and a desire to demonstrate the [4]_____ for controls to satisfy a public that is often [5]_____ offended by intrusions into the private lives of British citizens. Recent allegations of phone hacking, [6]_____ denied by some journalists and admitted by others, have served to [7]_____ awareness of an issue that should, according to Patel (2009), have been resolved in a much more timely fashion.

The fact that victims of press intrusion have been [8]_____ compensated by the newspapers responsible, and that these payments have been [9]_____ reported, is unlikely to lessen the demands for a legal framework to be established. Such a framework would need to give the public confidence that when journalists carry out an [10]_____, they [11]_____ carefully the penalties they face if it is later discovered that they have behaved improperly. As Wooller (2010) argues, the penalties that currently exist are regarded by many members of the public as barely [12]_____ .

---

**AWL GLOSSARY**

**demonstrate** to show something clearly by giving proof or evidence

**document** to prove or support something with documents

**assumption** a belief or feeling that something is true or that something will happen, although there is no proof

**evolution** the gradual development of plants, animals, etc. over many generations

---

**AWL GLOSSARY**

**contradictory** containing or showing a lack of agreement between facts, opinions, actions, etc.

**deny** to say that something is not true

**awareness** knowing that something exists and is important

**resolve** to find an acceptable solution to a problem or difficulty

**compensate** to pay somebody money because they have suffered some damage, loss, injury, etc.

**framework** the structure of a particular system

**C** Circle the more appropriate option to complete the text about educational achievement.

Family [1]*information/background* and social [2]*class/category* are two of the elements that are studied [3]*closely/completely* by researchers examining the likelihood that children will take advantage of the educational opportunities that are offered to them. As far as the first of these is concerned, the behaviour of a child's parents will inevitably have a [4]*large/considerable* influence on his or performance at school, but not always in the ways that might be expected. Billings (2003), for example, points out that an important [5]*contradiction/difference* between one set of parents and another may not lie in what they achieve in terms of their educational qualifications, but rather in their attitude to the concept of learning. Berryford (2006, cited in Morgan, 2009) confirms this, establishing a clear [6]*bond/connection* in her research [7]*findings/discoveries* between the positive views that some parents express at home towards the acquisition of knowledge, and improvement at school amongst their offspring. Some of the evidence that she [8]*thinks about/considers* may seem superficial: she notes for example, that in households where books are [9]*conspicuously/detectably* absent, the child's attitude towards the textbooks that are consulted in class appears to be 'less favourable' (ibid.), but in terms of [10]*naming/identifying* the causes of underachievement at school, the link between home and school seems to be clear.

**D** Match pairs of words in the box to create collocations, then use the collocations to complete the text about the decline in high-street shopping.

social   business   recently   respond   significant   economic   market
specific   inevitably   local   context   published   networks   reduction
community   positively   conditions   forces   result   authorities

The [1]_____ in Stockport is currently considering the options for reviving the shopping opportunities in the town centre. The [2]_____ in which discussions are taking place is a [3]_____ study that indicates that Stockport has one of the highest rates of town centre shop closure in the country.

There are conflicting views of the [4]_____ that have led to the closing of familiar high street shops. Peterson (2010) makes the simplest case, arguing that [5]_____ have attracted the mobile consumer to out-of-town retail outlets, and that this will [6]_____ in the decline of high-street shopping. Clark and Westbrook (2011) contend, in contrast, that [7]_____ treat small town centre retailers unfairly in the rates and rents that are charged.

An argument put forward by Smalley (2010) suggests that it is in our long-term interests to [8]_____ to the crisis facing the high street in order to preserve the [9]_____ that local shopping promotes. He claims that a [10]_____ in commercial town centre activity can lead to an increase in social alienation.

**E** Use collocations to write 100–200 words about the health services (hospitals, clinics, doctors, etc.) in your country. How do experts, commentators, and health workers view them? What position do politicians take? What do the general public feel about the quality of service?

**inevitably** as is certain to happen

**positive** thinking about what is good in a situation; feeling confident and sure that something good will happen

**acquisition** the act of getting something, especially knowledge, a skill, etc.

**evidence** the facts, signs, or objects that make you believe that something is true

## Introduction

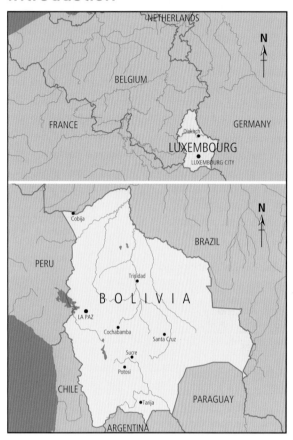

Cohesion describes the process of referring to other parts of a text, using words like *they*, *this*, and *some* to create a well-organized piece of writing. The careful and correct use of cohesive devices is important in academic English because of the likely complexity of the arguments being presented.

The most common cohesive devices are personal pronouns (*she, him, its, their,* etc.), demonstrative pronouns (*this, that, these, those*), and words such as *the same, both, some,* and *respectively*.

- *The refrigerated unit of a supermarket is often **its** single biggest area.*
- *The suburbs are considered to be safer than inner-city areas. **This** is why some people choose to live there.*
- *Not all eco-friendly business want to be labelled 'green'. **Some**, in fact, distance themselves from the term.*

Most of the time these devices are used to refer backwards to things already mentioned but, as you can see in the example below, it is also possible to refer forwards.

- *Placing a job advertisement on the internet may result in applications from around the world. Until **they** (refers forwards to the candidates) notice the opportunity, some of the candidates may never have thought of working outside their home country.*

This unit covers all of the reference words above and also looks at the role of ellipsis (leaving words out) in cohesion.

Other units that deal with cohesion are unit *5 Relative clauses*, and unit *7 Connectors* (because all connectors link one part of the text to another).

**Read the essay extract. What nouns or noun phrases do the underlined words and phrases (1–6) refer to?**

Luxembourg and Bolivia do not seem to have much in common. ¹The former is a comparatively prosperous European country; ²the latter is one of South America's poorest states. ³Both, however, are landlocked, and ⁴this has influenced ⁵their history in ways which will be explored ⁶below.

1 _____
2 _____
3 _____
4 _____
5 _____
6 _____

**Suggested answers: see page 212**

# 20.1 Personal pronouns

## 20.1 study

The following pronouns are all commonly used as cohesive devices in writing: the subject pronouns *he/she/it* and *they*; the object pronouns *him/her/it* and *them*; and the possessive adjectives *his/her/its* and *their*.

- *A new mother is most at ease when **she** feels that the hospital has given **her** all the information she needs.*
- *Some commentators talk as if markets were living beings, investing **them** with human characteristics such as greed.*
- *Staff may naturally become demoralized if **they** are told they may be losing **their** jobs. The manager's role in this situation is to ease tensions, although this may be difficult if **his** or **her** job is also at risk.*

**TIP** In spoken and less formal English, *his* or *her* (as in *his or her job* above) may be replaced by *their*, and *he or she* can be replaced by *they*.

Mistakes that are sometimes made with these pronouns include getting the number wrong (singular when it should be plural and vice versa) and not making it clear what the pronoun refers to.

- *Archiving files online has some advantages over storing material on disc. ~~Their~~ **Its** usefulness lies in employees being able to access information from any location.* (Although *files* is plural, *archiving files* as an idea is singular.)
- *English-English dictionaries are more useful for international students than bilingual dictionaries, because they do not have enough information on words.*

In the example above *they* could refer to either English-English dictionaries or bilingual dictionaries. The writer hasn't made it clear. It is better to keep to a single noun in the first clause so that it is clear what any pronoun in the second clause refers to. Assuming that the writer was using *they* to refer to bilingual dictionaries, the sentence could be rewritten as:

- *English-English dictionaries have more information on words, and they are therefore more useful for international students than bilingual dictionaries.*

**TIP** Remember that the possessive adjective *its* is quite different from *it's* which means 'it is' or 'it has'.

## 20.1 test yourself

Complete the sentences, using a personal pronoun in each space.

1 When a job advertisement has been written, the question of where to place _____ must be addressed.
2 Steele argues that the police are wary of being used for political purposes, and that _____ impartiality is vital to _____ as an institution.
3 Webber (2007) was surprised at the lack of interest in specific policies that the ordinary voter displays when _____ or _____ is about to enter the polling station.
4 Businesses must try to anticipate the problems that _____ will face in _____ particular sector.
5 Staying in hotels can have _____ disadvantages for the business traveller in terms of isolation and loneliness.

# 20.2 *This, these, that, those*

## 20.2 study

**1 *This* and *these* in general**

*This* and its plural form *these* can refer to a specific noun phrase that has recently been mentioned.

- *The government is planning to introduce **a new law** on privacy. If it were to be passed, **this legislation** would add an extra layer of protection to the existing laws.*
- (in a presentation) *There are two **questions** we can ask about global warming: 'What will be the result if we do not act?' and 'What actions can we take?' I will try to provide answers to both of **these (questions)**.*

Frequently, however, *this* is used on its own to refer to a whole 'idea'.

- *Consumers now expect their favourite fruit and vegetables to be available all year round. **This** means that food must be imported from great distances.* (*this* = consumers expecting fruit and vegetables to be available all year round)

## 2 *This* and *these* with summarizing nouns

*This* and *these* are used with nouns that summarize a recent argument.

- *There have been several recent stories of parents overstepping the boundaries to help their children at school. **This phenomenon**, known as 'helicopter parenting', is satirized in the novel* May Contain Nuts.
- *Cities work best when the traffic flows freely. Workers are most productive when they feel fit and well. A city with a strong cycling programme can achieve both of* **these objectives**.

TIP Note that you can also refer forwards, as in this example from a presentation.

- 🗨 *And so we come, I believe, to* **this conclusion**: *the war against drugs is essentially unwinnable.*

Nouns regularly used with *this* and, in their plural form with *these*, include:

| | | |
|---|---|---|
| advance | discussion | policy |
| advice | drop | problem |
| amount | estimate | proposal |
| area | example | reduction |
| argument | explanation | remark |
| change | fall | report |
| claim | idea | rise |
| comment | increase | situation |
| conclusion | issue | subject |
| crisis | measure | suggestion |
| criticism | method | system |
| description | misunderstanding | trend |
| development | number | view |
| difficulty | objective | warning |
| disagreement | phenomenon | |

## 3 *That* and *those*

*That* and the plural form *those* can also be used to refer to a specific noun phrase that has recently been mentioned, but they tend to express a greater distance from the writer. The distance expressed by *that* and *those* may be in time, or it may be in 'emotional' distance.

- *In* **those** *days, women were unable to pursue careers as research scientists at Canadian universities. Maude Menten therefore left for the USA shortly after receiving her doctorate in medicine in 1911.*
- *Lang writes that longer prison sentences are an appropriate expression of the public view of criminal behaviour. If* **that** *argument is accepted, however, then the UK prison population will rise to an almost unmanageable level. (Using* **that** *argument indicates that the writer may not agree with it.)*

In academic writing, *that* and *those* are sometimes post-modified. (See page 028 for an explanation of post-modify.)

- *The process of making marmalade is similar to* ~~this~~ **that of making jam**, *except that a particular type of orange is required. (that = the process)*
- *The general public is made up of two distinct types of people:* ~~these~~ **those who see themselves as an important part of the political process**, *and* ~~these~~ **those who do not even trouble themselves to vote**. *(those = the people)*

## 20.2 test yourself

**A Replace part of the underlined sentence with the word or phrase in brackets.**

1 More and more businesses are going bankrupt in the second six months of their existence. The increased number of businesses going bankrupt needs to be examined in the overall context of the current economic situation. (this trend)

2 The arctic wolf would seem to be the natural predator of the buffalo. Mitchell (2009) argues, however, that the hunting of buffalo by wolves was not always how these two species behaved in the wild. (this)

3 Economic sanctions against the regime will be put in place shortly by the EU. Sanctions against the regime are likely to result in greater hardship for the general population. (these measures)

4 Consumer loyalty can be vital to the success of a company. The importance of loyalty was confirmed in a recent study by Stevens and Black (2011), who examined the recent performance of 23 companies. (this)

5 Anders and Silver do not share the same views on stem cell research. A series of articles published in 2010 first made the fact that they have different opinions public. (this disagreement)

**B Complete each sentence with *this*, *that*, *these*, or *those*.**

1 Throughout _____ report, we will refer to the experiments that took place at the Lever Laboratories in 2001.

2 In the early part of _____ century, during the 1820s, André-Marie Ampère was developing his groundbreaking theory of electrodynamics.

3 Armstrong (2001) criticized _____ who had withheld their taxes in support of unilateral nuclear disarmament.

**4** In her study Clements (2006) explores _____ two ideas: that most languages are much more complicated than they need to be, and that they change for sociohistorical reasons, rather than by chance.

**5** The argument put forward by Keller (2008) is different from _____ presented by Fischer and Bly (2004).

## 20.3 *The, such, the same, one, both,* etc.

### 20.3 study

**1** *The, such*

One of the uses of the definite article *the* is to show that information has already been mentioned.

- *Aruna Kumari set up a mail order business and two retail outlets in 1986. While* **the** *shops soon closed,* **the** *mail order business went on to become one of the region's most successful SMEs.*

*Such (a/an)* meaning 'of the kind already mentioned' is common in academic English. With singular nouns, use *such + a/an*; with uncountable nouns and plurals, use *such*.

- *Some quite small areas – Papua New Guinea, for example – account for a disproportionate share of the world's languages.* **Such places,** *unsurprisingly, are a magnet for linguistic study.*
- *Some writers on the subject have argued that time may be circular rather than linear, and that if* **such a** *theory holds true, then time travel itself is theoretically possible.*

**2** *The same, (the) other, another*

To emphasize that you are referring exactly to the person or thing mentioned before, you can use *the same.*

- *All of these small relief projects are endangered by a lack of water.* **The same** *problem affects the larger efforts required to improve the region's infrastructure.*

By using *(the) other* or *another,* you refer the reader to related examples of the thing mentioned.

- *There is a lack of housing in the south of England. In* **other** *parts of the country, improvement to the existing housing stock could offer a way forward.*

- *The publishing industry will inevitably be affected by the rise of the e-book. Cutting the price of the printed book is one solution.* **Another** *avenue that can be explored, however, is the redesigning of traditional bookshops.*

**3** *One, both,* etc.

The words *one(s), both, some, none, few,* and *many* can all refer to nouns previously mentioned.

- *Unlike previous economic bubbles, the* **one** *(= the bubble) in 1929 involved many different investment banks and trading houses.*
- *Many people visit religious retreats simply for a short period of quiet reflection.* **Some** *(= some of these people), however, speak of profound changes in their lives after spending time in retreat centres.*
- *Galileo and Einstein are the 'parents' of modern physics.* **Both** *(= both of these scientists) made discoveries that have led to the work now being undertaken by their 'children' in the research centres of the 21st century.*

### 20.3 test yourself

**Complete each sentence with one of the words in the box. One word is not needed.**

| | | | | |
|---|---|---|---|---|
| same | the | such | few | many |
| both | other | | | |

**1** The rumours of budgetary cutbacks may have two effects on staff: one is uncertainty; the _____ may be suspicion that senior managers know more than they are revealing.

**2** Early Himalayan climbers often returned with little to show for their efforts; _____ were ill-equipped for the sudden changes in weather.

**3** A casual employee may perform well in a post for months, but when _____ post is advertised, their candidacy is often unsuccessful.

**4** New York State is often confused with New York City, since both bear the _____ name.

**5** A bookshop these days can be made of bricks and mortar or be virtual or, increasingly, be _____ .

**6** An aging population has a profound effect on medical spending, because although younger people incur _____ expenditure, old people incur far more.

## 20.4 Former, latter, respectively, etc.

### 20.4 study

*The former, the latter, respectively, above,* and *below* are all used in formal writing to make specific references to other parts of the text.

**1 *The former, the latter***

When you mention two things and then want to refer back to them, *the former* means the first one you mentioned, and *the latter* means the second.

- *There is an immediate visible difference between **whale hunting** and **whale watching businesses**: **the former** use an expensive fleet of specialized factory ships, and **the latter** carry out their trade in small- to medium-sized vessels that are away from shore for only a few hours.*

**2 *Respectively***

*Respectively* means 'in the order in which I mentioned them'.

- *Michael Sims and Joanna Stevens, the owner and general manager of Border Wool Mills **respectively**, were both present at the meeting which agreed the final merger with Woolcraft plc. (= Sims is the owner; Stevens is the general manager.)*

**3 *Above*, etc.**

*Above* refers to something immediately before or something anywhere before.

- *In the graph **above**, it can be seen that sales of flats to first-time buyers declined by 20% in the first quarter.*
- *In the part of this essay **above** on endowment mortgages, it was suggested that ...*

*In the preceding section/paragraph, ...* refers the reader to the part of the text immediately before the one being read.

- *In the **preceding section** of this report, we attempted to explain the reasons for economic growth in South Korea; now we will try to predict the extent to which this growth is sustainable.*

*As we have seen, ...* is used for a general reference to what has been written up to that point in an essay, report, article, etc.

- *As we have seen, current planning laws present a number of barriers to new housing developments.*

The phrase *as we saw + in the first part of this essay/ on page 2,* etc. uses the past simple tense because reference is being made to a specific piece of previous text.

- *As we saw in Table 3.2, unemployment has affected young people disproportionately.*

**4 *Below*, etc.**

*Below* refers the reader forwards, to information that comes immediately afterwards or later on in the text.

- *In the example **below** from Branner (2009), we can see two competing aims at work. (You could also say In the **following** example from ...)*
- *All of the statistics **below**, in the final section of the report, are regularly updated on the website of the Office for National Statistics.*

*As we shall see in the next part of/later in,* etc. *this essay, ...* can also be used to refer forwards.

### 20.4 test yourself

**Complete each sentence with one of the words or phrases in the box.**

> the former   the latter   respectively
> above   below

**1** We shall see in the section _____ how this result was obtained.

**2** Funding for the new opera house came from the state and from private philanthropy; _____ source represents a major achievement by Barbara Hultz who visited hundreds of individuals in their homes and persuaded them to make donations.

**3** In the introduction to the report _____ we saw how the company was set up. In the following part, its merger with Pastel Inc. will be explored.

**4** Marten plc are now exporting electronic goods to Brazil and America. In _____ case, most of the sales are in Rio de Janeiro.

**5** Tate Britain and Tate Modern, both located in London, were opened to the public in 1897 and 2000 _____.

## 20.5 Ellipsis

### 20.5 study

Ellipsis (leaving words out) works as a cohesive device because readers can supply the missing words from the text they have just read.

Nouns accompanied by adjectives may be left out the second time they are mentioned, particularly where numbers and superlatives are used.

- *There are two reasons for the original growth in cities. The first (reason) was the process of industrialization, where factories required new workers.*
- *A number of psychological experiments were carried out at Yale University in the 1960s. Two of the most interesting (experiments) are explored by Blass (1999), who comments on their representation in film and TV.*

In formal writing, the expression *do so* can be used instead of repeating a verb phrase.

- *Individuals may not take responsibility for recycling waste, but government agencies should **do so**. (do so* = take responsibility)
- *The investigating body made three requests to Vector plc to produce their accounts. When Vector finally **did so**, it became clear that some information was missing. (did so* = produced their accounts)

### 20.5 test yourself

**A** Replace repeated verb phrases in the sentences with a form of *do + so*.

1 If a museum which was previously free decides to charge for admission, it should charge for admission in the knowledge that it is certain to receive a measure of bad publicity.
2 Hewlings Ltd agreed to improve their health and safety standards, but when inspectors arrived at their premises in April 2009, it was apparent that they had not improved their health and safety standards.
3 New traffic schemes will not solve all the problems of congestion, but they can help to solve them.
4 It is often difficult for a homeless person to secure a fixed address, but he or she will be able to apply for a job much more easily by securing a fixed address.

**B** Identify where the writer has avoided repeating a noun by leaving it out.

1 At the time, a government minister congratulated Unitech on the projects it had established. The most successful had succeeded in obtaining jobs for hundreds of unemployed people.
2 The first two trains of the day completed their journeys without incident, but the third was forced to stop outside London, when it was discovered that the theft of copper cables was causing signalling failures.
3 There have been many campaigns aimed at encouraging the public to eat more healthily. Some of the latest involved memorable catchphrases such as 'your five a day', a reference to the number of portions of fruit or vegetables people are recommended to eat.
4 With Tony Blair as their leader, the Labour Party, according to Garfield (2007), entered their third general election with a surprising lack of confidence, given their success in the previous two.

# 20 Challenge yourself

**A** Complete the text about British supermarkets, using the words and phrases in the box. Three of the words and phrases are not needed.

> another  respectively  between them  both  its  one  the one
> some  this remark

Overseas visitors are often astonished by a few particular aspects of British supermarkets. [1]_____ is the market penetration of the main brands. The four leading chains [2]_____ take over 80% of the money spent in the UK on groceries; [3]_____ currently at the top of the pile, Tesco, takes over 10 pence of every consumer pound. [4]_____ is the amount of packaged and prepared food sold in supermarkets. The refrigerated section of the supermarket is often [5]_____ single biggest area. A third aspect is the relative cheapness of food. [6]_____ may provoke some controversy, given the current spikes in food commodity prices.

**B** Complete the introduction to an essay about home-grown fruit and vegetables.

**AWL GLOSSARY**

**analysis** a detailed study or examination of something in order to understand more about it

**attach** to connect something with something

**guarantee** to make something certain to happen

**briefly** in few words

The activity of growing one's own produce is enjoying a resurgence in popularity in cities throughout the industrialized world. The effects of [1]___ trend have yet to be fully studied. This essay will begin [2]___ an analysis from an economic point of view. Firstly, I will define the phenomenon, distinguishing between [3]___ two most prominent aspects, namely allotments and edible landscaping. The [4]___ are associated in the UK with individually held plots, whereas in the United States [5]___ often take the form of community gardens, and [6]___ divergence will be examined, since [7]___ has significant implications for the economies of the households and neighbourhoods where [8]___ allotments are situated. [9]___ leads into a discussion of the history of urban gardening, and the financial and economic importance attached to [10]___ activity when [11]___ was the main method of guaranteeing purity and continuity of supply at an affordable cost. [12]___ days are past, as [13]___ factors are no longer relevant for most of the population, so the question now is, why the resurgence? What needs does [14]___ activity fulfil? As mentioned [15]___ , this essay will concentrate on [16]___ economic factors, but other motivators will be mentioned briefly.

**C** Put the sentences in the correct order to make a cohesive paragraph about protest groups.

**a** This is not a label that many of these groups use themselves.
**b** They are often categorized under the heading of anti-capitalism or anti-globalization.
**c** In the past few years, many protest movements around the world have converged, partly assisted by internet-based technologies which allow easy communication.
**d** Some, in fact, disavow it.

**D** Put the sentences in the correct order to make a cohesive paragraph about data storage. List the words and phrases used to create cohesion in the text.

**a** DropBox and its competitors allow digital files to be stored online.

**b** These are items of hardware or storage media, respectively, that individuals or organizations own and maintain themselves.

**c** Another feature of this method of storage is its 'chat' feature, which enables those working on a file simultaneously to type to each other via a sidebar.

**d** This method of storage has distinct advantages over storing items in folders on hard drives or discs.

**e** When it comes to electronic storage, one can store data in different ways.

**f** One can save files on an internal or external hard drive, or on a portable storage device (CD, USB stick, etc.).

**g** However, there is another method: in the cloud.

**h** Its usefulness lies in individuals being able to access and edit files from any location with internet access.

**AWL GLOSSARY**

**item** a single article or object

**via** by means of a particular person, system, etc.

**distinct** used to emphasize that you think an idea or situation definitely exists and is important

**E** In this overview of one researcher's career, which would precede some extracts from her writing, add the missing words of cohesion.

Personal financial management (PFM) was a long-term interest of Korliovski. She made major contributions to the field; here we will look at three of [1]_____. First of all, [2]_____ made early contributions to the understanding of the psychology of PFM. A second strand of [3]_____ work was education, particularly getting the main concepts of PFM into the secondary school curriculum. The third aspect, a logical extension of the two [4]_____, focused on policy changes. [5]_____ three key aspects of Korlovski's work overlapped throughout her life. The [6]_____ extracts have been chosen to show [7]_____ range of her contributions in [8]_____ areas.

**AWL GLOSSARY**

**logical** seeming natural, reasonable or sensible

**overlap** if two events overlap or overlap each other, the second one starts before the first one has finished

**extract** a short passage from a book, piece of music, etc. that gives you an idea of what the whole thing is like

**F** Rewrite the underlined phrases, using some of the cohesive devices in unit 20, to complete the text about the education system in Quebec.

The education system in Canada reflects [1]Canada's history by containing elements borrowed from the United Kingdom, France, and the United States. Canadian schools, for example, seek to ensure that all pupils possess at least a minimum oral and written competency in both French and English. In Quebec, [2]ensuring that pupils can speak and write in English and French is achieved by mandating lessons in [3]English and French in elementary and high school, [4]elementary school lasting six years and high school lasting five years.

After high school, the vast majority of young Quebecois students progress to a general and vocational college called a CEGEP. In [5]progressing to a CEGEP, [6]young Quebecois students follow a path which is different from [7]the path taken by their British equivalents, because students who are preparing for university and [8]students who wish to enter the job market as eighteen-year-olds are all taught in the same building. [9]A system where students are all taught together may, according to educational theorists, have the advantage of promoting the integration of different social classes.

**AWL GLOSSARY**

**majority** the largest part of a group of people or things

**theorist** a person who develops ideas and principles about a particular subject in order to explain why things happen or exist

**integration** the act or process of mixing people who have previously been separated, usually because of colour, race, religion, etc.

**G** Write 150–250 words about a famous person. Use as many of the cohesive devices covered in unit 20 as possible.

# PUNCTUATION

## Apostrophes
- with 's' is used to show possession after singular nouns, and after plural nouns that do not end in 's'.
  *Picasso's paintings, London's new Mayor, Keynes's economic theories, people's rights*
- without 's' is used after plural nouns that end in 's'.
  *Teenagers' problems, ships' navigation systems*
- is used in contracted forms.
  *It's difficult (= it is), who's won? (= who has), you mustn't enter (= must not)*
- is <u>not</u> used for decades, plural numbers or plural abbreviations.
  *in the 1920s, people retiring in their 50s, DVDs*
- is <u>not</u> used for the possessive form of *it*.
  *When Dalco plc was set up, its ambitions were modest.*

## Brackets
- are used around sources of information and cross-references.
  *Some emotional responses appear to be innate (Eibesfeldt, 2004).*
  *Most of the results show a marked improvement in performance (see Appendix 1).*
- are used when giving additional but not essential information.
  *The term 'Barbary' (derived from the Berber people) was used to describe the North African coastal states of Morocco, Algeria, Tunisia, and Libya.*

## Capital letters
- are used for the names of people and titles; places, days, months, and festivals; organizations, brands, laws and treaties; nationalities and languages.
  *after Professor Blake had spoken; Wales, Saturday, February, the New Year; the University of Warwick, Sony, the Maastricht Treaty; a Brazilian city, a Portuguese speaker*
- are used for the first and main words in the titles of books, films, etc.
  *A Short History of the English People; Travels with a Donkey*
- are used for job and course titles, but <u>not</u> for types of jobs or subjects of study.
  *Emily Wong was appointed Chief Accountant at Hills plc; students training to be accountants; a BSc in Computer Science; fewer students are studying physics*
- are <u>not</u> used for seasons or for north, south, etc. unless they are part of a place name.
  *in winter; to the east of the mountains; East Java*
- are <u>not</u> used for ordinary nouns such as *society, poetry,* or *childhood.*

## Colons
- are used to introduce lists and direct quotations, and to give explanations.
  *Three cities were suggested to the organising committee: Bristol, Leeds and Manchester.*
  *As Greer (2009) points out: 'There is insufficient data to support a change in policy'.*
  *Rothko's bid ultimately failed: most board members felt that it lacked long-term potential.*

## Commas
- have many uses, some of which are optional. Key information is given below.
- are used in clauses with participles, and with non-defining relative clauses.
  *Stevenson plc lost the contract, leading to a sharp downturn in their business.*
  *Sebastian Coe, who won four Olympic medals, was appointed chairman of the London Organizing Committee for the Olympic Games.*
- are used after clauses beginning with connectors such as *when, although* and *if.*
  *Although the fire caused no fatalities, the damage to the factory was extensive.*
- are used with connectors such as *consequently, however, therefore* and *moreover.*
  *There are, however, several reasons to doubt that the latest experiment will be a success.*
  *Moreover, the continuing storms prevented relief workers from rescuing the villagers.*
- are used to separate items in a list.
  *The play completed a very successful tour of Hungary, Bulgaria(,) and Romania.*
- are used, like colons, to introduce quotations.
  *As Foll (2010) states, 'The competence of the Competition Commission was questioned by MPs'.*
- are used with the words and phrases *of course, for example* and *namely.*
  *There were, for example, two sightings of the bird in 2011 in the Scottish Highlands.*
- are used when giving additional useful information (in a similar way to brackets).
  *The journalist who investigated the incident, Mike Sams, was nominated for a Pulitzer Prize.*
  *The oil tanker ran aground on Taransay, an island in the Hebrides.*

## Dashes

- are not common in academic English, but may sometimes be used instead of commas or brackets to give additional information.
  *Hideo Suzuki – one of Japan's leading entrepreneurs – was Senco's main financial backer.*

## Full stops

- Apart from indicating the end of a sentence, full stops are usually used in Latin abbreviations such as *a.m., p.m., e.g.* and *i.e.*
- A series of three full stops (called an ellipsis) shows that some words are missing from a quotation.
  *Dixon (2012) points out that 'there is a tendency ... for price and quantity to change.'*
- Full stops are <u>not</u> used in abbreviations such as *BBC, NATO* or *USA*, or for titles such as *Dr, Mr* or *Ms.*

## Hyphens

- are used in compound adjectives, particularly when they come before nouns.
  *peace-keeping forces, high-tech designs, a sugar-free diet, an Anglo-American agreement*
- are used after some prefixes, such as *anti-, co-, counter-, e-, ex-,* and *self-.*
  *anti-aircraft guns, co-author, counter-productive, e-commerce, ex-employee, self-conscious*
- are normally used in expressions relating to ages and dates.
  *a 25-year-old woman, a 300-year-old bridge, pre-1800, post-war prime ministers*

## Inverted commas (quotation marks)

- Inverted commas, single (') or double ("), are used at the beginning and ending of quotations from other writers.
  *As Higson (2001) states, 'The risk of injury can be reduced by the use of a safety harness'.*
- Note that the writer's words may contain another quotation; in this case, double inverted commas are used for the secondary quotation (or single commas, if double commas were used for the main quotation).
  *Norman points out that 'few people nowadays accept that Fry's "situational dialogues" can be the basis for a language learning syllabus'.*
- Inverted commas are used to highlight or separate out a specific word or phrase.
  *The term 'passive resistance' is sometimes open to misinterpretation.*
- Inverted commas are used for the titles of articles, book chapters, reports etc.
  *Barbara Castle's paper 'In Place of Strife' was an early proposal to restrict the power of trades unions.*

## Semi-colons

- are used to separate two sentences which are very closely linked in meaning. Note that the semi-colon in the example below could be replaced by a full stop (but not by a comma).
  *Most food industry workers have no form of health insurance; as a result, more than half, according to Samson (2008), continue to work when they are sick.*
- are used to separate grammatically complex items in a list, where a comma would not be as clear.
  *For an expedition of this type, a number of pieces of equipment are required, including a high-performance satellite phone; specialist food rations that will last at least a week; emergency signalling devices; and a hospital-standard first aid pack.*

# GLOSSARY OF GRAMMATICAL TERMS

**active voice** a verb form that describes what the subject of a sentence does: *Jane Austen **wrote** 'Pride and Prejudice'*. The **passive voice** uses the past participle + *be* to describe what happens to the subject: *'Pride and Prejudice' **was written** by Jane Austen.*

**adjective** a word that modifies or describes a noun: *a **recent** article; this issue is **complex**.*

**adverb** a word or phrase that modifies verbs, adjectives, other adverbs, and sometimes sentences: *write **quickly**; **extremely** hot; run **very fast**; **in fact**, most experts agree that there is a third possibility.*

**agent** in passive sentences, the agent is the person or thing that the action is done by: *The building was destroyed by **fire*** (fire = the agent).

**article** *a/an* are the indefinite articles. *The* is the definite article.

**auxiliary verb** a verb (*be*, *do* or *have*) that combines with the main verb in tenses and questions: ***Have** you finished?* **Modal verbs** also act as auxiliary verbs: *The plan **could** fail.*

**clause** a group of words that contain a subject and a verb. Longer sentences may have two or more clauses, sometimes linked with connectors such as *because*. A **subordinate clause** is a clause that depends on a main clause for its meaning: *The company was forced to close, **despite winning several new contracts in its last year of business.***

**cohesion** the way in which parts of a text refer to other parts of a text, sometimes by using words like *they*, *this* or *some*.

**collocation** the way in which some words work naturally together: *latest figures; highly skilled; computer age.*

**comparative form** a form of an adjective or an adverb with *–er* or *more* used to make a comparison: *longer, more effective*. The **superlative form** is made with *–est* or *most*: *longest, most effective.*

**compound adjective** an adjective formed from two words: *a **right-wing** politician; a **cutting-edge** design.*

**conditional sentence** a sentence with two clauses, often linked with the word *if*, in which one clause describes a condition and the other a result: *The town will flood* (result) *if the water level rises any higher* (condition).

**connector** (also known as **conjunction**, **connective** or **linking/connecting word**) a word or phrase such as *because*, *in spite of* or *however* that links ideas or sentences.

**contracted form** or **contraction** a short form such as *I'll*, *we've* or *couldn't*.

**countable noun** a noun with a plural form such as *car/ cars*. **Uncountable nouns** have no plural forms, e.g. *advice, music, information.*

**demonstrative pronoun** *this, that, these* or *those*.

**determiner** a word normally used before a noun, or adjective + noun, which forms a noun phrase: *the, this, some, each, his.*

**ellipsis** leaving words out instead of repeating them: *There are a number of mountains in the Lake District; the highest (mountain) is Scafell Pike.*

**gerund** an *-ing* form of a verb used as a noun: *Not all managers are good at **delegating**.*

**gradable** the words *easy* and *small* are gradable because you can say *fairly easy* or *very small*. Words such as *perfect* or *female* are normally **ungradable**.

**infinitive** the basic form of a verb: *(to) write, (to) study, (to) understand.*

**intransitive verb** (see **transitive verb**)

**inversion** a structure where a verb or part of a verb comes before its subject. Inversion occurs, for example, in questions and emphatic patterns: ***Is it** correct? Rarely **do they** agree.*

**modal verb** a verb (*can, could, may, might, must, shall, should, will*, or *would*) which modifies the meaning of a main verb. **Semi-modal verbs** are *ought to, need, have to, have got to, had better, be supposed to, be going to*, and *used to*.

**modifier** a word or phrase which strengthens or weakens another word, such as ***a great deal** (harder)* or ***almost** (complete)*.

**nominalization** the process of forming nouns or noun phrases from other types of words and phrases: *very carefully → with great care. People soon began to lose faith in the government. → **Disillusionment** with the government soon set in.*

**noun** a word for a person or a thing: *mother, president, bird, table, London, beauty, chemistry.*

**noun clause** a subordinate clause that acts like noun: *The announcement that the factory was about to close came as a surprise to most of the workers.*

**noun phrase** a phrase based around a noun: *an interesting argument*; *research into alcoholism*; *back pain*.

**object** (see subject)

**preparatory subject** (also known as **empty subject**) the words *it* or *there* when used at the beginning of a sentence when there is no clear subject: *It is often suggested that entrepreneurship skills are acquired early in life.*

**participle** a verbal form: *working, taking* (present participles); *worked, taken* (past participles); *having worked, having taken* (perfect participles); *Finding the winters too cold* (participle clause), *Keats left England for Italy.*

**passive voice** (see active voice)

**phrasal and prepositional verbs** verbs that combine with a 'particle' (adverb or preposition): *look up, check into.* Phrasal verbs can separate from their particles, e.g. *look a word up.* Prepositional verbs cannot, e.g. *check into a hotel.*

**pronoun** a word that replaces a noun or noun phrase: *she, it, them* etc.

**quantifier** a **determiner** that describes the amount of something: *some, enough, all* etc.

**reflexive pronoun** *myself, yourself* etc.

**relative clause** a clause that normally starts with a **relative pronoun**, giving extra information about a **noun** or **noun phrase.** Relative clauses can be 'defining' (*the problem that researchers encountered*) or 'non-defining' (*Aluminium, which is a relatively soft metal, has an atomic number of 13.*).

**relative pronoun** the words *who, which, that, whose* and *whom* when they introduce a **relative clause.** The words *where, when, why* and *what* can also act as relative pronouns.

**semi-modal verb** (see modal verb)

**state verb** (also known as **stative verb**) a verb that describes a state or situation rather than an action, e.g. *believe, like, own, contain.* State verbs are not normally used in continuous verb forms.

**subject** a **noun, noun phrase** or **pronoun** that normally comes before the verb, and describes who or what performs the action. The **object** is a **noun, noun phrase** or **pronoun** that normally follows the verb, and is affected by the action: *The flood* (subject) *destroyed the bridge* (object).

**subordinate clause** (see clause)

**superlative form** (see comparative form)

**tense** the form of the verb that indicates the time of an action or situation. English has a present tense, e.g. *she works* and a past tense, e.g. *she worked*, but expresses future time in a variety of ways, such as by using modal verbs, e.g. *she will work.*

**transitive verb** a verb that normally takes an object, e.g. *they found a solution.* An **intransitive verb** does not take an object, e.g. they *arrived.* Some verbs can be used transitively and intransitively, e.g. *she ran the company* for six years (transitive use); *they had to run* from the fire (intransitive use).

**uncountable noun** (see countable noun)

**ungradable** (see gradable)

**verb** a word such as *go, walk* or *show* that normally follows the **subject** of a **clause**, and usually describes an action, event or situation. (See also **auxiliary verb, modal verb** and **transitive verb.**)

**word family** a group of words with a common base, e.g. *predict* (verb), *prediction* (noun), *predictable* (adjective).

# ACADEMIC WORD LIST (HEADWORDS)

*These are the headwords included in the Academic Word List. For more information on word families and frequency see www.victoria.ac.nz/lals/resources/academicwordlist.*

| | | | |
|---|---|---|---|
| abandon | assure | compile | corporate |
| abstract | attach | complement | correspond |
| academy | attain | complex | couple |
| access | attitude | component | create |
| accommodate | attribute | compound | credit |
| accompany | author | comprehensive | criteria |
| accumulate | authority | comprise | crucial |
| accurate | automate | compute | culture |
| achieve | available | conceive | currency |
| acknowledge | aware | concentrate | cycle |
| acquire | behalf | concept | data |
| adapt | benefit | conclude | debate |
| adequate | bias | concurrent | decade |
| adjacent | bond | conduct | decline |
| adjust | brief | confer | deduce |
| administrate | bulk | confine | define |
| adult | capable | confirm | definite |
| advocate | capacity | conflict | demonstrate |
| affect | category | conform | denote |
| aggregate | cease | consent | deny |
| aid | challenge | consequent | depress |
| albeit | channel | considerable | derive |
| allocate | chapter | consist | design |
| alter | chart | constant | despite |
| alternative | chemical | constitute | detect |
| ambiguous | circumstance | constrain | deviate |
| amend | cite | construct | device |
| analogy | civil | consult | devote |
| analyse | clarify | consume | differentiate |
| annual | classic | contact | dimension |
| anticipate | clause | contemporary | diminish |
| apparent | code | context | discrete |
| append | coherent | contract | discriminate |
| appreciate | coincide | contradict | displace |
| approach | collapse | contrary | display |
| appropriate | colleague | contrast | dispose |
| approximate | commence | contribute | distinct |
| arbitrary | comment | controversy | distort |
| area | commission | convene | distribute |
| aspect | commit | converse | diverse |
| assemble | commodity | convert | document |
| assess | communicate | convince | domain |
| assign | community | cooperate | domestic |
| assist | compatible | coordinate | dominate |
| assume | compensate | core | draft |

184

drama
duration
dynamic
economy
edit
element
eliminate
emerge
emphasis
empirical
enable
encounter
energy
enforce
enhance
enormous
ensure
entity
environment
equate
equip
equivalent
erode
error
establish
estate
estimate
ethic
ethnic
evaluate
eventual
evident
evolve
exceed
exclude
exhibit
expand
expert
explicit
exploit
export
expose
external
extract
facilitate
factor
feature
federal
fee
file

finance
finite
flexible
fluctuate
focus
format
formula
forthcoming
foundation
found
framework
function
fund
fundamental
furthermore
gender
generate
generation
globe
goal
grade
grant
guarantee
guideline
hence
hierarchy
highlight
hypothesis
identical
identify
ideology
ignorance
illustrate
image
immigrate
impact
implement
implicate
implicit
imply
impose
incentive
incidence
incline
income
incorporate
index
indicate
individual
induce
inevitable

infer
infrastructure
inherent
inhibit
initial
initiate
injure
innovate
input
insert
insight
inspect
instance
institute
instruct
integral
integrate
integrity
intelligence
intense
interact
intermediate
internal
interpret
interval
intervene
intrinsic
invest
investigate
invoke
involve
isolate
issue
item
job
journal
justify
label
labour
layer
lecture
legal
legislate
levy
liberal
licence
likewise
link
locate
logic
maintain

major
manipulate
manual
margin
mature
maximise
mechanism
media
mediate
medical
mental
method
migrate
military
minimise
minimum
ministry
minor
mode
modify
monitor
motive
mutual
negate
network
neutral
nevertheless
nonetheless
norm
normal
notion
notwithstanding
nuclear
objective
obtain
obvious
occupy
occur
odd
offset
ongoing
option
orient
outcome
overall
overlap
overseas
panel

paradigm
paragraph
parallel
parameter
participate
partner
passive
perceive
percent
period
persist
perspective
phase
phenomenon
philosophy
physical
plus
policy
portion
pose
positive
potential
practitioner
precede
precise
predict
predominant
preliminary
presume
previous
primary
prime
principal
principle
prior
priority
proceed
process
professional
prohibit
project
promote
proportion
prospect
protocol
psychology
publication
publish
purchase
pursue
qualitative

quote
radical
random
range
ratio
rational
react
recover
refine
regime
region
register
regulate
reinforce
reject
relax
release
relevant
reluctance
rely
remove
require
research
reside
resolve
resource
respond
restore
restrain
restrict
retain
reveal
revenue
reverse
revise
revolution
rigid
role
route
scenario
schedule
scheme
scope
section
sector
secure
seek
select
sequence
series
sex

shift
significant
similar
simulate
site
so-called
sole
somewhat
source
specific
specify
sphere
stable
statistic
status
straightforward
strategy
stress
structure
style
submit
subordinate
subsequent
subsidy
substitute
successor
sufficient
sum
summary
supplement
survey
survive
suspend
sustain
symbol
tape
target
task
team
technical
technique
technology
temporary
tense
terminate
text
theme
theory
thereby
thesis
topic

trace
tradition
transfer
transform
transit
transmit
transport
trend
trigger
ultimate
undergo
underlie
undertake
uniform
unify
unique
utilise
valid
vary
vehicle
version
via
violate
virtual
visible
vision
visual
volume
voluntary
welfare
whereas
whereby
widespread

# Answer Key

## 01 Tense review

**Suggested answers (page 006)**

1    present perfect: to describe an activity that started in the past and has continued up until the present

2, 3, 4  past simple: to describe finished past actions or events

5    past perfect: to describe a past event that happened earlier than the one just mentioned

6, 7  present simple: to describe regular activities that still happen

### test yourself

**1.1**

1  is looking for
2  place
3  operates
4  are establishing
5  notes
6  watches
7  recognize
8  is working
9  prefer
10  are changing

**1.2**

1  struck, were sleeping
2  asked
3  would (*or* used to)
4  launched
5  were investing
6  was making, destroyed

**1.3**

1  have discovered, was made
2  have been building
3  emigrated, wrote, has just been filmed
4  has had, started
5  has demonstrated
6  have moved, have arrived

**1.4**

1  had just left
2  had expected
3  had participated
4  had been leaking
5  had signed
6  had announced

**1.5**

1  is going to double
2  will be
3  was to prove (*or* would prove to be)
4  will be driving
5  will
6  will take *or* takes
7  were about to
8  is opening (*or* will open)

### Challenge yourself

**A**

1  has grown (1.3)
2  is (1.1)
   (*or* has been) (1.3)
3  began (1.2)
4  gained (1.2)
5  became (1.2)
6  fought (1.2)
7  won (1.2)
8  had changed (1.4)
   (*or* changed) (1.2)

**B**

1  c (1.2)
2  d (1.2)
3  a (1.2)
4  e (1.1)
5  b (1.2)

**C**

1  b (1.2)
2  c (1.1)
3  a (1.2)
4  b (1.2)
5  d (1.4)
6  a (1.4)
7  b (1.2)

**D**

1  poses (*or* is posing) (1.1)
2  used to serve (1.2)
3  is (1.1)
4  take (1.1)
5  is needed (1.1)
6  are contributing (1.1) (*or* have contributed) (1.3)

**E**

1  which seeks to develop (1.1) (*or* which sought to develop) (1.2)
2  it transformed construction (1.2)
3  The pyramids of Egypt were built (1.2)
4  A corollary of this argument is that (1.1) (*or* a corollary of this argument would be that) (1.5)
5  it is certain to migrate to another (1.1) (*or* will be certain) (1.5)
6  Technology, on the other hand, has encountered (1.3)
7  these innovations have already been invented. (1.3)
8  incremental improvements will be the path of the future. (1.5) (*or* incremental improvements are the path of the future) (1.1)
9  we are not capable (1.1)
10  Before the wheelbarrow existed (1.2)
11  The second argument points to (1.1)
12  our future inventors may be working at (1.5)

**F**

1  has been (1.3)
2  to be (1.1)
3  have lived (*or* have been living) (1.3)
4  endured (1.2)
5  changed (1.2)
6  had become (1.4)
7  had developed (1.4)

**G**

1  is (1.1)
2  share (1.1)
3  shared (1.2)
4  have (1.1)
5  look (1.1)
6  suffer (1.1)
7  is caused (1.1)
8  enables (1.1)
9  lies (1.1)
10  will be (1.5)
11  is (1.1)
12  is (1.1)
13  evolves (1.1)
14  is (1.1)

**H** Sample answer

Oxford is well known for being a university city. Although it is a small city, the population increases during university terms and during the summer, because it is a popular tourist destination.

The university was first established in the twelfth century but has grown over the years as new colleges have been added. For example, Nuffield College was founded in 1937 by Lord Nuffield, a local businessman who made his wealth from car manufacturing. There is still a car factory in Oxford which makes the Mini. However, the city is most famous for its 'dreaming spires' and academic traditions, and the university will continue to be at the heart of the city for years to come.

## 02 Comparing and contrasting

Suggested answers (page 016)
more, than, While, freshest, as, as, biggest, unlike, in common, differ from

| the freshest items | (sales of) prepared meals |
|---|---|
| to cook from a recipe | to place a cook-chill meal in the microwave |
| ready-to-cook section | other sections/areas of the supermarket |
| two countries (where home cooking seems to have retained its appeal) | the UK |

### test yourself

**2.1 A**
1 hotter, hottest
2 more complex, most complex
3 further (or farther), furthest (or farthest)
4 more helpful, most helpful
5 simpler, simplest
6 more optimistic, most optimistic
7 luckier, luckiest

**2.1 B**
1 later, latest
2 worse, worst
3 more realistically, most realistically
4 better, best

**2.2**
1 The water in Tank B is not as cloudy as the water in Tank A.
2 Howton argues that basic products are not as cheap in towns as in big cities.
3 Changes in micro-climates frequently occur too quickly (for anyone) to predict.
4 Excel plc did not return a profit last year because they did not export enough of their helicopters.
5 French is as difficult to learn as English.
(or English is as difficult to learn as French.)

6 Some of the roads in this region are too dangerous (for you or anyone) to travel on.
7 It was not as complex a formula as most mathematicians had expected.
8 Campbell's *Bluebird* was fast enough to break the water speed record several times.

**2.3**
1 Critics have complained that school exams are less difficult than they used to be.
2 The closer an institution gets to a financial crisis, the more it feels the pain. (*or* ... the more pain it feels.)
3 Campaigners hoping for change within the country have become more and more pessimistic.
4 The Swiss wind turbines have worked less efficiently than the Italian ones.
5 The heavier the particles are, the easier they become to observe.
6 Introverts absorb information less quickly than extroverts, according to research.

**2.4 A**
1 the easiest of the many routes
2 the furthest city on the planet
3 the best film of the decade
4 (the) most efficiently
5 the most socially responsible companies in Canada
6 the least effective of all leadership styles
7 the most carefully planned expedition
8 the highest climbing snakes in North America

**2.4 B**
1 oldest
2 lightest
3 least
4 Japan
5 least, populated, on
6 the, most, of
7 the wettest, in
8 the second most, on

**2.5**
1 22%
2 considerably
3 almost
4 not nearly
5 just
6 one of
7 twice
8 approximately

**2.6**
1 similar
2 that
3 like
4 as
5 similarities
6 similarly
7 same
8 in

**2.7**
Sentences 1, 4, 7 and 8 are correct.
2 ... differs **from** the humid interior ...
3 **On the contrary**, he argues, ...
5 A significant political difference **between** the USA and the UK ...
6 **in contrast** *or* **on the other hand**, others argue for ...

## Challenge yourself

**A**

1 the most up-to-date (2.4)
2 higher (2.1)
3 faster (2.1)
4 more integrated (2.1)
5 more profitable (2.1)
6 happier (2.1)
7 more comfortable (2.1)
8 less problematic (2.1)
9 the lowest (2.4)
10 the best (2.4)

**B**

Sentences 3, 5, 7, and 10 are correct.
1 the greatest show on earth (2.4)
2 in the world (2.4)
4 than athletes (2.3)
6 differ from (2.7)
8 on the other hand (2.7), as high profile (2.2)
9 easy enough (2.2)

**C**

1 its worst (2.1)
2 by far the longest (2.5)
3 More and more (2.3)
4 oldest (2.1)
5 highest (2.1)
6 stronger (2.1)
7 the strongest (2.4)
8 In contrast to (2.7)
9 Like (2.6)
10 The highest (2.4)
11 unlike (2.7)
12 almost twice as heavy (2.5)
13 nearest (2.1)
14 three times heavier (2.5)
15 The best (2.4)
16 fast as (2.2)
17 the sooner, the better (2.3)

**D**

1 one of (2.4)
2 easily, by far (2.5)
3 Likewise, Similarly (2.6)
4 many (2.5)
5 controversial enough (2.2)
6 a product as before, a product as it was (2.2)
7 On the contrary (2.7)
8 most (2.4)
9 dissimilar (2.7)
10 from (2.7)

**E**

1 easier (2.5)
2 older (2.3)
3 more (2.3)
4 unlike (2.7)
5 exactly (2.6)
6 much (2.5)
7 quickly (2.5)
8 younger (2.3)
9 quite (2.7)
10 from (2.7)
11 better (2.3)
12 nearly (2.5)
13 before (2.5)
14 more (2.3)
15 more (2.3)
16 longer (2.3)
17 easily (2.5)
18 best (2.4)

**F**

1 in common with many (2.6)
2 similar to other (2.6)
3 the same as hundreds (2.6)
4 The most noticeable (2.4)
5 to the most junior (2.4)
6 more efficient than it was (2.3)
7 use less space (2.3) (*or* to use space better) (2.1)
8 work more effectively (2.1)
9 in contrast to the (*or* in contrast with) (2.7)
10 of the biggest (2.4)

**G**

1 have much in common (2.6)
2 there are obvious similarities between (2.6)
3 there is one significant difference (2.7)
4 London is the UK's most populous city (2.1)
5 although the situation is not exactly alike (2.6)
6 a striking similarity in (2.6)

**H**

1 is strong enough to draw in (2.2)
2 it could have been realized more successfully (2.1)
3 was too cautious to do justice to its theme (*or* was too cautious and did not do justice to its theme) (2.2)
4 technology at the time of the source film was not as advanced as it is today (*or* technology was not as advanced at the time of the source film as it is today) (2.3)
5 the new version is similar to the original film (2.6)

**I** Sample answers

1 It is normally cheaper to study in a local college, particularly if it is located in a student's home town. Capital cities tend to be the most expensive places in the country. On the other hand, the right type of education is an investment in one's future, and it may therefore be worthwhile taking out a loan to fund the additional expenses that studying in the capital would incur.

Another important consideration is the length of time the degree would take. Sometimes local colleges make it easier to study part-time, so although it would take longer, a student studying locally might be able to work at the same time as completing the qualification. A university in the capital city may not be as flexible.

The most important thing, however, is the qualification itself. There is no doubt that the best paid jobs go to graduates from the most prestigious institutions. Unless the local college can indicate that its degree will carry the same weight as the one offered in the capital city, this might be the deciding factor.

2 A tourist researching a short cycling holiday in England needs to consider several factors. Norfolk is the flattest county, so it is ideal for beginners, in contrast to Yorkshire, which is hilly enough to satisfy the more experienced. The weather is also important. Some foreign visitors hold the view that the English climate is always cold and wet. On the contrary, nothing could be further from the truth: in summertime, Norfolk may suffer from drought. Yorkshire tends to be wetter year-round. The tourism market is more developed in Yorkshire, where their bed and breakfast establishments are used to catering to hungry cyclists. The breakfasts tend to be bigger in northern counties.

# 03 Noun phrases

Suggested answers (page 028)

1 The underlined words and phrases modify or change the noun, making its meaning more precise and giving more information about it.

2 *Metaphorical* and *economic* are adjectives; *globalized* is a past participle; *resource* and *production* are nouns.

## test yourself

**3.1**

Sentences 2, 5 and 6 are correct.

1 ... in ~~the~~ a research project ...

3 ~~A~~ Good advice ... (*or* A **piece of** good advice ... *or* **Some** good advice)

4 ... in 1993. ~~A~~ **The** factory ...

7 ... in ~~the~~ hospital ...

8 ... across **the** Thames ...

**3.2**

| | | |
|---|---|---|
| 1 little/no | 4 Both/Each | 7 both |
| 2 enough | 5 some | 8 all |
| 3 Any | 6 either | |

**3.3**

| | |
|---|---|
| 1 and private | 5 -divided |
| 2 -renowned | 6 -distance |
| 3 -fitting | 7 -up |
| 4 and secondary | 8 -boosting |

**3.4**

| | | |
|---|---|---|
| 1 cash | 5 European | 7 Water |
| 2 Law and | Union | 8 arts research |
| 3 Protest | member | |
| 4 market | 6 family | |

**3.5**

| | |
|---|---|
| 1 on (*or the less formal* about) | 5 for |
| | 6 to/towards |
| 2 to | 7 of |
| 3 into | 8 in |
| 4 of | |

**3.6**

| | |
|---|---|
| 1 proposition | 4 view |
| 2 rule | 5 news |
| 3 conclusion | 6 assumption |

## Challenge yourself

**A**

| | |
|---|---|
| 1 child (3.4) | 6 recent (3.3) |
| 2 long-term (3.3) | 7 three-year (3.3) |
| 3 humanitarian (3.3) | 8 demobilized (3.3) |
| 4 government (3.4) | 9 vocational (3.3) |
| 5 completion (3.4) | 10 financial (3.3) |

**B**

| | | |
|---|---|---|
| 1 b (3.6) | 3 f (3.6) | 5 c (3.6) |
| 2 e (3.6) | 4 a (3.6) | 6 d (3.6) |

**C**

| | |
|---|---|
| 1 any well-run (3.2) | 6 well-maintained (3.3) |
| 2 obvious (3.3) | 7 virtually (3.3) |
| 3 Paper (3.4) | 8 very little (3.2) |
| 4 comprehensive (3.3) | 9 storage (3.4) |
| 5 considerable (3.3) | 10 of obsolescence (3.5) |

**D**

1 regional arts funding (3.3, 3.4), government grants (3.4)

2 summer riots (3.4)

3 long-held beliefs (3.3)

4 Press freedom (3.4)

5 recently-broadcast documentary (3.3), care home residents (3.4)

6 Bribery allegations (3.4), oil-trading companies (3.3)

7 fuel tankers (3.4), fire safety test (3.4)

8 Broken-down trucks (3.3)

9 Plastic products (3.4)

10 life-expectancy statistics (3.4)

**E**

1 f the collapse of the housing market (3.4, 3.5)

2 a the piercing of the banking bubble (3.4, 3.5)

*The answers to 1 and 2 are interchangeable.*

3 g Some of these failing banks (3.2, 3.3)

4 e This use of public funds (3.3, 3.5)

5 b a higher level of public scrutiny (3.1, 3.3, 3.5)

6 c which were much higher than the average (3.3, 3.4)

7 d Protests at all levels of society (3.2, 3.5)

**F** Sample answer

The founder of Apple, Steve Jobs, was one of the most influential entrepreneurs of recent history. As long ago as 1990, he recognized **the importance of** the personal computer as the communication device of the future. He was a very talented engineer, of course, but more than that, he attracted to himself and to his **ground-breaking** company some of the world's most talented **hardware and software engineers**. He was above all a leader: where he went, others followed.

Apple made its name selling **relatively high cost products**, but it maintained **customer satisfaction** by paying attention to the user experience. Jobs was passionate about this. He was at the forefront of three related revolutions: the re-conception of computers (previously perceived as boring business machines) as devices of playfulness and creativity; the integration of digital music – and, later, videos – into everyday life; and smartphones. Unsurprisingly, **demand for** the products that Apple produced grew year on year while Jobs was in control.

## 04 Being formal and informal

Suggested answers (page 038)

The first text might be from a popular magazine, or it could even be the transcript of an introduction to a TV or radio programme. The second sounds as if it is piece of academic writing, perhaps from a student on a human resources course. These are the main differences:

1 The first text uses *you* to address the reader directly. The second has a more impersonal style, using the third person, e.g. *Many young people ...*
2 The first text uses informal language e.g. *guy, gal, a lot of, look (each other) over*, while the second uses more formal vocabulary, such as *embark* (rather than *start*); *assess* (rather than *look over*); *offer a contract of employment* instead of *hire*; and *probationary basis* rather than *trial period*. In the informal first text, the writer also uses contractions (e.g. *you're, they're, it's*) and direct questions, one with a question tag (*isn't it?*), which a formal writer tends to avoid.
3 Much of the second text is based around nouns rather than verbs, which is characteristic of formal English; *the main concern* is used, for example, rather than *You're probably worried ...*, and *makes a decision* instead of *they decide*.
4 The second text takes a more cautious approach, using expressions such as *In most cases* (rather than *of course*) and *usually*.

### test yourself

**4.1**
1 communication
2 preservation, development
3 relevance
4 prediction
5 stability/stabilization, elimination

**4.2**
1 There
2 It
3 It
4 There
5 There
6 It

**4.3**
1 We
2 one is
3 I would
4 We have
5 I understand
6 agree

**4.4**
1 deteriorated
2 occupation
3 administered
4 advisable
5 occasions, negotiations
6 accelerated
7 catalogued
8 unacceptable

**4.5**
1 is little
2 virtually/practically
3 vice versa
4 status quo
5 primarily/principally/ predominantly
6 are no

### Challenge yourself

**A**
1 set out (4.4)
2 to examine (4.4)
3 optimum (4.4)
4 growing conditions (4.1)
5 with regard to (4.4)
6 two separate variables (4.1)
7 namely (4.4)
8 were exposed to (4.4)
9 a strong correlation (4.1)
10 growth rates (4.1)
11 in the range of (4.5)
12 showed less influence on (4.1)
13 no matter what (4.5)
14 the same growth (4.1)

**B** Sample answer

Demonstrating the link between the burning of fossil fuels and the world's increasingly erratic weather patterns is not always straightforward. Expert opinion holds that the former is a primary cause of the latter. The science, however, depends on the accurate measurement and complex analysis of data. Mistakes can be made in the conduct of these studies, and there are scientists who dissent from the majority opinion, despite the mounting evidence.

**C**
1 b (4.1)
2 a
3 b (4.1)
4 c (4.1)
5 c (4.1)
6 a (4.4)
7 c (4.1)
8 b (4.1)

**D**
1 b There ... many interpretations (4.2)
2 a The disproportionate youthfulness (4.1), demographics (4.4)
3 a The confusion (4.1), the conflation (4.1)
4 b Not only ... but also (4.5)

**E** Sample answer

The transportation system of greater London has always balanced private and public initiatives. The movement of millions of commuters from the hinterland into the metropolis, and the related travel between the concentric rings of central, inner and outer London, are worthy of extensive study. Although precise measurement is beyond the scope of this evaluation, it is clear that many of these journeys are by private vehicle: mainly cars, but to a lesser extent motorcycles, scooters, and bicycles; and likewise many are by public systems of transport: notably the Underground, better known as the Tube, the overground trains, and the bus system. (The Thames riverbus, while formally a part of London Transport, forms such a neglible fraction of commuter transit that it can safely be left out of the equation.)

This essay will examine the changing patterns of use of these private and public systems over the past twenty years. There is no doubt, for instance, that the introduction of the congestion charge - a tax on cars and vans entering a specified zone of central London - has had a significant effect on traffic patterns. It remains a question for further study, however, whether the initial decline in vehicle movements has been compensated for in other ways.

## 05 Relative clauses

### Suggested answers (page 046)

a Clause 1 is essential to the meaning of the first part of the sentence; clause 2 contains useful additional information, but the sentence would remain meaningful without it.

b The relative pronouns in clauses 1, 3 and 4 could all be replaced by *that*. The meaning wouldn't change, but in 3 and 4, the use of *that* would make the style slightly less formal.

c *Which* could be left out. Neither the meaning nor the style would change.

### test yourself

**5.1**

1 Some doubts were raised about the quality of the questionnaire which/that the group used in the research.

2 The shoe company which/that made the largest profits was based in Dundee.

3 The folding bicycle which/that/- they designed at their workshop in York is selling very well.

4 Hewitt questioned the experience of the software engineers who/that Wentworth plc recruited.

5 The director who pioneered the tracking shot later wrote a memoir.

6 The region is crossed by two main roads which/that require substantial repairs.

**5.2**

1 In a case of gross misconduct, which includes theft, an employer may fire an employee immediately.

2 Bill Grayson handed his small pharmaceutical business to his daughter, who transformed it into a multinational corporation.

3 Turkey has land borders with eight countries, which has frequently led to a kind of diplomatic balancing act.

4 Vegetable oils, which are traded as commodities, have seen recent volatility in their spot price.

5 Barbara Hepworth, who critics regarded as a key Modernist sculptor, created *Single Form* for the United Nations building in New York.

**5.3**

1 whom
2 whose
3 -
4 of which
5 who (*or* whom)
6 to whom

**5.4 A**

1 in which
2 neither of which
3 with whom
4 at which
5 from whose
6 three of which

**5.4 B**

1 A jury may have to listen to several expert witnesses, some of whom may seem to contradict each other.

2 The oil leak may destroy the local fish stocks on which the coastal villages depend.

3 The newspaper chain was inherited by Forster's daughter, one of whose first actions was to sell two of the titles.

4 Several of the paintings were owned by Massine, with whom Picasso collaborated in a number of projects.

5 The Pianura Padana is the plain in northern Italy through which the river Po flows to the Adriatic sea.

6 The fear is that thousands of local people will begin to move out of the area, in which case refugee camps will need to be established.

**5.5 A**

| | | |
|---|---|---|
| 1 where | 4 what | 7 when |
| 2 why | 5 when | 8 What |
| 3 where/when | 6 where | |

**5.5 B**

| | | |
|---|---|---|
| 1 when | 4 when/where | 7 when |
| 2 why | 5 what | 8 what |
| 3 where | 6 why | |

**5.6**

| | | |
|---|---|---|
| 1 arising | 3 used | 5 consisting |
| 2 given | 4 based | 6 caused |

### Challenge yourself

**A**

| | | |
|---|---|---|
| 1 e (5.2) | 5 i (5.5) | 9 d (5.1) |
| 2 b (5.1) | 6 c (5.1) | 10 f (5.5) |
| 3 j (5.1) | 7 a (5.6) | |
| 4 h (5.4) | 8 g (5.2) | |

**B**

Sentences 6 and 8 are correct.

1  with **which** they (5.4)
2  Britannica, **which** used (5.2)
3  time **when** businesses (5.5)
4  writers, **who** are (5.2)
5  of **which** is (5.4)
7  access, **which** makes (5.2)
9  figure, **who** copy (5.1)
10 topics **which** would (5.1)

**C**

1  ~~which were~~ (5.6)
2  containing (5.6)
3  ~~which are~~ (5.6)
4  ~~that are~~ (5.6)
5  requiring (5.6)
6  ~~which are~~ (5.6)
7  using (5.6)
8  involving (5.6)

**D**

1  Klein writes about adbusters and culture jammers, who add graffiti to billboards or create their own fake advertisements. (5.2)
2  British banks were bailed out by the government, which considered their rescue as the least worst option. (5.2) (*or* British banks, whose rescue was considered as the least worst option, were bailed out by the government.) (5.3)
3  The inquiry reported on the mechanical failures which/that had caused the accident. (5.1)
4  According to a report from Goldman Sachs, the so-called 'next eleven' countries, which have the potential to become the world's largest economies, have now been identified. (5.2)
5  The two factories which/that introduced a flexi-time policy boosted their production. (5.1)
6  The polar bear, which is a vulnerable species, is threatened in its habitat because of global warming and rising sea levels. (5.2)

**E**

1  in which (5.4)
2  in whose (5.4)
3  to whom (5.4)
4  whose (5.3)
5  to which (5.4)
6  from whom (5.4)

**F**  Sample answer

In deciding which career to follow, many students choose to prioritize features such as job security and financial reward, in which case actuarial science, combining both of these, might be a good fit for them. An actuary is a financial professional who assesses risk. The way in which they do so depends very much on the circumstances of the case. For example, before issuing any form of insurance, a broker needs to calculate what the chances are of having to pay out. A ship owner who wants to insure against piracy or a farmer who needs to protect a crop against bad weather both depend on the actuary.

Actuarial skills are useful in many areas, which means that someone who holds them is rarely unemployed. It is also a well-paid profession. However, anyone considering it should bear in mind that the initial training is rigorous and long. Trainee actuaries usually seek employment with large companies which offer to support their professional development. Typically, junior actuaries stay with this firm until they are fully qualified, which may take some years, depending on which specialism they choose.

## 06 Stating facts and opinions

Suggested answers (page 054)

Facts:

1  The number of adoptions in England and Wales has fallen by 4.1% in the past two years.
2  In the same period, the number of couples applying to adopt has risen.
3  The number of UK adoptions from developing countries has risen.

Opinions:

1  The process of adopting in the UK currently presents an unreasonable barrier.
2  Changes in the way that UK adoption agencies operate are overdue.

**test yourself**

**6.1**

1  Fresh, demonstrates/demonstrated
2  issued, statistics
3  evaluated, empirical
4  attacked, flimsy
5  relevant, emerged
6  leaked, vital

**6.2**

1  by 11%
2  of 22%.
3  highest level
4  from the pie chart
5  in births
6  risen rapidly
7  remained constant at
8  tripled between

**6.3**

1  According to Escher, it should be possible
2  Stevens has pointed out that Mexican politics
3  As Nikura maintains, some species of insect
4  Bostock's view is that crime statistics
5  In Metstrom's opinion, corporate lawsuits

**6.4**

1  concerned
2  agree
3  seems
4  may
5  believe
6  indicates

## Challenge yourself

**A**

1 Spot prices for metals remained stable in this period despite the turbulence in the oil and textile markets. (6.2)
2 There was an increase of 14% in the number of visitors at the Sizewell education centre in the period 2007–9. (6.2)
3 It seems plausible that modern medicine will continue to extend human life. (6.4)
4 The sales totals for fine art at the auction house reached a twenty-year peak in 2009. (6.2)
5 House prices fell slightly in Cumbria in the first half of 2012. (6.2)
6 'You may have a point, but I disagree with your order of priority.' (6.4)
7 Payday loan companies reported that demand for their services trebled during the Christmas period in 2012. (6.2)
8 There was a steep rise in the number of complaints to the BBC over offensive language throughout the 1990s. (6.2)

**B**

1 obvious (6.4)
2 collected (*or* collated) (6.1)
3 valuable (6.1)
4 absolutely (6.4)
5 interesting (6.1)
6 examine (6.1)
7 compiling or comparing (6.1)
8 indicates (6.1/6.4)
9 longest (6.2)
10 information (6.1)
11 by (6.2)
12 of (6.2)
13 sharp (6.2)
14 fall (6.2)
15 may/might (6.4)
16 agree (6.4)
17 more (6.2)
18 explain (6.1)
19 what (6.4)
20 absorb (6.1)
21 right (6.4)
22 support (6.1)

**C**

1 Companies that withhold information … (6.1)
2 … does not support the conclusions … (6.1)
3 … argues that there is no hard evidence … (6.1)
4 Timely information … (6.1)
5 .. should produce statistics … (6.1)
6 … revealed some disturbing facts … (6.1)
7 The preliminary data … (6.1)
8 The facts did not emerge … (6.1)
9 There was extensive evidence … (6.1)
10 … did not allow them to retrieve data … (6.1)

**D**

1 observes (6.3)
2 accurate (6.1)
3 gradual (6.2)
4 seen (6.2)
5 gathered (6.1)
6 show (6.1)
7 twice as (6.2)
8 suggests (6.3)
9 opinion is (6.3)

**E**

Graph A: sample answer

The statistics show that the number of one-person households in the UK almost doubled between 1971 and 2001, reaching a final figure of 30% of all households. Between 1971 and 1991, there was a steady increase in the number of such households, but, as can be seen from the graph, the peak was reached in 1991, and the figure then remained stable for the last decade of the thirty-year period. It seems likely that rising divorce rates and the trend for later marriage could explain these figures. Another possible explanation could be an overall increase in the number of older people, some of whom will inevitably have found themselves living alone in the last period of their lives.

Graph B: sample answer

We can see from the graph that there were three times as many households with more than five people resident in 1971 as in 2001. The figure of 9% of UK households with this number of residents dropped gradually to 7% in 1981, and then more steeply to 3% in 1991, where it stabilized until 2001. The evidence suggests that couples in the UK were choosing to have fewer children in this period. The greater availability of means of contraception may have played a part in this trend. It also seems plausible that, as a result of changing UK life and work patterns, more elderly parents were looked after in care homes rather than as part of extended families.

The period from 1971 to 1991: sample answer

The data in these two graphs indicates that the period from 1971 to 1991 was one of significant change within UK society. Most people, looking at the figures, would agree that by 2001 the position of the traditional family unit had been noticeably weakened by new social pressures.

# 07 Connectors

Suggested answers (page 062)
1 Adding information: not only…, but also…, as well as
2 Expressing reason and result: due to, because of
3 Expressing time: first, then, as

## test yourself

**7.1 A**

1 a result
2 to
3 because
4 therefore/consequently
5 because/as/since
6 the fact

## 7.1 B

1 The pressure of water was so great that the dam broke.
2 The nuclear facility was damaged by the tsunami and for this reason the local area had to be evacuated. (*or* The nuclear facility was damaged by the tsunami; for this reason the local area had to be evacuated.)
3 Most of the bridges in the region have such a strong structure that they can survive serious earthquakes.
4 Since the business had made a late surge in sales, the redundancy programme was cancelled.
5 Her first novel was such a success (*or* such a successful one) that she immediately gave up her job.
6 There were so many complaints that the company withdrew the product.

## 7.2

1 labelled so that
2 in order to communicate
3 call to let
4 In order to demonstrate
5 in order for mechanics
6 so as not to disturb

## 7.3

| | | |
|---|---|---|
| 1 Although | 4 though | 7 whereas |
| 2 however | 5 While | 8 in spite of |
| 3 Despite | 6 Despite | |

## 7.4 A

| | |
|---|---|
| 1 until | 4 Meanwhile, |
| 2 finish. | 5 eventually |
| 3 has received | 6 is |

## 7.4 B

| | | |
|---|---|---|
| 1 First | 3 After | 5 Then/Next |
| 2 Then/Next | 4 same | 6 Lastly |

## 7.5

1 As well as losing the Battle of Naseby, *Charles I* was also forced to give up his crown.
2 The company was declared bankrupt. Moreover, the CEO was imprisoned for fraud.
3 Not only did Edison patent many new inventions, (but) he also developed systems for the mass distribution of electricity.
4 In addition to its main site in the UK, the University of Nottingham has campuses in Semenyih, Malaysia and in Ningbo, China.
5 Not only will the centre's research increase our understanding of the brain, (but) it may also help to fight diseases such as cerebral palsy.
6 The National Theatre's production of *Hamlet* ran for two years in the West End. What is more, it toured in India, Australia and Canada, winning several awards.

## 7.6

1 Needing to regain California, the Democrats launched a series of aggressive TV ads.
2 Before beginning his expeditions, Amundsen always made meticulous preparations.
3 Refused access to the nuclear facility, Hans Blix and his team had to return to their hotel.
4 Having worked through the night, Professor Ancram was able to announce her results before the midday deadline.
5 After exploiting (*or* Having exploited) known reserves around the world, oil companies began to look to the Arctic for new sources of petroleum.
6 The bridge rises automatically on the approach of tall ships, allowing them to pass safely through.

## 7.7

| | |
|---|---|
| 1 such as | 4 namely |
| 2 i.e. | 5 To sum up |
| 3 for example | |

## Challenge yourself

### A

1 that is to say (*or* in other words) (7.7)
2 namely (7.7)
3 subsequently (7.4)
4 in other words (*or* that is to say) (7.7)
5 but (7.3)
6 Since (7.1)
7 consequently (7.1)
8 In brief (7.7)

### B

Phrases 1, 3, 7, 8, and 10 are correct.

| | |
|---|---|
| 2 e.g. (7.7) | 6 At the same time (7.4) |
| 3 As (7.4) | 9 By (*or* In) (7.4) |
| 5 such as (7.7) | |

### C

| | | | |
|---|---|---|---|
| 1 c (7.4) | 2 b (7.4) | 3 a (7.4) | 4 d (7.4) |

### D

| | | |
|---|---|---|
| 1 e (7.4) | 3 d (7.5) | 5 a (7.1) |
| 2 f (7.4) | 4 b (7.5) | 6 c (7.4) |

### E

1 as well as → so that (7.1)
2 and → but (7.3)
3 whereas → therefore (7.1)
4 however → but (7.3)

### F

| | | |
|---|---|---|
| 1 c (7.7) | 6 a (7.5) | 11 d (7.4) |
| 2 d (7.3) | 7 d (7.3) | 12 c (7.4) |
| 3 a (7.4) | 8 b (7.4) | 13 b (7.3) |
| 4 a (7.4) | 9 c (7.3) | 14 b (7.3) |
| 5 b (7.7) | 10 c (7.4) | 15 d (7.7) |

**G** Sample answer

I am going to talk about my last school because it's the organization I know best. To give you a general impression of the school I'm going to use three words: friendly, active, and inspiring. Even though it's a big school, all the teachers know the students' names and whenever there's something to celebrate, the whole school always joins in. As well as this, the teachers encourage the students to work hard. Having got the best exam results in the city last year, the teachers were very proud and they showed this by giving out awards and prizes, for example.

# 08 Being emphatic

Suggested answers (page 074)

1 For the first time in history, more people live in cities than in the country. In fact, this has been true of industrialized countries for a century at least. Now it is also true for the rest of the world. As these conurbations grow ever larger, it is vital that their transport infrastructures keep pace. What we see too often these days are cities grinding to a halt under the pressure of traffic jams. Only by stepping back and taking a fresh approach to our transport systems will we be able to ensure that the places where most of us now live can actually function.

2 These changes all emphasize parts of the text.

## test yourself

### 8.1 A

1 What a business requires for its long-term viability is a healthy reserves account.

2 It was a fundamental change that the Americans were seeking in the presidential election of 2008.

3 What the advocates of a traditional encyclopedia contend is that its research is more objective than that of Wikipedia.

4 It is the police who/that were accused of breaking the law during their investigation.

5 What none of the focus groups did was place priority on the privacy rights of celebrities. (or What none of the focus groups placed priority on were the privacy ...)

6 It is value for money rather than luxury that that travellers are generally looking for in an airline operator. (or It is value for money in an airline operator that travellers are generally looking for rather than luxury.)

### 8.1 B

1 arrived **were** hundreds
2 that **it** was; physics **that** allowed
3 argues that **what** some
4 to do **was** provide
5 explains, **it is** the tropical
6 Ramsay **who/that** first

### 8.2

1 At no time did Prime Minister Eden appear to be in control of the Suez crisis.

2 Not since the recession of the early 1990s has business confidence been so low.

3 Rarely has the capital witnessed such a large protest march.

4 Only when people buy more local produce will the amount of food transportation decline.

5 Under no circumstances should doctors be employed without a full check of their qualifications.

6 No sooner did talks break down than fighting began once again in the region. (or No sooner had talks broken down than ...)

### 8.3

| | |
|---|---|
| 1 indeed | 5 entirely/quite |
| 2 Only | 6 emphatically |
| 3 completely | 7 Even |
| 4 unfailingly | 8 Obviously |

### 8.4

| | |
|---|---|
| 1 is ... to | 4 can ... no |
| 2 is ... to | 5 is ... for |
| 3 is ... that | 6 is ... that |

## Challenge yourself

**A**

1 it is the ash from a volcano, rather than the heat and fire, that often causes more damage to human life. (8.1)

2 no sooner had the residents of St Pierre emerged from their houses, believing they were safe, than they were enveloped in a cloud of poisonous ash, resulting in 29,000 fatalities. (8.2)

3 What she focuses on is the fine ash that is drawn up into the atmosphere, (8.1)

4 Only by decreasing power can a pilot hope to limit the risk; (8.2)

5 what they had to do was (to) close the airspace over much of Europe (8.1)

6 it is our health and safety culture that makes us overreact in situations such as these. (8.1)

**B**

| | |
|---|---|
| 1 certain (8.4) | 5 crucial (8.4) |
| 2 particularly (8.3) | 6 quite (8.3) |
| 3 obvious (8.4) | 7 clearly (8.3) |
| 4 Indeed, (8.3) | 8 even (8.3) |

**C**

1 What she discovered was a pattern of behaviour (8.1)

2 Rarely are qualifications required (8.2)

3 Not until they have spent at least six months in these positions do they make their first attempt to act as doctors. (8.2)

4 However, it is the behaviour of members of the public and senior staff towards these impostors that is the most interesting aspect (8.1)

5 There can be no doubt that (*or* There is no doubt that) (8.4)

6 At no time during his two-year period as a hospital doctor was he asked (8.2)

**D**

| | |
|---|---|
| 1 undoubtedly (8.3) | 5 invariably (8.3) |
| 2 essentially (8.3) | 6 wholly, utterly (8.3) |
| 3 absolutely, quite (8.3) | 7 inevitable (8.4) |
| 4 in fact (8.3) | 8 actually (8.3) |

**E** Sample answer

On no account should the electric car be dismissed as the vehicle of the future. Despite its low sales, it can be argued that the long-term case for an alternative to the internal combustion engine remains entirely convincing. Petrol prices are indisputably rising year on year, and it is clear to most observers that the need to reduce greenhouse gas emissions is still a global priority.

What the government should do, as environmentalists point out, is offer greater incentives to the potential buyers of electric cars. Without doubt, this must include an increase in the number of recharging points throughout the country, further subsidies on price at the point of purchase, and greater support for the research that is certain to result in cheaper battery technology. Only by taking these measures can the government play its part in creating a system of sustainable private transport.

# 09 Passives

Suggested answers (page 082)

1 The Chrysler Building is currently the third tallest skyscraper in New York City. It was designed in Art Deco style by William Van Alken, and work was started in September 1928. The tower was completed less than two years later, after nearly four million bricks had been laid manually. In 2007, it was ranked ninth on the 'List of America's Favorite Architecture' by the American Institute of Architects.

2 By using the passive voice, the writer is able to keep the building – the main topic – as the subject of the sentences, and also to leave out the unimportant agents *building contractors* and *bricklayers*.

**test yourself**

**9.1**

1 A new device for measuring the purity of water was launched at a conference in Manchester last year.

2 Most of the spare parts for the car are made abroad.

3 Some new urban roads are built without pavements.

4 Four laptops were stolen from the offices of the research team.

5 Copies of the company's annual report can be obtained from reception.

6 The new brochures are printed, packed, and distributed to all the retail outlets.

**9.2**

1 Twelve new species of Peruvian insect were identified (*or* ... were identified last year ...) by a team of Swiss naturalists last year.

2 *Guernica* was painted by Pablo Picasso in 1937 as a direct response to the bombing of the Basque town. It was first exhibited as part of the Spanish display at the World's Fair in Paris in 1937.

3 10,000 new jobs in the UK electronics industry have been created by hi-tech companies since 2008.

4 The Menier Chocolate Factory was converted into a theatre in 2004. Over the last few years, a number of award-winning productions have been staged there.

**9.3 A**

1 is being restructured

2 was being planned

3 will have been occupied

4 had been released

5 will be carried out

6 has been observed

**9.3 B**

1 The hostages were being transported to the airport when they made their escape.

2 Six of the region's smaller clinics are going to be demolished and replaced with two new hospitals.

3 Emphysema is characterized by enlarged lungs and breathing difficulties.

4 For hundreds of years, hurricanes in the West Indies were named after the particular saint's day on which the hurricane occurred.

5 New species of plant such as the *Berlinia korupensis* are being discovered every year in Cameroon's rainforest.

6 'Atomic time' has been used since 1972 as the primary reference for all scientific timing.

**9.4 A**

Sentences 3 and 6 are correct.

1 must ~~to~~ be carried out

2 resented being **met** by

4 should not **be touched**

5 deserves **to** be criticized

## 9.4 B

1 Simple changes can be made by local communities to aid biodiversity, according to Shalmi (2012).
2 Most people would prefer to be consulted before a flight path is permanently re-routed over the area where they live.
3 Middleton (2011) argues that more than 100,000 deaths per year in the UK could be prevented by better quality healthcare.
4 Holstein (2009) describes being questioned for three hours in a threatening manner at Los Angeles International Airport.
5 BAA are piloting a system that will allow hand luggage to be examined more efficiently.
6 If an accident victim is unconscious, his or her breathing should be checked regularly.

## 9.5

1 It has been estimated that the cost of repairing the fire damage to the port will be £60m.
2 Oil companies are reported to be exploring parts of Antarctica.
3 Athens in Ancient Greece is believed to be (or believed to have been) the site of the first democracy.
4 Juan Olmo, who died in 2009, is thought to have been Europe's most skilful brain surgeon.
5 It was claimed that the drug had been tested on soldiers without their knowledge.
6 Passengers on the new jet are said to experience a slight feeling of weightlessness.

## 9.6

| | | | |
|---|---|---|---|
| 1 in | 3 with | 5 as | 7 on |
| 2 by | 4 by | 6 by | 8 of |

## Challenge yourself

**A**

1 have been hunted (9.3)
2 was joined (9.3)
3 was generated (or was being generated) (9.3)
4 was imposed (9.3)
5 is justified (or has been justified) (9.3)
6 are consumed (9.3)

**B**

1 are diagnosed as (or have been diagnosed as) (9.3, 9.6)
2 are associated with (or have been associated with) (9.3, 9.6)
3 be classified as (9.6)
4 are entitled to (9.6)
5 to be admitted to (9.1)
6 (to be) confined to (9.6)
7 to be located at (9.6)

**C**

| | | | |
|---|---|---|---|
| 1 h (9.2) | 4 j | 7 f (9.6) | 10 g (9.1) |
| 2 d (9.6) | 5 a (9.4) | 8 c (9.3) | |
| 3 i (9.5) | 6 b (9.6) | 9 e (9.1) | |

**D**

Verb forms 2 and 8 are correct.

1 is growing (or grows) (9.3)
3 might be expected (9.4)
4 was conducted (9.3)
5 are increasing (9.3)
6 are expected (9.3)
7 are affected (9.3)
9 is known (9.3)

**E**

1 Environmental legislation has been passed (9.3)
2 environmental legislation as being imposed on them (9.4)
3 know what is expected of them (9.2)
4 Member states are obliged to pursue this (9.3)
5 business having its factory insulated (9.5)

**F**

1 is caused by mining (9.3, 9.6)
2 has been extracted (9.3)
3 will be abandoned (or is abandoned) (9.3)
4 are perceived to be avoiding paying (9.5)
5 were bailed out by the state (9.3, 9.6)
6 continue to be felt (9.4)
7 is borne by the poor (9.3, 9.6)
8 will be targeted (9.3)

**G**

1 has been called (9.3)
3 are packed (9.3)
4 It was described (9.3)
5 were awarded (9.3)
7 has already been made (9.3)
8 are currently being invested (9.3)
9 will have been fulfilled (9.3)

**H** Sample answer

### Fire evacuation procedure

Make sure that you are aware of the location of the fire exits. If there is a fire anywhere in the building, the fire alarm will be set off. When you hear the alarm, make your way immediately to the nearest fire exit. The lifts should not be used. Fire doors will be automatically unlocked. The rallying point is situated in the front car park. Please ensure that access gates for emergency vehicles are not blocked. When the fire has been dealt with you will be informed when you can re-enter the building. Do not go back into the building until the 'all-clear' has been given. An analysis of the event will be undertaken by the building supervisor and circulated for information.

# 10 Arguing and persuading

Suggested answers (page 092)

1 The five phrases are: It seems obvious that; As Seiber argues; According to Norman and Martinsen; While it is clear that; it might be argued.

2 In the first text, the writer uses the view of another writer to support her own; in the second, she introduces another view as a counter-argument to her own, and comments on it.

## test yourself

### 10.1

| | | |
|---|---|---|
| 1 of all | 5 on to | 8 for the |
| 2 will | 6 Lastly | 9 refer |
| 3 identify | 7 conclude | |
| 4 Next | with | |

### 10.2

| | |
|---|---|
| 1 must, because | 4 can, argue |
| 2 However | 5 defend |
| 3 If | 6 Although |

### 10.3

1 ... a case in point **is** tobacco, ...
2 ... this **is** exemplified in planning law.
3 There **is** no doubt that, ...
4 ... prison **is** its deterrent effect ...
5 ... to be considered **is** that ...

### 10.4

| | |
|---|---|
| 1 pointed | 4 Although/While |
| 2 According | 5 cause (or produce) |
| 3 however | 6 less |

### 10.5

| | |
|---|---|
| 1 drawback | 4 second, of |
| 2 favour | 5 advantage |
| 3 serious, to | |

### 10.6

1 **It** follows that ...
2 ... it can be conclud**ed** that ...
3 **In** conclusion, ...
4 ...is therefore recommend**ed**.
5 ... it would be advis**able** to ...
6 ..., **it** may be said that ...

## Challenge yourself

### A

| | |
|---|---|
| 1 introduces (10.1) | 5 argued (10.4) |
| 2 considers (10.1) | 6 Firstly (10.1) |
| 3 examine (10.1) | 7 Next (10.1) |
| 4 describe (10.1) | 8 Lastly (10.1) |

### B

| | |
|---|---|
| 1 b, 5th sentence (10.3) | 4 a, 3rd sentence (10.3) |
| 2 f, 4th sentence (10.3) | 5 d, 6th sentence (10.3) |
| 3 e, 2nd sentence (10.3) | 6 c, 1st sentence (10.3) |

### C

1 Although there are many benefits to owning a car (10.4)
2 I will evaluate both of these (10.1)
3 are beyond the scope of this essay (10.1)
4 Instead, it will focus on the environmental consequences (10.1)
5 I will argue that it is vital for (10.2)

### D

1 exemplifies (10.3)
2 will argue (10.2)
3 On the other hand (2.7)
4 contention (10.2)
5 Studies have shown (10.3)
6 It therefore follows (10.6)
7 In summary (10.6)
8 To conclude (10.6)
9 will consider (10.1)
10 For the purposes of this discussion (10.1)
11 will begin (10.1)
12 then move on (10.1)

### E Sample answers

1 This essay will examine the necessity for the media to come under tighter legislative control. For the purposes of this essay, I will restrict my enquiry to newspapers, not broadcasters. I will argue that the most recent scandals, of political interference in suppressing major stories of public interest, prove that the industry's system of self-regulation has failed. Despite years of warnings, and more than one cycle of reforms, this system is manifestly not fit for purpose. My contention is that the only practical alternative is a clear set of laws, setting out what is and what is not permitted in relationships between journalists on the one hand and politicians, civil servants, and the police on the other. It is obvious that more transparency is needed, in order to rebuild public trust in these essential institutions. Critics of increased legislation claim that it will have a disturbing effect, leading to self-censorship on the part of editors, and thus the non-appearance of certain important stories. I believe that the very opposite is the case.

2 It is vital that healthcare be provided by the state, because a publicly-operated system will work to the benefit of the whole country. First of all, I will look at the impact of comprehensive healthcare on the working population. Once it becomes a right of citizenship rather than being tied, as now, to employment, it lessens the burden on employers, as well as freeing employees to move around the labour market more efficiently. Secondly, although it has long been recognized that workers are entering the labour force later, not enough thought

has gone into the ramifications of this extended adolescence on the healthcare system. Virtually all developed countries provide healthcare to children, independent of parents' means; the proposed system would ensure that young adults continuing their education are not forgotten by the system.

Finally, and arguably most importantly, public health emergencies can best be taken care of within a holistic system of public healthcare: epidemic and highly contagious diseases can be contained most effectively when the treatment of individuals is not less important than the treatment of the population as a whole. It follows that there is an urgent need for healthcare provision to be understood as a national, public responsibility. It is beyond the scope of this essay to consider which of the various economic models is best suited to our needs, but it is clear that we need to agree quickly on a system of basic healthcare provision.

# 11 Modal verbs

Suggested answers (page 100)
<u>should</u> consider, <u>will</u> fall, <u>will</u> flow, <u>can</u> bring, <u>must</u> also think, <u>can</u> easily satisfy

| | | | |
|---|---|---|---|
| 1 must | 2 can | 3 should | 4 will |

## test yourself

### 11.1
Sentences 3, 4 and 8 are correct
1  … rescue ships **were able to** remove/**managed to** remove/**succeeded in removing** …
2  The government **could have** bailed out …
5  No one **has ever been able** to prove …
6  … from IBM Zurich **were able to** produce/ **managed to** produce/**succeeded in producing** …
7  … be shared out …

### 11.2
| | | |
|---|---|---|
| 1 might be | 3 could soon | 5 may explain |
| 2 may focus | 4 might have | 6 could not |

### 11.3
| | |
|---|---|
| 1 could not | 4 had to stop |
| 2 must | 5 do not have to |
| 3 ought | 6 should |

### 11.4
1  needed/had
2  does not need to (*in written English* needn't *is not appropriate*)
3  need not have gone
4  must/need to
5  needn't/don't need to (*in spoken English both are possible*)
6  did not need to build

### 11.5
| | | |
|---|---|---|
| 1 would | 3 will | 5 would |
| 2 would | 4 will | 6 will |

### 11.6
1  Shall **I** start …
2  I **could** contact …
3  … society **has** got to
4  … we'd **better** look …
5  … supposed **to** include …
6  Would it be **possible** for …
7  … were **supposed** to be …
8  Could **we** present …

## Challenge yourself

### A
1  The science of logistics can be illustrated (*or* We can illustrate the science of logistics) (11.1)
2  Anyone planning a serious expedition needs to be aware (11.4)
3  Modern climbers can use (11.1)
4  had to do (11.3)
5  ought to serve (11.3)
6  Nile Brangwen and his team need not have failed (11.4)
7  The two lead climbers could have waited (11.1)
8  managed to descend (11.1)
9  they must have regretted (11.3)

### B
1  should (11.3)
2  might (11.2)
3  will be able/could (11.1)
4  could (11.1)
5  should (11.3)
6  will (11.5)

### C
| | | |
|---|---|---|
| 1 needs to (11.4)/ should (11.3) | | 7 would (11.5) |
| | | 8 will (11.5) |
| 2 may (11.2) | | 9 need (11.4) |
| 3 could/might (11.2) | | 10 will (11.5)/ could (11.2) |
| 4 would (11.5) | | |
| 5 will (11.5) | | 11 would (11.5) |
| 6 must (11.3) | | 12 can (11.1) |

### D
1  senior staff ought to have been aware (11.3)
2  FoodExpress could not have predicted (11.2)
3  conflict would lead (11.5); the charity managed to withdraw (*or* succeeded in withdrawing *or* was able to withdraw) (11.1)
4  FoodExpress cannot be blamed (11.1); it could be argued (11.2)
5  they ought not to overlook (11.3); can be satisfied (11.1)
6  that could/might/may not have been achieved (11.2)

**E**

| | |
|---|---|
| 1 Shall/Should (11.6) | 6 mind (11.6) |
| 2 could/should/can (11.6) | 7 better (11.6) |
| | 8 got (11.6) |
| 3 supposed (11.6) | 9 could/can (11.6) |
| 4 Shall/Should/Could (11.6) | 10 think (11.6) |
| | 11 supposed (11.6) |
| 5 can/could (11.6) | 12 have (11.6) |

**F** Sample answer

Aberdeen could not have become the prosperous city it is today without the discovery of North Sea oil in the 1970s. Like other towns and cities that depended on shipbuilding, fishing and other failing industries such as paper-making, Aberdeen might have declined quite rapidly in the latter part of the 20th century; instead, it would become what is known as a 'boom' town, benefiting from high levels of employment, a skilled workforce and two well-regarded universities.

Even if, as predicted, oil supplies finally begin to decline, modern industries in which the city has taken an interest, such as renewable energy projects, will be stimulated by a 'technology transfer' from the oil industry. Recently named one of the five cities that could lead the UK out of recession, Aberdeen should remain an economic success story for many years to come.

# 12 Talking about cause and effect

Suggested answers [page 108]
The essay questions all require a discussion of causes and effects. Question 2 focuses on effects and question 3 on causes.

## test yourself

### 12.1
| | |
|---|---|
| 1 led to | 4 bring about |
| 2 produce | 5 causing, to return |
| 3 resulting in, creating | 6 responsible for |

### 12.2
1 be produced by
2 result from
3 is caused by (*or* can be caused by)
4 stem from
5 be triggered by
6 is brought about by (*or* can be brought about by)

### 12.3
| | |
|---|---|
| 1 such | 4 meant/means |
| 2 therefore/ consequently | 5 as |
| 3 As/Since | 6 so |

### 12.4
1 ... because **of** a lack ...
2 ... made **on** account of the fact that ...
3 If an employee ...

4 ... as a result **of** ...
5 ... California **because**/**as** they ...
6 Due **to** a lack ...

### 12.5
1 ... result **of** an excessive ...
2 ... reason **for** the female ...
3 ... consequences **of** people ...
4 ... cause **of** mental illness. ...
5 ... contribute **to** poor performance ...
6 ... outcome **of** the growth ...

## Challenge yourself

**A**

1 If a new training course is evaluated continuously, the organizers are able to measure its success in detail. (12.4)
2 One consequence of war and the resulting political turmoil is an acute shortage of food. (12.5)
3 Stein (2007) argues that the lack of print archives in modern governmental department offices has resulted in a kind of institutional memory loss. (12.1) (*or* Stein (2007) argues that a kind of institutional memory loss results from the lack of print archives in modern governmental department offices.) (12.2)
4 A surge southwards of economic migrants from the (former) communist state would be triggered by the reunification of the two Koreas, according to Masefield (2010). (12.2)
5 One factor that contributed to the successful conclusion of the deal was the hiring of professional negotiators. (12.5)
6 A dioxin spill further up the river led to high fish mortality. (12.1)
7 One outcome of the experiment with advertising methods was a noticeable change in the demographics of Centra's customers. (12.5)
8 Medium-term economic growth may stem from tax cuts, in the view of Conway (2009). (12.2)

**B**

1 give rise to (*or* are responsible for) (12.1) (*or* have brought about) (12.2)
2 because (12.4) (*or* as/since, *though they normally come at the start of a sentence*) (12.3)
3 on account (12.4)
4 as a result (*or* as a consequence) (12.4)
5 so (12.3)
6 that (12.3)
7 This means (12.3)
8 causing (12.1)
9 consequently/therefore/so (12.3)
10 because (12.4)

**C**

1 One probable result of the pollution generated by road vehicles is (*or* will be) a rising level of childhood asthma. (12.5)

2 Very little rain fell in the early part of the year, which explains why the government banned people from using domestic hosepipes. (12.3) (*or* The fact that very little rain fell in the early part of the year explains why the government banned people from using domestic hosepipes.) (12.4)

3 Since some new urban roads are built without pavements, pedestrians are unable to reach their destinations. (12.3)

4 The disparate attitudes of the American people may be caused by the huge size of the United States. (12.2) (*or* The huge size of the United States may have caused the disparate attitudes of the American people.) (12.1)

5 There has been such public anger over tax avoidance schemes that parliament has tightened the appropriate financial regulations. (12.3)

6 As a consequence of overspending its budget, the marketing department was forced to make three account managers redundant. (12.4)

7 Under-regulation allowed some banks to make risky loans, producing uncertainty in the financial markets when the loans were not repaid, and finally causing an economic collapse. (12.1)

8 Charities may suffer during a recession due to the fact that people have less disposable income. (12.4)

**D** Sample answer

The 1990s are regularly described as 'the lost decade' in Japan. In the late 1980s, falls in real estate value and bad bank loans brought about a rapid drop in prices, leading to a period of economic stagnation. Continuing deflation caused the government to reduce interest rates to zero in the early 1990s. This policy did not, however, produce a revival in the country's economic fortunes, which continued to decline throughout the decade. Moreover, signs of improvement in the Japanese economy towards the end of the 1990s were short-lived as a result of the global slowdown in the closing year of the millennium.

**E** Sample answer

Violent shivering, caused by the body's need to produce heat, is one of the first probable effects of hypothermia. Mild confusion may follow as a consequence of a decrease in blood pressure and heart rate. Lips, ears, fingers, and toes may then become blue, resulting from the body's attempt to draw warm blood back towards the vital organs. Next, as an inevitable outcome of the closing down of the body's metabolic systems, victims will find it almost impossible to walk or use their hands.

**F** Sample answer

The high-street fashion chain Farflung went into liquidation last year, as a result of difficulties that had been predicted by business analysts for the preceding two years. Its downfall began, arguably, with its policy of continual special offers, which meant that shoppers expected a bargain every time they visited. This unrealistic goal was the main reason for Farflung's need to cut its profit margins.

In addition, the chain ran into difficulties with its suppliers, who were also feeling the effects of the recession. In July, the central bank devalued the currency, causing Farflung to change its payment terms. This resulted in its fulfilment houses becoming financially unstable. For many of them, their line of credit could not cope with the new terms of business, and, as a consequence, they cancelled their contracts. Thus, Farflung found itself without sufficient stock, and under pressure from investors.

The final disaster occured when its CEO's emails were leaked to the press, which gave rise to much criticism from financial analysts, fashion experts, and the public, as the amount of mismanagement came to light.

# 13 Verb patterns

Suggested answers [page 116]
Verb + infinitive: start, enable
Verb + infinitive without 'to': can, may
Verb + –ing form: enjoy, justify
Verbs + that: argue, contend
Verb + wh-: ask, explain

## test yourself

**13.1**

| | |
|---|---|
| 1 taking | 5 doing/to do |
| 2 to discourage | 6 to win |
| 3 to divide/dividing | 7 to hesitate/hesitating |
| 4 seeing | 8 lowering |

**13.2**

| | | |
|---|---|---|
| 1 reminded | 3 refused | 5 invited |
| 2 managed | 4 agreed | 6 helped |

**13.3**

| | | |
|---|---|---|
| 1 made | 3 will | 5 let |
| 2 would | 4 watch | 6 must |

**13.4**

1 ... carries **on** making ...
2 Zantec plc **delayed** launching ...
3 ... anticipate **losing** money ...
4 ... acknowledge **not** having ...
5 ... risk **being** overtaken ...
6 ... proposed **offering** research ...

## 13.5

| | | |
|---|---|---|
| 1 when | 5 that | 9 how |
| 2 that | 6 that | 10 that |
| 3 whether | 7 who | |
| 4 what | 8 why | |

### Challenge yourself

**A**

| | |
|---|---|
| 1 setting up (13.4) | 7 to allow (13.2) |
| 2 spending (13.4) | 8 establishing (13.4) |
| 3 to make (13.2) | 9 looking (13.4) |
| 4 to suggest (13.2) | 10 to acquire (13.2) |
| 5 making (13.4) | 11 expanding (13.4) |
| 6 to open (13.2) | |

**B**

| | |
|---|---|
| 1 persuade (13.2) | 5 spending (13.1) |
| 2 operate (13.3) | 6 would rather (13.3) |
| 3 to turn (13.2) | 7 confirms (13.5) |
| 4 suspected (13.5) | |

**C**

1 enable consumers to post reviews (13.2)
2 means accepting (13.1)
3 contends that this phenomenon produces (13.5), appears to spend (13.2)
4 explain what (13.5)
5 goes on to discuss (13.1), threatened to take (13.2)

**D**

| | |
|---|---|
| 1 which (13.5) | 7 watch (13.3) |
| 2 expect (13.2) | 8 rather (13.3) |
| 3 let (13.3) | 9 enjoy (13.3, 13.4) |
| 4 accept (13.5) | 10 better (13.3) |
| 5 why (13.5) | 11 when (13.5) |
| 6 might (13.3) | |

**E**

| | |
|---|---|
| 1 how/that (13.5) | 6 to allow (13.2) |
| 2 why (13.5) | 7 that (13.5) |
| 3 to suspend (13.2) | 8 that (13.5) |
| 4 to build/building (13.1) | 9 what (13.5) |
| 5 had (13.5) | 10 that/how (13.5) |

**F** Sample answer

Martha Stewart began developing her business skills by opening a catering business in the basement of her house in Connecticut. She went on quickly to become the manager of a gourmet store, where her experience enabled her to produce the first of a series of cookery and lifestyle books in 1982. By the end of that decade she realized that she had achieved the kind of reputation that would allow her to move into magazine publishing and the making of TV programmes.

Everything appeared to change in 2003 when Stewart was accused of securities fraud over a stock sale. After denying that she had acted illegally, Stewart was brought to trial and ultimately imprisoned for six months. On release she described how she had occupied herself in jail by acting as a liaison assistant between the prison authorities and her fellow inmates. Commentators who predicted that her career was finished were proved wrong over the next five years as she continued to produce books, to appear regularly on TV, and even to launch new lines in furniture, homeware and wine.

# 14 Hedging

Suggested answers (page 124)
The underlined words and phrases all make the text more cautious or tentative. The writer uses them because he or she is making an argument, rather than simply presenting facts, and wants to avoid making claims that appear too strong.

### test yourself

**14.1**

1 It has been estimated that 25% of homeless adults suffer from some form of mental illness.
2 The practice of short selling contributed to the collapse of Lehman Brothers.
3 Drought appears to be the major problem in some parts of Sub-Saharan Africa.
4 Wasps with a greater number of black spots on their heads tend to be more aggressive, according to research.
5 The report indicates that in some parts of the country bipolar disorder is being overdiagnosed.
6 It looks as if/though smaller electronics companies are doing better than their larger rivals.

**14.2**

| | |
|---|---|
| 1 slightly | 6 supposedly |
| 2 necessarily | 7 typically, usually |
| 3 quite | 8 rather |
| 4 relatively/reportedly | 9 approximately |
| 5 normally | 10 sometimes |

**14.3 A**

1 The latest research **appears to** indicate …
2 Most people **would say** that …
3 It is possible **to argue** that …
4 Statistics have **demonstrated** that …
5 It has **been** suggested that …
6 It **would** seem that …

**14.3 B**

Sentences 4 and 5 are correct.
1 fair **to** include
2 the **evidence** would
3 been **argued** that
6 It **is** widely (or It **has been** widely)

## 14.4

1 These new studies into brain function **can** help us to understand cases of slow development in some children.
2 **It is possible that** high-speed rail travel in Europe will take more market share from short-haul flights.
3 Scientists **may** have found a way of changing the immune system to prevent food allergies.
4 Medical research **is unlikely to** determine (*or* It **is unlikely that** medical research will determine) the cause of autism.
5 There **will probably be** a worldwide shortage of rare earth metals in the near future.
6 Sparks from electric power lines **are likely to have** caused (*or* It **is likely that** sparks … caused) some of the forest fires in the region.
7 Space debris **could** damage key communications satellites.
8 The amount of cybercrime in the USA and Europe **should** decrease as security software improves.
9 Recent government campaigns are unlikely to have had any long-lasting impact on levels of adult obesity.
10 The latest fall in unemployment might improve consumer confidence in the economy.
11 A horse that is deprived of sensory stimulation will possibly stop eating.
12 Changes in the chemical composition of the material could have occurred as a result of careless handling in the laboratory.

## 14.5

1 The new antibiotic has **in principle** …
2 … has improved **to the extent that** …
3 The new CEO Jackie Dell has **in one sense** …
4 There are **on balance** …
5 The advertising campaign worked **in the sense that** …
6 The new law will **to some extent** …

## Challenge yourself

### A

1 can be difficult to obtain (14.4)
2 the latest research appears to show (14.1)
3 It is estimated that the figure now stands at approximately 4,500. (*or* The figure is estimated to stand at approximately 4,500.) (14.1, 14.2)
4 The recession is likely to be responsible (*or* It is likely that the recession is responsible) (14.4)
5 Unemployment may cause relationships to break down (14.4)
6 economic stress has a tendency to increase levels of alcohol abuse (*or* there is a tendency for economic stress to increase levels of alcohol abuse) (14.1)

7 The situation seems to have been made worse (14.1)
8 notes the relatively high proportion of young people (14.2)
9 It is possible that apart from their obvious economic problems (14.4)

### B

1 arguably (14.2)
2 reasonably (14.2)
3 typically (14.2)
4 widely (14.3)
5 balance (14.5)
6 extent (14.5)
7 rule (14.5)
8 respects (14.5)

### C

1 Most/Many people (would) agree that economic sanctions against a country are preferable to war. (14.3)
2 it can be argued/it is argued/it has been argued that a properly calibrated system of sanctions should normally be implemented (14.2, 14.3)
3 the evidence suggests/indicates that the situation on the ground, where sanctions are actually experienced, is rather more complicated. (*or* the evidence from/provided by the situation on the ground, …) (14.2, 14.3)
4 tend to unify the people affected (14.1)
5 and thus help to strengthen the regime in power. (14.1)
6 It seems as if this was the case (14.1)
7 sanctions are only effective insofar as the blame for their effects (14.5)

### D Sample answers

No changes are necessary to sentences 3 and 7.

1 According to Harper and Maxwell (2009), approximately one third of Londoners believe that … (14.2)
2 It has been suggested that support for Scottish home rule will increase, the longer a referendum on independence is delayed. (14.3)
4 It is relatively unusual for salts to melt at low temperatures. (14.2)
5 As a rule, the supply of new money, known as quantative easing, stimulates medium-term growth in the economy. (14.5)
6 New insights into the causes of dementia should emerge from a doubling of government research funding. (14.4)
8 There appears to be an increase in the level of crime in poorly-maintained city centres. (14.1)

### E Sample answer

Obesity, the medical condition where an excess of body fat may cause (14.4) an adverse effect on health, is now the focus of a great deal of media attention. This interest is perhaps explained (14.4) by research that appears to show (14.1) that the incidence of obesity in higher income countries is now rising at its fastest ever rate. Stories in the press, however, are <u>likely to be accompanied</u> (14.4) by photographs designed to shock rather than by statistics designed to educate.

The pictures that draw attention are <u>typically</u> (14.2) those of children, and the background narrative <u>tends to concentrate</u> (14.1) on the diet of junk food that younger people <u>seem to</u> (14.1) enjoy. If space allows, there <u>may also be</u> (14.4) a reference to a lack of exercise, often with a graphic example, such as the children who are driven to schools <u>that appear to be</u> (14.1) within easy walking distance of their homes. <u>It is possible to argue, however, that</u> (14.4) the overall result of this kind of coverage is a distortion rather than a clarification of the problem.

# 15 Phrasal and prepositional verbs

Suggested answers [page 132]
wipe out, rely on (object: particular species), carry out (object: certain functions), die out, carry on, adapt to (object: another language)

## test yourself

### 15.1
| | | |
|---|---|---|
| 1 finish | 5 bail | 9 pick |
| 2 draw | 6 take | 10 laid |
| 3 take | 7 strike | |
| 4 set | 8 make | |

### 15.2
| | | |
|---|---|---|
| 1 slowed/went | 4 speak | 7 eat |
| 2 take | 5 carry/go | 8 ring |
| 3 bounced | 6 dying | |

### 15.3
| | | |
|---|---|---|
| 1 on | 4 with | 7 from |
| 2 with | 5 for | 8 to |
| 3 of | 6 for | |

### 15.4
| | |
|---|---|
| 1 looked, pointed | 4 engaging |
| 2 suffering | 5 qualify/apply |
| 3 go, led | |

### 15.5
| | |
|---|---|
| 1 comparing, with | 4 explain, to |
| 2 invested, in | 5 Protecting |
| 3 blamed for | (or To protect), from |

### 15.6
| | |
|---|---|
| 1 face up to | 4 get out of |
| 2 come up against | 5 running out of |
| 3 cut back on | 6 come up with |

### 15.7
| | |
|---|---|
| 1 be regarded as | 4 is based on |
| 2 be prejudiced against | 5 is associated with |
| 3 be required for | |

## Challenge yourself

### A
| | |
|---|---|
| 1 to (15.5) | 9 on (15.1) |
| 2 back (15.2) | 10 on (15.4) |
| 3 into (15.7) | 11 out (15.1) (or to (15.4) |
| 4 out (15.1) |    or up (15.1)) |
| 5 in (15.2) | 12 to (15.3) |
| 6 at (15.7) | 13 with (or on) (15.6) |
| 7 about (15.3) | 14 of (15.3) |
| 8 out (15.1) | |

### B
1 about (15.3)
2 as (15.7)
3 Drawing (15.3)
4 set (15.2)
5 up (15.1)
6 objecting (15.4)
7 known (15.7)

### C
| | |
|---|---|
| 1 accounted (15.3) | 4 points/pointed (15.1) |
| 2 defined (15.7) | 5 provided (15.5) |
| 3 transformed (15.3) | 6 vote (15.4) |

### D
1 taken **off** (15.2)
2 based **on** (15.7)
3 **go** along with (15.6)
4 sets **out** (15.1)
5 **set** up (15.1)
6 hand **out** (or **over**) (15.1)
7 **put** off (15.1)
8 prejudiced **against** (15.7)
9 **ends** up (15.2)
10 **cut** back (15.6)

### E
1 consists of (15.3)
2 carried (15.1)
3 agree (15.3)
4 concentrate on (15.3)
5 came (or comes) (15.3)
6 used (15.7)
7 added (15.3)
8 differ from (15.3)
9 specialized (15.4)
10 protected (15.5)

### F Sample answer

The first step is to check out the local area, find out what kind of restaurants already exist, and work out if there is a gap in the market. The time that a potential restaurateur invests in research is unlikely to be wasted. Once the new owner has decided on the type of restaurant, the next step is to hire the right kind of head chef. Taking on a chef with vision and drive may prove to be the key to success. It is also important to remember that, as well as being able to cook, a chef needs to be able to deal with staff and local suppliers.

With a head chef appointed, the next task is to weigh up the options for the menu. Key advice in this area is not to offer too many dishes. Long menus are likely to lead to waste.

Instead the focus should be on a short list of high quality local produce, with the flexibility to try out one or two new dishes every month. The final quality that the new restaurateur is required to possess is patience: new businesses start slowly and it may take months to build up a regular clientele.

# 16 Paraphrasing

Suggested answers (page 142)

1 techniques
2 with the characteristics we want to see
3 for thousands of years
4 (which ...) was the way in which agriculture developed
5 last
6 scientists created more efficient techniques
7 The latest (form of)

Selective breeding, radiation, genetic modification and genetic engineering are repeated because these are the technical terms in general use.

## test yourself

### 16.1

| | | |
|---|---|---|
| 1 criticizes | 3 demonstrate | 5 characterizes |
| 2 identified | 4 states | 6 argued |

### 16.2

1 High speed trains; economy
2 The Asian tiger; on safari; traditional medicine; skin
3 share price; January; financial year
4 copyright; the music industry (but you could say, for example, 'the music business')
5 water meters; the consumer (but you could say, for example, 'customers' or 'householders')
6 school governor; a member of the public (but you could say, for example, 'a member of the community'); school

### 16.3

1 visible/discernible
2 produce/publish
3 climax/main feature/high point
4 temporarily/briefly
5 worry/anxiety/stress
6 invariably/habitually
7 praised/flattered
8 indifferent/uninterested/lukewarm/half-hearted/disappointing

### 16.4

1 There is no direct link between a CEO's remuneration (or the remuneration a CEO receives) and the success of a company.
2 The mineral wealth of the Ural mountains has fundamentally affected the region's history.
3 South Korea is able economically (or is economically able) to buy its way out of any regional recession.
4 Students benefit from having undergraduates and postgraduates studying some of the same courses.
5 Self-adjustment by markets (or Market self-adjustment) can bring inflation under control.
6 Self-publishing ventures are often successful because of the power of the internet.
7 The rise of national pride in post-colonial countries is ultimately positive.
8 It is essential for the sole trader to thoroughly investigate the different ways to collect payment.

### 16.5

1 The effects of the very long-term use of computer games have yet to be studied by psychologists.
2 Economists tend not to be (or do not tend to be) as optimistic as politicians.
3 Subsidized house insulation schemes are likely to become more popular as energy prices rise.
4 Although they have many advantages, lithium-ion batteries have some drawbacks.
5 Before writing her first novel, Agatha Christie worked as a First World War nurse.
6 Cancer can result from long-term exposure to radiation.
7 It is possible that data loss will occur while the virus is being eliminated.
8 Temperatures rose so high in Kansas in July 2010 that more than 2,000 cattle died.

### 16.6

1 designing a building
2 is now an important element
3 the plans must
4 To meet this requirement
5 by taking into account how
6 the effect of the structure
7 natural or built
8 the architect has to assess

## Challenge yourself

**A** Sample answers (16.1–16.6)

1 If, at a small cost per citizen, the public provided funds for political parties, no one could accuse the government of changing their policies to suit large private donors, according to Smith (2010).

2 Sutcliffe (2011) argues that the BBC relies too much on costume drama in its effort to gain viewers at peak times.

3 Alberge (2010) maintains that private and public arts funding in the UK focuses too much on London, which means that the rest of the country does not normally get the support that it needs.

4 It makes no sense, according to Gardner (2011), for parents to borrow much more than they can afford to buy a house close to a top-performing primary school.

5 Hamilton (2009) suggests that critics have paid less attention to the British painter Keith Vaughan because, unlike other artists of his time, he portrays people rather than abstract forms.

6 Prosser (2011) suggests that poor advice is more likely to make a new business fail than a shortage of money.

**B** Sample answers (16.1–16.6)

1 As Asher (2006) indicates, there are still claims that Shakespeare did not write the plays that appear under his name. Despite this, no one has been able to provide convincing proof to support any other writer and the basis for these claims seems to be the rather weak assumption that his literary genius could not have originated from such an ordinary background. In fact, as Asher concludes, the documents that exist, such as official records and statements from people living at the time, indicate with the same force as for other writers of the age that Shakespeare was the author.

2 There are more productive ways of raising the level of fresh fish that the public can buy than by farming salmon, as Nye (2006) demonstrates. It is essential first of all to understand that the salmon requires other fish as part of its substantial diet. In fact, a farmed salmon eats more fish than it produces. Furthermore, the use of a vegetable protein as a substitute food lowers the quantity of important omega-3 fatty acids. The second point is that disease and sea lice can pass from farmed salmon to wild salmon in the area through the open-net procedures required by farming (ibid.).

3 May (2010) warns that there are three disadvantages to the method known as 'kettling', where the police hold protestors inside a restricted area for a period of time. First, law-abiding citizens with no connection to the protest may be detained. Next, the members of the public who are affected may be unable to access food, water, or toilets; and finally, as May points out, the possibility of a breakdown in order may in fact be increased by the conditions created by the 'kettle'.

4 As the intentions behind the garden city remain unrealized in their original form, there is no way, according to Patel (2008), of measuring how successful the project might have been. Sir Ebenezer Howard, who began the campaign for garden cities, envisaged towns that would be planned within detailed guidelines, which included maximum populations of 32,000 covering areas of 6,000 acres. Being dependent, however, on the financial backers of First Garden City Ltd, he could not afford to employ the kind of architects who might implement his plans, as Patel explains.

5 Martoff (2007) contends that the arguments made in support of gated communities do not stand up to criticism. In claiming that it is possible to reduce the risk of crime by keeping non-residents out, defenders of these communities fail to understand that these outsiders are unlikely to be criminal, and that by having people passing by, illegal acts may be discouraged. As Martoff explains, statistics from the USA show that there is as much crime in gated communities as there is in similar unsecured areas.

6 According to Weaver (2009), Margaret Thatcher's experiences as a child in Lincolnshire can explain the thinking behind the policies she implemented in the 1980s. As a grocer's daughter, she wanted to ensure a balanced national budget; the Methodist faith of her family resulted in her belief that people, in place of the government, are responsible for their own destiny, and, in the same way, her father's time as a prominent local politician gave her a belief in public service, as Weaver suggests.

**C**
Students' answers

# 17 Conditionals

Suggested answers (page 152)
1 c   2 a   3 d   4 b

## test yourself

### 17.1
1 Local authorities are fined **if** they do not …
2 **If** you translate poetry into another language, you lose …
3 Phosphorus burns **if** you expose it to air.
4 Some travel companies … **if** you pay online.
5 **If** they overtrain, athletes …
6 Transport costs are reduced **if** most produce sold is grown locally.

### 17.2 A
1 If you **do** not give people …
2 … if banks **do** not perform …
3 If you **ask** managers …
4 … if you **do** not evaluate …
5 … if the two sides **enter** into dialogue …

## 17.2 B

1 can increase
2 may suffer
3 should become
4 are likely to be
5 are going to lose

## 17.2 C

1 Stress levels **will increase** ...
2 ... the habitat that it lives in **will suffer** as well.
3 South Korea **will become** a major world economy ...
4 ... there **will be** significant delays...
5 Supermarkets **will lose** business ...

## 17.3

1 provided that
2 home unless
3 on condition that/provided that
4 If
5 even if
6 individuals; otherwise

## 17.4

Sentences 1 and 5 are correct.
2 If the UK **were** committed ...
3 ... if it **had** a more flexible recruitment policy.
4 If the government were **to introduce** or If the government **introduced** ...
6 If **it** were not for ...

## 17.5

1 **If** Hamlin Brothers ...
2 ... the centre of the city had **been** better designed ...
3 ... if they **had** produced ...
4 **Had** Max Brod ...
5 ... they might **have** won the case.
6 If it had **not** been for ...

## Challenge yourself

### A

1 had increased; third (17.5)
2 need; zero (17.1)
3 were; second (17.4)
4 (may) encounter; zero (17.1)
5 had listened; third (17.5)
6 will/may not see; first (17.2)

### B

1 (will) place (17.2)
2 (will) present (17.2)
3 would not renew (17.4)
4 is (17.3)
5 would act (17.4)
6 wished (17.4)
7 would not label (17.4)

### C

1 what if (17.4)
2 Suppose (17.4)
3 need (17.4)
4 as long as (17.3)
5 can (17.1)
6 improve (17.2)
7 likely (17.2)
8 might not have (17.5)
9 going to (17.2)
10 have to (17.2)
11 Unless (17.3)
12 won't (17.2)

### D

1 users switched from cars; would have an impact (17.4)
2 if there were a switch; would lead to a measurable reduction (17.4)
4 90,000 cars do so; can be postponed (17.3)
6 if they had invested; they might have saved (17.5)

### E

1 may have to (17.2)
2 if/provided that (17.3)
3 had advertised (17.5)
4 might have (17.5)
5 exists (17.1)
6 can be (17.1)
7 otherwise (17.3)
8 needs (17.1)

### F Sample answer

If Eatwell had focused on their long term strategy, rather than their day-to-day concerns, they might have turned their business around some time ago. Although senior staff undoubtedly worked hard and obtained some new contracts, the company's goal was unclear. If they had decided, for example, that they were going to concentrate on the catering needs of art galleries and museums, they could have built up a good level of return business in that sector.

Their new sales director needs to supply that kind of vision. If he or she lets the business community know what Eatwell stands for, the company may lose some contracts in the short term, but they will be able to find their place in the market. Brand identity is the key element. Eatwell would be in a stronger position today if they had spent more time developing this aspect of their business.

## 18 Using defining language

Suggested answers (page 160)
The writer is giving the reader a definition of the South Sea Bubble. Since this event forms one part of the comparison, it is important that the writer makes clear what he or she means or understands by the phrase.

## test yourself

### 18.1

1 A virus is a program
2 Perishables are food products
3 A parasite is an organism
4 The summer solstice is the day of the year
5 A carcinogen is a substance
6 An injunction is a court order

### 18.2

Sentences 2 and 5 are correct.

1 ... the system **by which/whereby** money is moved ... (*or* **for moving** money)
3 ... an instrument **for** screening ...
4 a method **by which/whereby** goods ...
6 ... for brea**king** up and smoo**thing** the soil.

### 18.3

1 literacy is defined as
2 The term 'stainless steel' describes an alloy
3 diseases is known as a pathogen
4 'People power' could be defined as the force
5 The word 'ethics' refers to the moral principles
6 The term 'climate change' designates statistical alterations

### 18.4

1 coined
2 is an example
3 are four main types
4 was first recognized, observed
5 can be exemplified

## Challenge yourself

### A

1 is (18.1)
2 which (18.1)
3 describes (18.3)
4 coined (18.4)
5 means (18.3)
6 which (18.1)
7 refer (18.3)
8 Examples (18.4)

### B

1 The term 'domestic violence' may be defined as a pattern of (18.3)
2 It can take many forms, such as (18.4)
3 It is defined more narrowly by the *Oxford Dictionary of Law* as (18.3)
4 it can also mean (18.3)
5 All of these types of violence can be expressed in various ways (18.4)
6 Verbal abuse is a form of abusive behaviour which (18.1)

### C

Phrases 1, 7, 8, and 10 are correct.

2 was coined (18.4)
3 was exemplified by (18.4)
4 for delivering (18.2)
5 whereby (18.2)
6 does not refer to (18.3)
9 refers to (18.3)

### D

1 b referring to (18.3)
2 d mean by (18.3)
3 c to describe (18.3)
4 d which (18.1)
5 a for example (18.4)
6 c means making (18.3)
7 b refers to taking (18.3)
8 d known as (18.3)
9 c means (18.3)
10 a called (18.3)

### E Sample answers

A wolf is a large canine animal which is the top predator in many temperate and arctic ecosystems. It is well known to have interacted with humans since prehistoric times, when we began to domesticate it and turn it into the dog. The wolf features in folktales and mythology in many cultures, and its image has changed significantly over the past half-century. It is not an endangered species, although many areas in which it was once widespread, such as Western Europe, are now devoid of wolves.

Tobacco is a word used for both a plant and the product of that plant. It is grown as a cash crop around the world, and is an important element of the economies of countries from southern Africa to China. Most tobacco is smoked as cigarettes; other forms of human consumption include cigars and snuff. In addition, tobacco can be used for completely different purposes; for instance, it has long served as a pesticide. It is highly addictive and is a leading cause of mortality globally.

President's Day is celebrated on the first Monday in June. It became a national holiday in Freelandia in 1972, on the twentieth anniversary of independence. It was intended to commemorate our first president, Dr Miriam Hakim, who had died in the previous year. President's Day quickly became a time to celebrate other events and characters in our nation's story, and in particular the struggle for independence. It is marked by parades, picnics, political speeches, and fireworks.

Marketing is the branch of business which deals with the customer's needs. It is allied with, but not synonymous to, the function of sales. Marketing exists to find out what the customer wants or needs, in some cases before they are even aware of it themselves, and to fulfil that need by ensuring that relevant goods or services are commissioned and produced.

## 19 Collocation

Suggested answers (page 166)

1 government officials, Travel disruptions
2 latest figures, significant reduction, economic hardship
3 establish conclusively

## test yourself

### 19.1

| | |
|---|---|
| 1 theme | 4 influence |
| 2 example | 5 belief, mobility |
| 3 stability | 6 impact, prosperity |

### 19.2

| | | |
|---|---|---|
| 1 casually | 3 deeply | 5 barely |
| 2 wrongfully | 4 severely | 6 mainly |

### 19.3

| | |
|---|---|
| 1 resolved | 4 demonstrated/demonstrates |
| 2 raise | 5 denied |
| 3 suppressed | 6 considered |

### 19.4

1 environment
2 animation
3 background
4 grants
5 workers
6 forces

## Challenge yourself

### A

| | |
|---|---|
| 1 considerable (19.1) | 6 carefully (19.2) |
| 2 clearly (19.3) | 7 conclusively (19.3) |
| 3 immensely (19.2) | 8 fiercely (19.2) |
| 4 sceptical (19.2) | 9 widespread (19.1) |
| 5 proposal (19.3) | 10 important (19.1) |

### B

| | |
|---|---|
| 1 policy (19.4) | 7 raise (19.3) |
| 2 detail (19.3) | 8 generously (19.2) |
| 3 political (19.1) | 9 extensively (19.2) |
| 4 need (19.3) | 10 investigation (19.3) |
| 5 deeply (19.2) | 11 consider (19.3) |
| 6 strenuously (19.3) | 12 adequate (19.2) |

### C

| | |
|---|---|
| 1 background (19.4) | 6 connection (19.3) |
| 2 class (19.1) | 7 findings (19.4) |
| 3 closely (19.3) | 8 considers (19.3) |
| 4 considerable (19.1) | 9 conspicuously (19.2) |
| 5 difference (19.1) | 10 identifying (19.3) |

### D

1 business community (19.4)
2 specific context (19.1)
3 recently published (19.2)
4 economic conditions (19.1)
5 market forces (19.4)
6 inevitably result (19.3)
7 local authorities (19.1)
8 respond positively (19.3)
9 social networks (19.1)
10 significant reduction (19.1)

### E Sample answer

There are major concerns about the state of the National Health Service in the UK. Experts from the health industry regularly point up the inconsistencies in the quality of treatment across the country; commentators write convincingly of the growing financial burden on hospitals as the population ages; health workers complain that NHS reforms are politically motivated and do not serve the interests of local people.

At the same time, however, there is a widespread belief amongst the public that the NHS, as it currently operates, is one of the UK's major post-war achievements, and a desire that it should remain in its current publicly financed form. The age of the family doctor may have passed, but local communities still have faith in the clinic or health centre in the part of town where they live.

## 20 Cohesion

Suggested answers (page 172)

1 Luxembourg
2 Bolivia
3 Luxembourg and Bolivia
4 the fact that Luxembourg and Bolivia are landlocked
5 the history of Luxembourg and Bolivia
6 in the rest of the essay

## test yourself

### 20.1

| | | |
|---|---|---|
| 1 it | 3 he, she | 5 its |
| 2 their, them | 4 they, their | |

### 20.2 A

1 **This trend** needs to be examined in the overall context of the current economic situation.
2 Mitchell (2009) argues, however, that **this** was not always how these two species behaved in the wild.
3 **These measures** are likely to result in greater hardship for the general population.
4 **This** was confirmed in a recent study by Stevens and Black (2011), who examined ...
5 A series of articles published in 2010 first made **this disagreement** public.

### 20.2 B

| | | |
|---|---|---|
| 1 this | 3 those | 5 that |
| 2 that | 4 these | |

### 20.3

| | | |
|---|---|---|
| 1 other | 3 the | 5 both |
| 2 many | 4 same | 6 such |

## 20.4

| | |
|---|---|
| 1 below | 4 the former |
| 2 the latter | 5 respectively |
| 3 above | |

## 20.5 A

1 ... for admission, it should **do so** in the knowledge ...
2 ... . in April 2009, it was apparent that they had not **done so**.
3 ... congestion, but they can help to **do so**.
4 ... but he or she will be able to apply for a job much more easily by **doing so**.

## 20.5 B

1 The most successful **(projects)** had succeeded ...
2 ... but the third **(train)** was forced ...
3 ... Some of the latest **(campaigns)** involved ...
4 ... given their success in the previous two **(general elections)**.

## Challenge yourself

### A

| | |
|---|---|
| 1 One (20.3) | 4 Another (20.3) |
| 2 between them (20.1) | 5 its (20.1) |
| 3 the one (20.3) | 6 This remark (20.2) |

### B

| | |
|---|---|
| 1 this (20.2) | 9 This (20.2) |
| 2 such (20.3) | 10 the (20.3)/this (20.2) |
| 3 its (20.1) | 11 it (20.1) |
| 4 former (20.4) | 12 Those/Such (20.2) |
| 5 they (20.1) | 13 those/these (20.2) |
| 6 this (20.2) | 14 the (20.3)/this (20.2) |
| 7 it (20.1) | 15 above (20.4) |
| 8 these/such (20.2) | 16 the (20.3) |

### C

1c, 2b, 3a, 4d

### D

1e, 2f, 3b, 4g, 5a, 6d, 7h, 8c
These (20.2), respectively (20.4), this (20.2), its (20.1), those (20.2), This (20.2), however (7.3), Its (20.1)

### E

| | |
|---|---|
| 1 them (20.1) | 5 These (20.2) |
| 2 she (20.1) | 6 following (20.4) |
| 3 her (20.1) | 7 the (20.3) |
| 4 above (20.4) | 8 these (20.2) |

### F

1 its (20.1)
2 this objective/aim (20.2)
3 these two languages (20.2)
4 which last five and six years respectively (20.4)
5 doing so (20.5)
6 these (young) students (20.2, 20.5)
7 that (20.2)/the one (20.3)
8 those (20.2)
9 Such a system (20.3) (*or* This system) (20.2)

**G** Sample answer

Mohandas Karamchand Gandhi was born in India in 1869. He was known by several names, such as Mahatma and Bapu, meaning 'Great Soul' and 'Father' respectively. He started work as a lawyer in South Africa after training for this profession in London, and he campaigned for civil rights for Indians living in that country. He believed firmly in ideas of peace and freedom and these ideas became more and more important to him.

When Gandhi returned to India in 1915 he was already a well-known Indian Nationalist. At that time India was ruled by the British and Gandhi fought against them by using a policy of non-cooperation. He also organized protests. Both led him to be imprisoned on several occasions. Such experiences only made him more determined.

After independence from Britain, India was troubled by conflict between Hindus and Muslims. Gandhi was assassinated in 1948 by a Hindu extremist who thought he was too sympathetic to Indians of the other religion.

# INDEX

## A

*a/an*, indefinite article  29, 161

*a case in point is*, presenting arguments  95

*a great deal* + comparative adjective + *than*  20

*a great deal of*, quantifier  30

*a little* + comparative adjective + *than*  20

ability, modal verbs  101

*above*, cohesion  176

*absolutely*, emphatic adverb  77

*accept*, reporting verb  143

*according to* (name), using others' opinions  58, 95

actions
  describing in present continuous tense  7
  in the past  8
  reasons for  63
  results of  63

activities
  in future tense  11
  tense emphasizing effect/length of  9

*actually*, emphatic adverb  77

additional information, expressing  67

adjective + *enough* + infinitive  18

adjective synonyms  145

adjectives
  + nouns  31-2
  comparative  17, 18, 20
  comparing  16-20
  compound  31
  connected with areas of influence  167
  coordinated  32
  describing trends  56-57
  formal  42
  gradable/ungradable  126
  limiting  167
  nominalizations from  39
  order before noun  32
  as pre-modifying words  28
  of size and impact  167
  superlative  17, 19

*advantage*, collocations and synonyms  96

advantages and disadvantages, expressing  96

adverb + adjective combinations  31, 167

adverb synonyms  145

adverbs
  adding own specific meaning  167
  comparing  16-20
  describing trends  56
  emphatic  77-8
  strengthening meaning of adjectives  167
  using for hedging  126

advice, giving  105

*after* + *-ing* form of verb  147

*afterwards*, sequencing events  66

agent of passives, avoidance of  83

*agree*, reporting verb  143

*agree with/to*  135

agreeing, in speaking  59

*albeit*, formal word  43

*alike*, expressing similarity  21

*all* + countable/uncountable nouns  30

*almost as* + adjective  20

*almost the same as*, expressing similarity  21

*almost the* + superlative adjective  20

*also*, expressing additional information  67

*although*, expressing contrast  64, 147

analysis verbs, stating scope of essay  93

*another/other*, cohesion  175

*any* + countable/uncountable nouns  30

*apart*, phrasal verb particle  133

*appear*, hedging verb  125

*apply for/to*  136

*argue*, reporting verb  143

*argue about/with*  136

arguing  92-7

arguments, words and phrases  94

articles  29
  as pre-modifying words  28
  SEE ALSO *a/an*, *the*

*as*, connector  63, 110

*as* + adjective/adverb + *as*  17, 20, 57

*as a consequence of*, connector  111

*as* (name) + reporting verb  58

*as a result*, expressing result  63, 110

*as a result of*, connector  111, 147

*as a rule*, hedging expression  129

*as soon as*, expressing time  65

*as we have seen*
  cohesion  176
  conclusion phrase  97

*as well as*, expressing additional information  67

*as...as*, expressing comparison  147

*assert*, reporting verb  143

*associated with*  87

*at first* and *first/ly*  66

*at last* and *last/ly*  66

*at no time*, emphatic inversion  76-7

*at which point*, at start of relative clause  49

*at work/university*, article omitted  29

*attributed to*, passive with preposition  87

## B

*based on*, passive with preposition  87

*be*, used in nominalized sentences  39

*be* + relative clause, defining language  161

*be able to*  101

*be about to*, immediate future  11

*be defined as*  162

*be going to* SEE *going to*

*be known as*  162